Soul Journey through the Tarot

"This book contains so many gifts. For starters, it showcases both deep subject knowledge and John's quicksilver way of weaving facts and insights across different fields. His love of poetry, music, and visual art is also here. His deep connection with the cosmic and elemental realms also shines through. Most charmingly of all, the text is peppered with very playful yet nonetheless practical advice for how to work with the tarot and its lessons in everyday life. For who else but John would think of creating essences out of imaginal or theoretical flowers?"

Ysette Guevara, Ph.D., contributor to *Ascension* by William Henry

"John Sandbach delves into the intricate realm of decoding symbolism and esoteric practices, ensuring that readers do not overlook even the most subtle aspects of richness and depth of insight. A captivating and enlightening synthesis of interpretations and a testament to his thoroughness, extensive research, insight, sensibility, authenticity, and innovation, this book opens up a gateway to a unique new perspective. The quest to gain insight from esoteric practices is not only approached as a set of rituals with a remedial effect on one's soul but also proposed and reviewed as a tool for understanding ourselves and the world around us."

Eleni Kostika, astrologer and architect

"This book is an alchemical fire itself that can ignite your creative imagination to practice and deepen inner work. It is dynamic and alive, because how you interact with the content of each card, portrayed from many different aspects, can open the door to infinite meaning—making for your self-understanding. This is not a fortune-telling pseudo New Age book. Sandbach's insights in this book are both traditional and unconventional, because they are multidimensional. Each symbol will lead you to both answers and questions with childlike wonder and old sage-like reverie."

Akiko Kinney, LMHC, founder of Soundscape Counseling

"An instant classic that will be returned to over and over again. The illustrations of the cards are beautiful and have a timeless quality about them. All of time and every human condition is contained within this book and its images. From the beginning you know you are in the hands of a master who will take you deeper into the tarot with the Kabbalah, numerology, and the exciting Language of Space."

SANDRA LEE SANDY, ASTROLOGER AND TAROT READER

"I was fortunate to study the tarot with John Sandbach forty years ago, using his personal and learned methodology. It was quite the journey. John's approach to understanding this historic and remarkable system of occult knowledge is, quite simply, superior to any other that I have encountered in years of spiritual learning. It is way beyond fortune-telling; it is a pathway to the sacred, enabling one to encounter their very soul. I reread his book regularly, as it is a ready aid for personal growth in these difficult times. I shall be forever grateful that John continues to share his learning."

ELISABETH KIRSCH, WRITER FOR *KC STUDIO* MAGAZINE

"*Soul Journey through the Tarot* works on subtle levels in magical, mystical ways. The author invites readers to absorb his ideas into their being as if they were poetry. Open-minded aspirants on diverse spiritual paths will gain rich reward from dedicated study of the deep wisdom contained in this one-of-a-kind book. For tarot neophytes there's a treasure trove of profound information to set them firmly on the right path, while more advanced practitioners will gain fresh insights. Students of numerology and astrology will also discover provocative new ideas that will illuminate their practice."

PAUL SWANN, ASTROLOGY STUDENT AND RESEARCHER

"What Joseph Campbell constructed for mythology, John Sandbach composes for the metaphysical: a harmonic illumination of the astral orchestra. More than a mere reference book, John provides a poetic key to a profound exploration of esoteric mechanisms. This book is a voyage into the subconscious cocoon, where an evolution of conceptual traditions emerges, bright and wonderful."

ADAM ELLIOTT RUSH, DESIGNER AND EDITOR AT SCIQI

SOUL JOURNEY THROUGH THE TAROT

Key to a Complete Spiritual Practice

A Sacred Planet Book

JOHN SANDBACH

Destiny Books
Rochester, Vermont

Destiny Books
One Park Street
Rochester, Vermont 05767
www.DestinyBooks.com

Text stock is SFI certified

Destiny Books is a division of Inner Traditions International

Sacred Planet Books are curated by Richard Grossinger, Inner Traditions editorial board member and cofounder and former publisher of North Atlantic Books. The Sacred Planet collection, published under the umbrella of the Inner Traditions family of imprints, includes works on the themes of consciousness, cosmology, alternative medicine, dreams, climate, permaculture, alchemy, shamanic studies, oracles, astrology, crystals, hyperobjects, locutions, and subtle bodies.

Originally self-published in 1976 and re-issued in 1981 by Aires Press under the title *The Golden Cycle: A Text on the Tarot*
Original edition co-written with Ronn Ballard

Cataloging-in-Publication Data for this title is available from the Library of Congress

ISBN 978-1-64411-709-5 (print)
ISBN 978-1-64411-710-1 (ebook)

Printed and bound in the United States by Lake Book Manufacturing, LLC
The text stock is SFI certified. The Sustainable Forestry Initiative® program promotes sustainable forest management.

10 9 8 7 6 5 4 3 2 1

Text design and layout by Kenleigh Manseau
This book was typeset in Garamond Premier Pro with Albertus MT Std and Trenda used as Display typefaces
aUI alphabet from www.auilanguage.org
22 Cubes drawing by Tom Gomersall
Major arcana illustrations for "The Oracle of Hermes" by Daehee Son (www.DaeheeWorld .com)
Creative assistance for the three-card spread, the seven-card spread, the Tree of Life, and the gematria diagrams provided by Adam Elliott Rush (www.sciqi.com)

To send correspondence to the author of this book, mail a first-class letter to the author c/o Inner Traditions • Bear & Company, One Park Street, Rochester, VT 05767, and we will forward the communication, or contact the author directly at www.JohnSandbach.net.

This book is dedicated to Teresa Anderson,
Arthur W. Ballard, Ronn Ballard,
Tom Gomersall, Antoinette Kaufman,
Elisabeth Kirsch, Adam Elliott Rush,
Brenda Smith, and Dr. John Weilgart

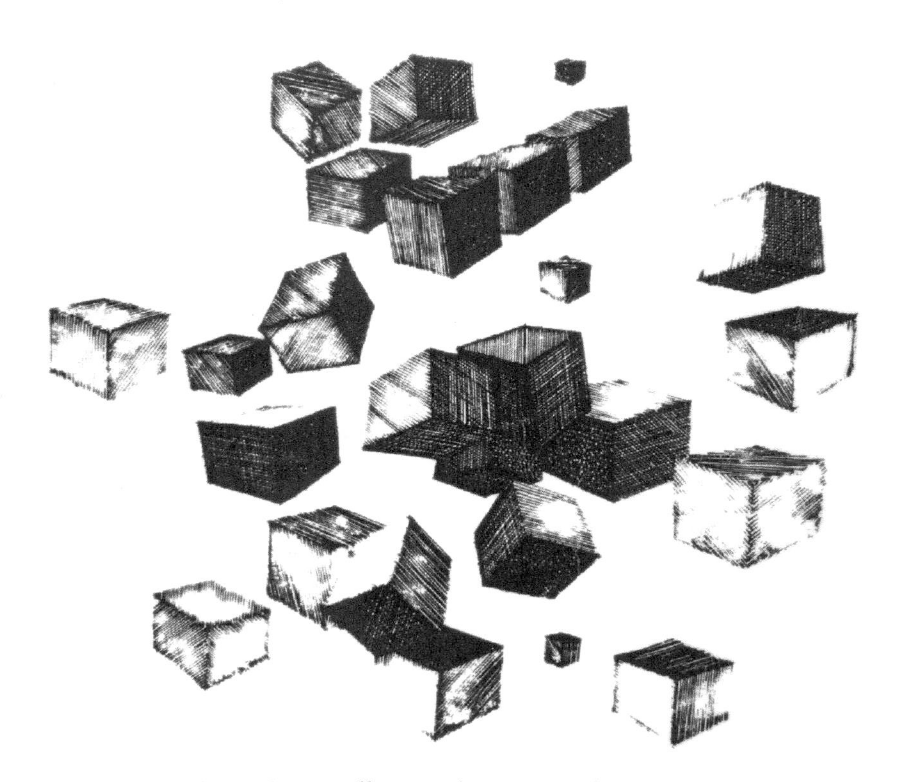

Tom Gomersall, 22 Cubes, *pen and ink, 1974*

Contents

PART FOUR
Advanced Practices

INTRODUCTION

The Nature of the Tarot

How many tarot decks are there out there anyway? Back in the 1970s I remember when the James Bond 007 Tarot of the Witches Deck came out. And then just recently my friend Elisabeth showed me a limited-edition tarot deck by a feminist artist collective inspired by the spiritual abstractionist Hilma af Klint. I braced myself for another piece of mediocrity and instead was blown away when she laid out for me a seventy-eight-card set of wonderfully profound abstract paintings, which were activated by the spirits of women artists no longer alive, according to the artists who painted them.

Heaps and heaps of decks and systems. And, of course, lots of arguing among aficionados about what means what. Ever since I first began studying the tarot more than fifty years ago I've had to psychologically keep a shovel handy so I could push all this stuff off to the side to make a place for myself where I could build my own tarot laboratory in which I could work, think, and dream about the cards. That's not to say I haven't been deeply influenced by some golden sources out there. It is to say, though, that it's easy to get lost in a labyrinth of the innumerable thoughts and pictures that have been piling up around this magical system.

In fact, there have been literally mountains written about the tarot. Some of these writings are good as gold, and other writings, in my estimation, are worthless or even misleading. So as you study the tarot I encourage you to always follow your own intuition and take the gold where you find it, from any source where you discover it. The purpose of this book is to promote a crystalline, therapeutic, and spiritual understanding of the tarot in this New Age we've been in the process of entering now for a good while. As I throw light on the cards, I hope many of the conflicting ideas around their interpretation will become clear. In many cases it will probably be seen that ideas that seem to be in conflict need not necessarily be mutually exclusive, but rather are simply different ways of looking at the same thing.

In this book I'm not so much interested in the words and concepts that allude to the things spoken of as I am in the things themselves—the energies and vibrations that weave the tapestry of our phenomenal world.

THE TAROT AS A REVELATION OF ARCHETYPAL FORCES

What is the tarot? We fool ourselves if we think that we can invent one best definition. If you look in a dictionary you will see that the word *pomegranate* has a relatively short definition, whereas the word *love* has many definitions. This is because the concept of a pomegranate is less universal or archetypal than the concept of love. In like manner, the tarot is universal more than particular, and hence a short definition can never address all the facets of this most sparkling of gems. And besides, who wants short definitions when there's poetry to be had?

As an arrangement of archetypes and the embodiment of sacred knowledge, the tarot is a complete system. As a tool or functional structure it is also complete, but it's more than just a system of knowledge and more than a simple tool—it's a dynamic arrangement of living archetypes, each having an evocative potential that grows and changes constantly, meaning that it's never definable in any ultimate sense. The tarot is a microcosm of the universe, and as we use or talk about it we can define some aspects of it, but its potential is infinite.

The limitations of the tarot as a functional system are the same limitations inherent in the person or persons using it. As you, the initiate, progress on your journey toward enlightenment, you become more and more fulfilled, and your appreciation of the tarot thus approaches the potential of the tarot, which is infinite: living wisdom, as opposed to mere knowledge.

It is this moving toward completion that we call evolution. Today we understand the tarot in certain ways, and tomorrow we will understand it more fully, in ways even more light-filled. It's an understanding and knowledge that one grows into and doesn't become filled up until you've attained the full potential of your being.

There's an infinite amount of information that can be harvested from studying the cards—literally too much to ever be taken in by one person, or even a group of people. This is as it should be, because we should not be so much interested in the accumulation of knowledge as we are in its uses. As you study these chapters you will perceive them in your own unique and special way—from your own perspective—for who else's perspective could you perceive them from? What you understand and can relate to will never be exactly the same as what anyone else experiences.

You may sometimes feel that you don't see how the knowledge you're gaining here is to be used. It's important to remember the great truth that everything we learn we always use in some way. This is one of the many ways of declaring the truth of divine order, which is the ultimate economy and efficiency of the universe. It doesn't free us from the need to make attempts to apply and use knowledge, but it does promise that all attempts, if persistent, will result in victory.

THE ARCANA: MAJOR AND MINOR

The tarot has two major divisions, the major arcana and the minor arcana. The word *arcana* is Latin and means "mysteries," while the singular form is *arcanum,* "mystery." These words derive from the Latin *arcanus,* meaning "shut in" or "hidden," and this word originally comes from the Latin for the English word *chest,* signifying a place where something is stored. The word has also come to mean a secret remedy or elixir, signifying that whatever is shut up and hidden in this symbolic chest has healing properties. Later, the words *arcanum* and *arcana* came to mean a card or the cards of the tarot deck, to signify that these cards hold lots of information as well as certain mysteries, which we can contemplate to advance our knowledge of life.

We have to be careful when thinking about the words *major* and *minor* in this context. We must not confuse these terms with "greater" and "lesser," or "more important" and "less important." All these mysteries are equal. The minor arcana, or minor mysteries, are more accessible and approachable, or we could say *seemingly* not as mysterious. They are one-pointed, whereas the major mysteries, as the major arcana, are always dualistic and hence enigmatic. Each of the major arcana thus has a double quality.

In the tarot, the minor arcana are depicted as numbers and only four visual symbols, whereas all the major arcana are depicted as full-blown visual images that are sometimes portrayed with great complexity, along with numbers and other symbols. The major arcana are sometimes referred to as the "picture cards" of the deck, whereas the earliest known minor arcana cards had no pictures. Some modern decks employ pictures on the minor arcana, but this is a recent development that for some people can sometimes be more confusing than revealing.

In this book we will start with an analysis of the major arcana, mainly because they require more work to understand and also because they help to explain the nature of the minor arcana. It may seem strange that we would start with the complicated and proceed to the simple, and yet, if you will remember the preceding example of the dictionary definitions of the words *pomegranate* and *love,* you will see how it is ultimately the simplest concepts that tend to require the greatest number of words to explain. Oftentimes people equate simplicity with easiness, but this is not necessarily an accurate way to look at it, for simplicity can sometimes be the most difficult thing to attain.

You may note that many of the names of the major arcana cards in this book are different from the traditional names you may be more familiar with. The names I have chosen were carefully thought out over a long period of time and were selected to mirror the highly specific meanings pertaining to the cards. For instance, the name of the card commonly known as Judgment, Arcanum XX, has been changed to The Awakening. One of the reasons for this change was to get away from the Christian idea of the Last Judgment and instead refer to the process of becoming enlightened, that is, awakening. My spirits tell me that the cards may carry many names, and do, and what is most important about these names is that they reflect the meaning of the cards. And since each card has many facets, the labels it can carry can potentially also be many.

THE CARD NUMBERS

The numbering system I use for the twenty-two cards of the major arcana is 1 to 22, but I also use 0 to 21 for the same range of cards. In both ways of numbering the cards, the numbers from 1 to 21 stay the same. It's the card known as The Fool that has two numbers, 0 and 22, for it can come at either the beginning of the major arcana or at the end. The Fool thus functions as a kind of hook that both ends and begins this group of cards, thereby turning the tarot progression into a circle rather than just a straight line.

The number 21 is generated from what is called a "triangulation" of numbers. To make this triangulation, we start by adding 1 to 2 to 3 to 4 and so on, until we have added the number 6. This can be represented in a visual diagram:

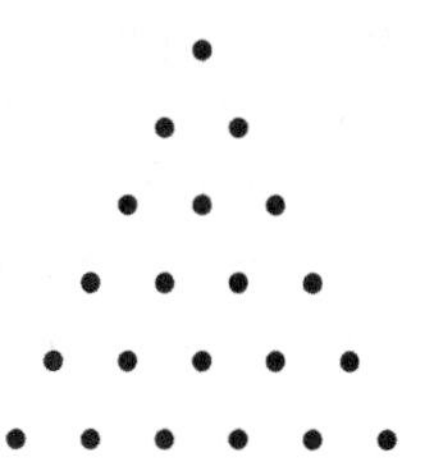

Each row of dots has one more than the last row, and the sum of the six rows of dots is 21. This makes a pyramid or a triangle of numbers. We start with the number 1 and move on to the number 2, but in the process we do not lose the concept of 1. When we conceive the number 2, we have based this conception on the number 1, and so we actually have three concepts: 1 by itself, 2 by itself, and 1 and 2 together.

We can take any number, such as 6, and say that 6 is a limited concept, but in terms of its underlying completeness it is 21, which is the sum of 1 + 2 + 3 + 4 + 5 + 6. So the 21 vibration of the major arcana is actually a filling-out or completion of the number 6 (kabbalists tell us the number 6 symbolizes the universe).

THE MINOR ARCANA, THE ELEMENTS, AND THE SUITS

The minor arcana consists of fifty-six cards, giving a total of seventy-eight cards in the complete tarot deck (fifty-six minor arcana cards plus twenty-two major arcana cards). The number 78 is also a perfect triangular number that is derived from adding all the numbers together from 1 through 12. Hence it's a triangulation, that is, a completion, of the number 12.

The two divisions of the tarot symbolize the inner and outer nature of experience, with the minor arcana corresponding more to the outer, or, let us say, the more directly visible part of our experience, while the major arcana corresponds to the more inner, intuitive part of our experience.

The minor arcana is further divided into four parts that correspond to the four traditional elements of astrology: fire, air, water, and earth. Fire is represented by the suit of Wands, water by Cups, air by Coins (which are sometimes called Pentacles, or sometimes Money), and earth by Swords.

The suit of Wands is usually depicted as sticks with sprouting leaves. This is a staff in the process of growth, or a magician's wand. Wands, or fire, represent the newness of life as a process of creativity; they are indicative of the evolutionary path of the spiritual self. The Wand is Moses's staff, for instance, which embodies the mystery of transformative spiritual power and magic.

The Cup, as pictured in the cards, is a vessel containing the nectar of life. The Cup represents the physical structure or material world through which the emotions flow. Cups, or water, signify the emotional or intuitive self washing over the world, dissolving and dispersing the baser elements in a process of purification. The Elixir of Life, the Holy Grail, the Communion chalice, and the Fountain of Youth—all of these are richly symbolic of the waters of life contained within the Cups.

The Pentacle, or Coin, a symbol of the element air and contrived by humans, is the currency of exchange between peoples. Out of primitive systems of barter and trade, the concept of money arose. Likewise, the air element resonates with concepts and systems formed through the mental activity of humans. The tarot as a system was conceived on the level of air. Pentacles express the flexible nature of humans and their ideas and point to their desire to order chaos through their inherent ingenuity. Thirty pieces of silver and "render unto Caesar" are two images of coins from biblical literature.

I'm aware that in many systems of rulership relating to the tarot, the suit of Coins is ascribed to the earth element and the suit of Swords is said to be ruled by air. My system is different from this in that it follows the system of astrologer and occultist C. C. Zain in his book *The Sacred Tarot,* where Coins are ruled by air and Swords by earth. The reasoning behind this is that in the Hindu *tattwa* system of philosophy, the air element is symbolized by a blue circle, and Coins, being circular, mirror this form. Also, money serves two main purposes: exchange and accumulation. The accumulation aspect of money is of an earthly nature most certainly, whereas money used for exchange is about relating, as in the passing of coins back and forth between people, a more airy activity, as air signifies relating and exchange. Money is not goods. Goods are earthly, yes, but money on the other hand is a concept invented by the mind (ruled by the air element)—it is born of thought processes, hence it belongs to the realm of air. The Sword, made of metal, sharpened to a point and honed to a cutting edge, is conceived as penetrating and slicing through the density of matter. The element earth, symbolized by the suit of Swords, displays its practicality. Early in humanity's emergence into a hostile world, the sword or its primitive equivalent permitted survival; thus by forming hard materials into weapons and hunting tools and later into agricultural implements, early peoples gained supremacy over their environment and whittled out a foundation on which to build. Swords are indeed evocative of the ultimate practicality of human nature. The sword is significant of both creative and destructive power. This is the sword, for instance, of Damocles, and Excalibur, King Arthur's magical sword.

Swords have in their symbology overtones of conflict, and the earth realm is the one filled with the most conflict, as it is the densest one. To penetrate this density, to see through the illusion of the earthly realm, requires the sharpness of a sword. Also, the form of a sword has a point at one end and at the other end the tip of the handle, with the hand guard forming two more points, making four points to mirror the four-sided yellow square that is the tattwa symbol for earth. It takes the sword's sharpness to cut through the thickness and darkness of earth, and this requires effort. Swords in this context may also be thought of as knives, just as pentacles may be thought of as round talismans that may be inscribed with magical pictures or symbols—once again, mental concepts.

At any rate, persuasive arguments certainly can be made for the opposite of what I've just said, reversing the elemental rulerships of the suits of Coins and Swords, so that Coins are ruled by the element earth and Swords by air. I consider these sorts of issues more stylistic considerations rather than matters of great importance. The kabbalistic approach would be inclined to say that both ways are valid, each yielding its own constellation of symbology, for Kabbalah maintains that everything is true, and it is interested in the relationships between all the parts of reality rather than rejecting any of them.

Ultimately what's most important is to understand the symbology you're working with and to be comfortable with it. If you feel more comfortable thinking of Coins/Pentacles as earth and Swords as air, then do so, for you can still use this book by simply using the card meanings I give for Coins to interpret the suit of Swords, and vice versa.

The irony of this issue is that the air element can signify a dualistic wavering back and forth (remember that Coins always have two sides), whereas the earth element can signify conflict, and so it seems somehow meaningful that this particular variance in rulership has arisen as the magi of the past have worked with the tarot.

The system using Coins as earth and Swords as air descends to us from the Celts, whereas the one using Coins as air and Swords as earth is from Vedic sources.

THE TAROT, THE TREE OF LIFE, AND THE CHAKRAS

Each suit of the minor arcana is composed of fourteen cards that fall into two categories, same as in an ordinary deck of cards: cards numbered 1 through 10 and four court cards. In tarot, the numbered cards correspond to the ten energy centers located in the core symbol of the kabbalistic tarot, which is the Tree of Life.

One of the key understandings of the tarot is that the twenty-two cards of the major arcana correspond to the twenty-two letters of the Hebrew alphabet. We do not know for sure exactly where the tarot came from, but we do know that it has always been closely associated with Kabbalah, the esoteric system that emerged with the ancient Hebrews. In Kabbalah there are rich associations surrounding all the Hebrew letters. Kabbalists believe that God created the letters first, and then it was the letters, which are living energies possessing consciousness, that became the tools he used to create everything else. So these letters are not just visually expressed concepts we use to communicate with, but actual living entities.

The ten energy centers that make up the Tree of Life are known as stations, or Sefirah. They correspond to the Sun, the Moon, and the eight planets. These ten centers are the planetary energy sources of our solar system (the macrocosm), which correspond to the energy centers called the chakras within the human body (the microcosm).

The numbered cards of the minor arcana are read by combining the meaning of the particular energy center, as shown by its number, with the meaning of the suit in which it's in, such as Wands or Coins, for instance.

Think of the stations on the Tree of Life as cities that pulsate with activity. These cities can be viewed from the top of a high building and seen wholistically as a network teeming with energy, but may also be seen by discerning the separate components of the city at work. The city has practical functions (earth = Swords), many complexes of systems (air = Pentacles), the pathos of the emotional relationships of its inhabitants (water = Cups), and spontaneous creativity everywhere at work (fire = Wands).

If a nation were compared to the Tree of Life and contained ten metropolitan centers as described, there would need to be some way of uniting the cities that for the nation's sake would permit a flow between them. Highways, railways, shipping lines, and air corridors have been devised for such purposes. Likewise in the Tree of Life, paths connect the ten stations, or Sefirot, thus forming a network of energy flow throughout the Tree. These arteries correspond to the twenty-two major arcana and channel the dynamic processes inherent within the body, the nation, and the solar system.

Whereas the four suits of the minor arcana represent the four elements, there's another element that has been perceived by sages of the past that transcends the other four in refinement. This fifth element corresponds to the major arcana as a whole, meaning that we can think of the entire major arcana as a fifth suit of the tarot. *Akasha* is the name some have given to this element. Akasha permeates all creation, as well as all the other elements, imbuing them with life. Its universal cosmic nature is the foundation of all else. The Greeks spoke of it as the *quintessence* (where *quint* means "five," and *essence* means "element"), referring to the ultimate substance of which the heavenly bodies are composed. This fifth element may be thought of as the perfect manifestation of God embodied in all creation. The major arcana, then, reflect the quintessential processes of universal order.

One of the primary concepts of the tarot is the inherent unity of the universe—the oneness of reality. Ultimately we must realize that the four physical elements are not four distinctly different things, but the same thing in different states. Thus ice is a solid, or earthly manifestation of water, whereas steam is an airy manifestation of it. The four elements are different levels of density, and density is an index of the amount of movement or excitation in matter. The less the movement, the greater the density.

The fifth element, the quintessence, or akasha, which means space, is the least dense. It's the subtlest level of physical reality yet the most powerful force in all creation. And because it's the least dense, it's the most active and hence the controlling factor of existence. From it is generated the energy known as *qi* (*chi*), which Eastern metaphysics says flows through and animates the entire human body and all living matter. Acupuncturists believe that all disease is caused by a damming up or blocking of this energy flow. The points or centers in the body where this can occur have the same relationship to the paths that qi takes through the human body as the relationship between the stations on the Tree of Life and the paths between them.

There are major and minor energy centers in the bodies of both humans and animals. These are the chakras. Vedic science says that there are seven major chakras as well as hundreds of minor ones. The Sanskrit word *chakra* means "wheel," and like a wheel, each energy center has a hub or vortex that generates a force field around it that spins the chakra. The Tree of Life has seven levels, which correspond to the seven major chakras. Some of these levels on the Tree consist of only one Sefirot while others have two. This accounts for there being ten Sefirah on the Tree and only seven major chakras.

The central idea of the tarot as well as the Tree of Life and the chakra system is *dynamic balance.* This is where evolution is taking us—to a complete dynamic balance of all energies and forces of the cosmos on both an individual microcosmic level, within each human being, as well as on a macrocosmic level. True balance is never static but always dynamic—a process rather than a product. Evolution never leads to an actual product that's permanently stable, but instead is aimed at kinetic harmony in which all elements operate together in beautiful perfection, and where change, death, and rebirth all dance together.

The universe is a growing work of art, always perfect and yet always reorganizing itself in terms of greater subtlety and coordination. Humans, as children of God, are co-creators in this process. They find themselves in a world of raw material they are learning how to work with, creating and destroying until the alchemical great work, or magnum opus, is complete. This great work involves spiritual transformation—the shedding of impurities, the overcoming of attachment to all polarities, and the refinement of materials. Exactly what the end result of this profound transformation may be varies according to different authors; it could be self-realization, union with divinity, escaping from the wheel of rebirth, or fulfillment of one's true purpose. In my opinion, all of these are different terms for the same thing: enlightenment. Completion of the great work will eventually lead to a cycle of nonmanifestation; this is the period, according to Vedic philosophy, when God rests, and then after a time awakens once again to begin all over the joyful cycle of play and creation.

THE LANGUAGE OF SPACE (AUI) AND THE TAROT

Finally, the most nontraditional aspect of this book on the tarot is the discussion of the Language of Space and how it relates to the tarot, found in chapter 18. This universal constructed language, known as aUI, was originally received from extraterrestrial beings by psychologist and linguist Dr. John Weilgart (1913–1981)* in the early 1950s.

The symbols depicted in the bottom right corner of each major arcana card depicted in this book are derived from this aUI language. The letters in the bottom middle of each major arcana card are the English letters that correspond to each card, and the letters in the bottom left corner of each major arcana card are the Hebrew letters that correspond to each card. In the same way that the major arcana have been associated with the letters of the Hebrew alphabet for centuries, I include this information about aUI in this book because I feel it helps to explain deeper and finer meanings of the cards, and provides you with a contemplative tool that is cosmic and uplifting, should you wish to delve more deeply into the esoteric message of the tarot.

Although Dr. Weilgart knew little about traditional occultism or the tarot per se, he was a giant of modern metaphysics, and his work is a fine example of the power of intuitive knowledge.

Many people who think of themselves as occultists are not really researchers, but rather just collectors of information. They read one another's works, and many of them are willing to read and believe anything so long as it has the occult label. The true occultist uses outer learning as a means to stimulate, guide, and enhance their inner knowing. We may think of Dr. Weilgart as a psychologist and linguist, but his real nature is that of a mystic in the deepest sense of the word.

Dr. Weilgart created aUI because he wanted to return language back to the root meanings of sounds themselves. Even though he wasn't schooled in conventional metaphysical thought, his work is an astounding breakthrough. aUI is based on sound. The correspondences between the sound of each letter and the meaning of that sound, which he came up with intuitively, enhance the traditional meanings of the letters of the Hebrew alphabet, which were given to us by ancient sages and which correspond to the twenty-two cards of the major arcana.

---

*Biographies of Dr. Weilgart can be found in *Leaders in American Science* and *Who's Who in American Education*. During his lifetime he was awarded the honorary title of Psychologist-in-Chief for the United Nations.

Dr. Weilgart calls the mouth "a sounding cave of wind and wave." The wind is the air moving through the vocal chords, and the wave is the tongue. The interrelations of their movements are a dance, and each gesture is symbolic. He starts with the idea that the linguistic sounds the voice makes are not just something arbitrary, but actually have meanings in and of themselves, and are based on the physical structure of the mouth—lips, tongue, teeth, palate, throat, and so on—and what those organs signify metaphysically. For instance, in English we have the words *dog, door,* and *duty.* They are related in that they all begin with the letter *d,* but to us the *d* sound is just an arbitrary convention. Dr. Weilgart starts from the premise that *d* always means "through," because it lies on the throughway between the deeper parts of the mouth (palate and throat) and the front and outer parts of the mouth, which are the teeth and the tongue. And so in aUI we have such words as *dav* (*d* = through, *a* = space, *v* = power; and so *dav* means "to go"). Having letters associated with specific meanings in aUI (like *d* always meaning "through") makes it so much easier to know what an aUI word means—if you know what the individual letters of aUI mean, you can look at how they are ordered in a word and often guess the word's meaning from that.

Dr. Weilgart told me that this language was given to him when he was a young boy by a green elf-like humanoid from outer space, so that the people of Earth would have an easy and effective way to communicate with all beings from other worlds. The little green space man told Weilgart that aUI was the universal language used by intelligent beings on all planets throughout the cosmos. In other words, aUI is an intergalactic language. As such, tuning in to each one of the aUI sounds associated with each major arcanum becomes another way to tune in to the vibration of that arcanum. This opens up tarot meanings that go beyond Earth history and lore to connect the tarot with meanings even more universal and inclusive than just terrestrial experience.

The ancient Hebrews believed that every letter of their alphabet has a particular vibration that corresponds to a number and a meaning. Dr. Weilgart's language is based on the same premise—that every letter expresses one of the root forces of the universe—but rather than being just an alternate system, aUI redefines for modern humanity the manifestation of God that emanates from sound. Exploring this relationship between sound and the deeper meanings of letters—be they English, Hebrew, or aUI letters—as they relate to the forces of the universe can deepen our understanding of the tarot.

SUMMARY OF "THE NATURE OF THE TAROT"

[I] The tarot is a *complete system,* which reflects both the evolutionary process of humans (microcosm) and the Universe (macrocosm). Greater self-knowledge may be attained through the study of this system as we achieve deeper insight and understanding by ascending to the subtler levels of the tarot.

[II] The tarot is comprised of seventy-eight cards. The two divisions of the deck are the twenty-two *major arcana* (mysteries) and the 56 *minor arcana.*

[III] The major arcana are dualistic in nature since each card is comprised of pairs of opposite concepts. The power of these cards resides in their dynamic quality, which creates a flow of energy and effects a balance between these polarized concepts.

[IV] The minor arcana are comprised of four suits that correspond to the four elements found in nature. Each of these elements is symbolic of a state of reality as we experience it; fire is represented by the suit of *Wands* and signifies pure creativity, spiritual transcendence, and newborn life; water is represented by *Cups* and signifies emotions, intuitional or astral experiences, and the universalizing nature of reality; air is represented by the suit of *Pentacles* or *Coins* and signifies mental activity, flexibility, and value systems; earth is represented by the suit of *Swords* and signifies ultimate practicality, material concerns, and sometimes affliction.

[V] The Tree of Life is the major symbol associated with the tarot. It depicts a tree with ten stations corresponding to the heavenly bodies in astrology and also to the chakras. Twenty-two paths connect the energy centers and are ruled by the major arcana. The major arcana may be understood as representative of the *quintessence* or life force.

MEET THE CARDS

The Oracles of Hermes

We start out by setting the tone for the rest of this book, for in all beginnings is planted the seed of all that is to unfold.

Each of the twenty-two major arcana cards is home to a great consortium of spirit beings of many different kinds: angels; plant, number, and gem devas; fairies; gnomes; salamanders; undines; elves; and trolls. These beings love to speak to our souls and use the great wealth of their creative resources to continually find new ways to connect to our human realm.

The great god Hermes of Greek mythology, who is said to have invented language and the alphabet as well as the art and science of healing, and who is known in Egypt as the god Thoth, is the author of this "Book of Moveable Pages" that we call the tarot, as well as the author of *The Emerald Tablet,* that shortest and greenest of alchemy texts. My own guides have told me that the tarot as a deck of cards was first put together in the city of Fez in Morocco, and that the ideas contained in it predate Egyptian history by a very long time. The Kabbalah states that the letters of the Hebrew alphabet were the first things to be created, and that it was these letters that then created the rest of creation. This set of twenty-two Hebrew letters are, in fact, the major arcana, which were later turned into cards with pictures on them to describe the individual essence of each one of them.

The Emerald Tablet is a short and cryptic alchemical writing that is said to have been inscribed on an emerald, a gem sacred to Mercury (the Roman version of Hermes), and was buried with Thoth when they laid him in his tomb. If you wish to read a translation of it you can find it online. It contains the famous aphorism "That which is above is as that which is below," which is a way of saying that heaven reflects Earth, and that our outer experience reflects our inner experience, and vice versa. You can think of the tarot as another version of *The Emerald Tablet,* for they both contain the same knowledge, but in different forms. I refer to *The Emerald Tablet* (and the tarot as well) as a "green" alchemical text because all the wisdom and knowledge contained in both works was discovered by the ancients as they observed how energies interact with one another in the natural world, and especially how numbers interact with one another, for even though numbers are in a sense abstract, they are also the basis for all natural phenomena. All branches of science depend on them.

The whole of this book you are now reading was made to hold the energy of the tarot, so that as you proceed through it your conscious mind will absorb its concepts; but I also hope that your inner knowing will resonate with this magical system. In essence, this book is meant as a tool for vibrational healing, and the tarot spirits hope that reading it will bring peace and light to your consciousness.

As you read the following twenty-two oracles, one for each of the major arcana, note those meanings that especially resonate for you, for whatever attracts you is always what you need. As time goes by, go back and read them again and see if what you're drawn to has changed.

Also I want you to know that I am the person who channeled these oracles. They first came through me in 1976, when the first version of this book was published, and very speedily—over a period of about two hours. When I was preparing this present edition for publication I was encouraged by the spirits who had helped me originally and assisted me in adding to what I had previously written to both clarify and enrich the descriptions. I cannot tell you exactly how much of this information came from me and how much came from the spirits who spoke to me (and are continuing to do so), and so I think of these descriptions as not coming solely from myself or other entities, but rather the result of a process of co-authoring. I have had many visions of how, as the New Age unfolds, humans will be doing more and more of this kind of co-creating with the wise ones of the spiritual realms. Increasingly it will become our way of tuning in to cosmic harmony and taking our place among the more advanced cultures of the cosmos, with which we are, in these times, making closer and closer contact.

THE ORACLE DECK

The major arcana cards depicted in an earlier version of this book were originally drawn in the 1970s by Klaus Zalinskis, who, at the time, was a student at the Kansas City Art Institute and a student of myself and fellow metaphysician Ronn Ballard. The illustrations have been re-done for this book by a South Korean artist named Daehee Son. I have named the major arcana cards in this book the Azoth Deck, as "azoth" refers to the spirit and energy of the planet Mercury, who in Egypt was the god Thoth, who was the inventor of the alphabet—the tarot being an alphabet of spiritual forces.

The names I give to many of the cards in this book, which vary from the traditional, more widely-used names for the cards, reflect aspects of the cards' energies that I feel are important to focus on. There are no right or wrong names for the cards, for names are labels, and each different label one can give a card can express a different facet of it. An example is The Devil, the traditional name given to Arcanum XV. I prefer not to use this name because it tends to give the person who encounters this card a negative feeling toward it. The great metaphysician Emanuel Swedenborg (1688–1772) refers to demons as "the judges and bailiffs of the universe," so we might call Arcanum XV The Judge. I have instead chosen the name The Musician for Arcanum XV to emphasize how the planet Saturn (the planet corresponding to this card) brings all energies into a state of greater harmony—though if there is much deeply ingrained discord in a person's being the path toward harmony can be fraught with great pain and suffering. In Vedic astrology Saturn is thought of as the most spiritual planet. The purpose of this most spiritual of planets is to reflect back to us the state of our inner harmony, or discord, so that we can know ourselves more completely and come into alignment with divine harmony. I feel that this energy in the past came to be thought of as demonic because people had a great fear of having to confront their own discord. This is one example of how the names of the cards function. If you prefer to think of any or all of the cards as having other names than the ones I include, it's fine to do so. If you are open to thinking of the cards as having multiple names, then that's good too. Later in this book I will say more about the different names and what they reveal.

Regarding the symbols in the border of each major arcanum card in this book: In the bottom left corner are the Hebrew letters associated with each arcanum. You needn't try to pronounce them, as many people do not know this language. But the kabbalists of antiquity tell us that we can take in the spiritual energy of these letters just by gazing at them—something that can be nice to do as you do readings—as a means of tuning in to the cards psychically. In the bottom middle of each card are the letters of the English alphabet associated with each arcanum. Note that some of these are double letters, since the English letter correspondences stem from the transliteration of Hebrew into English. This aspect of transliteration is also why the English letters don't proceed in the order of the English alphabet as the cards proceed numerically (for example, Arcanum III is associated with the English letter *G*, rather than *C*). In the top middle of each card is the Roman numeral that shows you the numerical value of the card, and if you aren't into Roman numerals you will find the Arabic number for the card in the top left corner. You can use these letters and numbers to convert letters into numbers and numbers into letters as you explore the meanings of different tarot cards during tarot readings and as you get to know the cards. In the bottom right corner of each card you will find the aUI symbol, which is the letter equivalent for the card in aUI. This symbol can also be gazed at too, to tune you into the various vibrations of the arcana. And last but certainly not least, in the top right corner of each card we find the astrological glyph associated with each arcanum—ten planet glyphs and twelve zodiac sign glyphs, corresponding to the twenty-two major arcana.

I. THE MESSENGER (THE MAGUS)

Come away from the past as well as the future. The present is the gold you seek and also an elusive nothingness, a dividing time, a chameleon forever changing. Capture it and recapture it if it slips away. Look neither backward nor forward, or else the gold of the present moment will escape you.

Above all, take everything as it comes. Life's a journey, its destination neither more nor less important than each moment's passing scenery. Every moment and every step is a destination.

The journey to Paradise is Paradise itself.

II. THE GUARDIAN OF THE GATE (VEILED ISIS)

Be watchful of what you "eat," whether it be food, thoughts, emotions, concepts, or vibrations. The mind and heart can be poisoned as easily as the stomach. Consider diet on all levels. You are what you eat. Should you choose to be wise, consume wisdom. Should you desire to be loving, feed on love.

III. THE QUEEN MOTHER (ISIS UNVEILED)

Act, and do not stop. Rejoice in the creative act more than in what you create. Love the doing's every moment rather than just the final accomplishment. Move with life's flow. It's better to travel the wrong road than to sit and wait at the crossroads.

IV. THE COMMANDER (THE SOVEREIGN)

Take charge of your realm. Map out kingdoms and conquer. The smallest challenge you overcome becomes a precious jewel, sparkling in God's eye. Befriend your desires, for if you ignore them they'll grow into fiery dragons. Tame them. Harness them. Beseech them nicely to do your bidding. They will rejoice in working for you.

V. THE PENTAGRAM (THE HIEROPHANT)

Feel your common ground with all life. You're an instrument of evolution, and evolution's a choir. Improvise songs wherever you go. Listen with crystalline ears to nature's melodies and to the countermelodies of the spirit realms singing forever with and within you.

Listen to and play at the same time the old music and improvisations as well, which are forever new. This is the key to harmony.

VI. THE CROSSROADS (THE TWO PATHS)

You always stand at a crossroads. You always have a choice. Find love and beauty in the higher realms and draw it down into yourself in ever-increasing abundance. Seek inner guidance for your choosing, for sometimes the most difficult path brings greatest value, while at other times the path of ease benefits most. Inner knowing lights the way.

VII. THE VICTORY (THE CONQUEROR)

Denial's sword cuts you free. Always refuse the lesser, and the greater will draw you up. Seek the gold of the highest thought shining in every idea, and victory will be yours in every action.

Your life is your friend, and when you see it with fresh eyes you become an adventurer in a foreign country.

VIII. THE BALANCE (JUSTICE)

Learn when not to react, and consider your action before you act. Life is giving and taking in balance. Should you always consider giving, you'll never lack in receiving. Make much from little, as flowers are made from air, light, and dirt.

Know that all that comes your way is a gift, though sometimes gifts are disguised as hard lessons.

IX. THE SEEKER
(THE SAGE)

If you seek for something particular, be it large or small, you're certain to find it eventually; but seek with a mind open to whatever it finds, and you'll discover everything. Be open so that your path will be lit by your inner light.

Think of and see friends everywhere. Each star is your friend. Light knows no remoteness.

X. THE CYCLE
(THE WHEEL)

The wheel of life is a storm, and stillness lies in its eye. The universe is a wheel, and inspiration waits at its center. The farther from the center you venture, the swifter and more chaotic the currents become. Strength is at the center, weakness at the edge. The hub is within you; shine the star of consciousness on this point of power.

XI. THE MAIDEN (THE ENCHANTRESS)

Gentleness accomplishes all. Delicacy is life's ultimate power. Tread softly, go peacefully, and you may journey anywhere, even on the surface of water and through walls. Become stiller and stiller to hear the voice of Spirit clearer and clearer.

It's all you, the whole luminous cloud of it, the only edges being those you imagine.

XII. THE DEVOTEE (THE MARTYR)

So many hidden knots inside, so many ties, so many bonds and binds no longer needed. Relax and let them go. Relax—give up control. Then the waters of love flood in, as more and more clearly you hear your true self's music, the dissolver of all illusion. In this way the fruit of you ripens and you drop your seeds, your one becoming many.

XIII. THE RAINBOW (THE REAPER)

Growth is only painful for those who strive against its potent current. Let change happen. Embrace it. Fear not death's face—it's but the mask that birth wears.

Seek new horizons before you, rejoicing in whatever disappears behind you as you move forth.

Soar like the rainbow whose life is often brief, except at the waterfall, where it waits, invisible, for the Sun's appearance.

XIV. THE ALCHEMIST (TEMPERANCE)

Remember, all buildings are built stone by stone. Work steadily and do not strive against slowness as the work proceeds, for sometimes offspring need time as a source of nourishment.

Work with patient diligence, like rocks that sit in the stream, parting the waters. Let your formulas change like waters, taking on arctic or tropical forms as needed.

XV. THE MUSICIAN (THE BLACK MAGICIAN)

Be like the stars; look into the darkness. Like the stars, look in all directions. Sometimes seeing takes light years. Sometimes the music is slow—a single note sounding a lifetime. But listen with your inner ears and you will hear the whole song with your heart; you will hear the akashic fugues of your music, music composed by you over many lifetimes.

XVI. THE PYRAMID
(THE POWER)

Whatever is stored away returns at last. Even a tomb grows bored and seeks an archaeologist.

It seems that lightning is new, a sudden thought blurted out by the sky; but lightning's an ancient sword that polishes itself in the using.

The forms of mind rise up and are destroyed, but mind is never ruined, only cleared with repeated washings until it comes from the vat of akasha, shining with unblemishable clarity.

XVII. THE LIGHT (THE STAR)

So many countless wavelengths, so many species of light. So many spectrums to roam. For the mind's darkness sees the night sky as a labyrinth of confusions, ways to nowhere. How can we ever find a certain path?

Then, sensing something within, we open our inner eyes and find in the dark a magic star of indescribable color, whose miracle is all colors and yet white, whose light nourishes with its galactic milk.

O light of the Inner Star, always within! Light of imagination undoing all the chaos of darkness!

XVIII. THE NIGHT (THE MOON)

Emerging from waters of sleep, a creature seeks home. That creature is you, your steps making a road beneath the full Moon. Seek home, nourishment, and places of protection.

Everywhere dogs of light and shadow roam. Some show you ways of brightness, others tempt with food that is not food. The light of the Moon is dim and sometimes shows "friends" who are not actual friends. It makes illusions walk the land.

If you come to live in your heart, then any outer abode will also serve, but first your home must be within you. Then those plays of light and shade will turn to fascination without confusion, proliferating wondrous roads.

XIX. THE DANCE (THE SUN)

Reflect the stars. Be a mirror redirecting the light. The Sun adores the lion, for it's the Sun's mirror, for both shine bright—the Sun bright with light, the lion alchemist turning the light into the gold of love.

The world is your stage. You act in the mystery play, feeding the audience with light.

XX. THE AWAKENING (THE SARCOPHAGUS)

Whatever comes up is what needs to come up. Be with whatever presents itself; observe its rising, and if it obstructs, observe the stasis. Let your attention be soft as the light of the Moon, for attention is your magic elixir. Your simple, direct observing, free of judgment, has the power to free you from all illusions.

Whatever returns again and again is seeking release. Have patience with such returns. It's easy to welcome whatever you love and enjoy. But also welcome as much as you can all sorrows and hardships, for they have the power to teach and connect you more deeply to all that is.

XXI. THE LORD OF THE DANCE (THE ADEPT)

Everywhere is gold. Some things, like the Sun, seem great and powerful, and so they are. But each dandelion in a field is also a Sun, and so are all the stars. Everything is important, rejoicing in the fullness and richness of its meaning. The lesser alchemist tries to make gold, but the greater one discovers it everywhere.

Whatever meanings you find and whatever uses you put them to are your own, for your attention shines on the gold that is found everywhere. Let it naturally select whatever it discovers.

XXII. THE TRAVELER (THE FOOL)

Vague? Insecure? Unsure? Wait, watch, and listen. The universe moves in and through you. If lost, you may find your way in no time. Cease thought and all becomes clear. Shut your eyes to the world and see it as is. Your blindness can be a magic, luminous light. See what it reveals.

PART ONE

The Major Arcana

CHAPTER ONE

The Four Elements and Major Arcana I–IV

In the eternity before creation, God was all there was. Because of this, the old scholars ask the question, "Since God was everything and everywhere, how could creation even appear?" Logically it seems there would be no room for creation to even exist. Some have thought that God created the universe out of him-, her-, or itself. Others have answered this conundrum by saying that God withdrew—pulled his, her, or its energy back so as to create an empty or conceptual space in which creation could happen. Technically, in what is known as the Lurianic Kabbalah, after Rabbi Isaac Luria (1534–1572), considered the most original and visionary of the theosophical kabbalists, this contraction is called the *tzimtzum*. This separation, then, between God and God's conceptual space, created a duality that naturally leads us to Arcanum II, The Guardian of the Gate/Veiled Isis.

But back to Arcanum I, The Messenger/The Magus. The number 1 is most like the element of fire, for fire is the lightest of the four elements. In fact, we might say that fire consists of two aspects: heat and light. The heat part is the earthly part. The light part is the heavenly part. Arcanum I is ruled by Mercury, representing the mind, the source of all our light and creativity. When we use the word *mind* to describe the energy of this card, we are not referring solely to the conscious mind, but also (and mainly) to the intuitive mind, which has created the vast and elaborate structure of our body and nervous system, together with all those etheric and unseen parts that animate us. This mind is our creative spirit and a part of all that is, or God. Maharishi Mahesh Yogi liked to call it "Creative Intelligence," and we use that term frequently throughout this book.

Arcanum I is the key to everything. To embrace the powers of this arcanum is to have access to all knowledge and wisdom that comes to us through inspiration. All we need do if we want to evolve is to cultivate our receptivity to this. Arcanum I is the ultimate seed of the Tree of Life, and what I have just described is the answer that lies within that seed, the answer to all questions and the solution to all problems.

Arcanum II, The Guardian of the Gate/Veiled Isis, ruled by Virgo, signifies relativity, all dualities, and hence all limitations. One of the greatest secrets of Kabbalah is this: through limitations we learn and grow, for limitations restrict us, and by pushing back against these restrictions we exercise our soul, which causes our light to burn brighter and brighter, until at last all restrictions fall away because we then no longer need them. Arcanum II most relates to the element of air, which feeds the fire.

Arcanum III, The Queen Mother/Isis Unveiled, is 1 plus 2, or mind (1) encountering dualities and restrictions (2), which is what relating (Arcanum III) is all about. Hence Arcanum III concerns *attention,* which is the mind focusing its energy on the limited phenomenal world around it.

Deepak Chopra has aptly expressed the secret of Arcanum III in this simple and beautiful statement: "You become what you focus on." Arcanum III most relates to the element of water, which signifies the emotions.

Think of how water, in its undisturbed state, is a natural mirror, and how when you look into it there are three things present: the you who is looking, your image looking back, and the reflective medium of the surface of the water, which provides you with a point of contact with your image. Arcanum III is about all our projections, for it is through projecting that we relate.

And then we come to Arcanum IV, The Commander/The Sovereign. The number 4 signifies the four elements, whose interaction with one another creates phenomenal reality, with all its striving and stresses. This reality provides a vehicle or matrix in which creative expression can occur. It gives rise to all the kingdoms of nature—plant, animal, and mineral, as well as many other unseen realms, such as the fairy, astral, and spirit kingdoms. Arcanum IV most relates to the earth element, which needs the other three elements to thrive.

In everything that's said throughout this book about the cards you're likely to find seeming inconsistencies, which are actually the basis of the tarot's poetry. The more you study it, though, the more I hope you'll see that these inconsistencies are actually deeply harmonious—or we could say wonderfully dissonant. This is because the tarot mirrors physical reality, which appears to be fraught with inconsistencies—such as how a light beam can crash into a mirror at 186,000 miles a second without harming it, and not only that, but immediately change direction without losing acceleration, take off in a new direction, and plunge into your eye. This is what happens when you look into a mirror that is directed at the night sky. To me, this is a phenomenon so bizarre I'm not surprised that science has yet to completely figure out what light is.

I wish, reader, that you take in my words with more than your rational mind. Allow what I say to enter your being as poetry, and though your logical mind may want to pore over the words, do not be disturbed by what you don't understand at first, for these inconsistencies can be openings to the deeper meanings lurking in all things. Let them work on you, and see what they might eventually create.

And now let's look at the first four major arcana individually.

ARCANUM I: THE MESSENGER (THE MAGUS)

Alternate names: The Juggler, The Magician
Number: 1
Planet: Mercury
Anatomy: thyroid
English letter: A
Flower: lavender, cilantro, peppermint
Angel: Gabriel
Color: purple, lavender

The Messenger/The Magus signifies the mind. It shows a magician standing before a wall with engravings. In his right hand is an upraised wand. His left hand points to the ground. He's the Egyptian god Thoth, known for the invention of the alphabet and numbers. To the Greeks he was the messenger god Hermes, and to the Romans, Mercury.

This card brings together the opposite ideas of unity and diversity. The mind, like quicksilver, which is the planet Mercury's traditional metal, is fluid at room temperature. The mind is the unifier of all realities. Through its flexibility and incessant activity it connects diverse ideas.

This card is often pictured with four implements laid out on the top of a stone cube. In this deck we see they are depicted on the wall behind the magician, with two on either side of him. These implements represent the magician's tools, which are the four suits of the tarot: a Wand, a Sword, a Cup, and a Pentacle. The magician coordinates, controls, and directs the forces of the four elements, as symbolized by these objects. In other depictions this magician stands ready to immerse himself in activity before the stone cube, which connotes the tangible and limited world of matter. The four implements are different aspects of this realm. The wand that the magician holds in his hand is symbolic of the quintessence, the fifth element—pure energy—with which he harmonizes the four lower elements.

In some decks this arcanum has been titled The Juggler, a name that has come down to us from tarot decks of the Middle Ages. The Juggler is a skillful person balancing and directing the active flow of the elements.

The mind is not depicted here as a thing that has parts, but rather as a focus moving through time and space—the attention. The art of juggling proves the importance of attention. One's attention is capable of seeing both the whole and the parts of a thing at the same time. The aspirant who wishes to begin to speed up their own evolution must first become aware of the nature and power of attention. The inability to focus one's attention is the single biggest obstacle to completing the magnum opus, or great work, of alchemy.

Some schools that teach metaphysical practices, such as meditation, astral travel, energy healing, and so forth, have tried to control the attention through concentration, which merely tires the mind and renders it less flexible. Other schools use contemplation, which, though effective on its own terms, doesn't really allow the mind to experience the subtlest level of reality at its core. The attention must be allowed to flow, and yet must be given something that will naturally attract it to deeper levels, like a magnet. Mantras can be such magnets.

The thyroid, which is the gland corresponding to this card, governs the speed at which bodily processes occur and so may be likened to a type of physical attention. If the thyroid is sluggish, the body does not pay attention to itself, and things like chronic colds and flu and a myriad of other pathologies can then take hold.

It is the present that is the source of creation, but the mind, unfortunately, likes to drift back into memories of the past or wander into fantasies of the future. It avoids the power of the present, possibly because in lower states of consciousness the body and its baggage of stored thoughts, emotions, and memories is not yet ready to handle this power.

Mercury is the eternal child who enjoys playing and exploring, even if it may mean getting into trouble—an unruly child, who, like the mind, likes to play tricks on us.

Occult doctrine holds that all things are alive. The average person thinks of aliveness as something that only plants and animals have, but the occultist sees life in all matter, even in time and space. Since God is infinite and everywhere at once, then everything must be alive. Such things as places, moments, and even concepts are just as alive as material beings.

Because of the principle that everything derives from mind, when we refer to Arcanum I as *mind,* we're referring to anything that can be conceptualized, rather than just the limited idea of thought as a biological process.

Usually The Magus is shown with one hand pointing up and one pointing down. This connects him or her to both heaven (the realm of abstraction) and earth (the realm of the tangible). It's mind that relates these two principles. Note that the concepts of high and low are associated with Arcanum I, whereas the concept of inner and outer is associated with Arcanum II.

High-low describes the interaction of forces in terms of different levels of being, whereas inner-outer signifies the interaction of forces that all exist on the same level. Veiled Isis, Arcanum II, guards the doors of a temple. The door is that point of passage between the inner and the outer. The veil she wears separates her face from the outside world.

It's also significant that The Magus is depicted standing. The three primary postures of a human being are lying, sitting, and standing. Lying is passive and unconscious, sitting is passive and conscious, and standing is active and conscious. The fourth possible state of mind is active-unconscious, which is the state of meditation. The Magus stands because he or she is ready for action.

Most journey myths originating in every corner of the globe begin with the arrival of a messenger, and this messenger can usually be construed as having been sent by the gods. The Christian and Jewish faiths have always spoken of angels being sent by God in order to relate a message from God to a chosen person. Mary, the mother of Jesus, was so honored, as were the shepherds later. The Bible is filled with such happenings. Within the context of the journey motif, angels represent the liaison between God and a favored person. As liaison, the messenger is actually communicating a call to adventure from a higher source. This call alerts the favored person to prepare for the journey, which is about to begin.

Arcanum I is ruled by the planet Mercury. Mercury, in Roman mythology, and his counterpart, Hermes, in Greek mythology, was the messenger of the gods. The Olympians would send him from the home of the gods with a message for a person living below. He was thought of by these cultures as the liaison between the mortal world and the worlds inhabited by the great immortals. His appearance was similar to that of the angels in that he also had wings, although his wings were described as being attached to his feet, which denotes swiftness.

The call to adventure within mythology is found in stories from all cultures, whether they are religious in nature or not (as in children's fairy tales). For instance, we're all familiar with the rabbit in *Alice in Wonderland*. What was the rabbit in the context of that tale other than a messenger who came to Alice to "awaken" her so that she might begin her incredible journey? He did not consciously mean to introduce Alice to her adventure, but nevertheless, he did. We know from this and many similar stories that the messenger is very often unaware of the role he or she has been sent (by a higher force) to play.

Experience teaches us that often we encounter someone who, for a brief moment and without their knowledge, changes the course of our life. This lack of conscious motivation doesn't make them any less an instrument or messenger from a higher source.

What the messenger actually says or does is not necessarily of the utmost importance; the importance, rather, lies in the fact that after the encounter with the messenger, the person's life has changed. This encounter can be described as changing the person's center of gravity, or pointing and directing the person toward a new world, a world that the person perhaps looks at in an entirely new way, or a subtle and indescribable way, or from some new perspective.

The adventure compels the person to work through a series of tests and challenges in order to learn, grow, and evolve to a higher level of consciousness. In a very real sense the message brought by the messenger summons the person to embrace their destiny.

At times, the messenger's function does not end with the call to adventure, but continues along with the person throughout their journey, or at least far enough into their journey so that the person is firmly grounded on the proper path. In this manner the messenger becomes a guide. In some myths this guidance comes in the form of a teacher, a ferryman, or a conductor of souls. In various meditation techniques the concept of the spiritual guide can be found. For instance, in the discipline of astral travel or projection, normally a guide is summoned from a higher or more spiritual plane to conduct the astral body through its journey.

I've engaged in this description of the role of messengers to show their diversity, as well as to give you an idea of how elusive they often are. Of all the cards of the tarot, I think Arcanum I may be the most difficult to describe, for as soon as we capture its essence it flits away and must be recaptured. In a profound sense this is the process of evolution, for the messenger is our attention, which we continue to capture and recapture over and over again until the moment of our enlightenment, when we finally emerge into completeness.

ARCANUM II: THE GUARDIAN OF THE GATE (VEILED ISIS)

Alternate names: The High Priestess, The Papess, The Female Pope
Number: 2
Sign: Virgo
Anatomy: intestines
English letter: B
Flower: centaury, green rose
Angel: Metatron
Color: yellow-green

Arcanum II, The Guardian of the Gate/Veiled Isis, is ruled by the sign Virgo, which has to do with work, problem-solving, and analysis. Virgo desires perfection and therefore can be a fault-finder, a nitpicker, or a microscope addict, because if we're going to perfect anything we need to first assess what's wrong with it. Virgo also wants to divide things, to take them apart to see how they work so that any problems they might have can be located and solved. This sign rules forensics.

Virgo also rules details. Through generality we approach universality, but through details we see particulars. Virgo is naturally drawn to perceiving differences in things, no matter how small these differences may be. It's the multitude of differences that any one thing can have from another that makes it unique. If Creative Intelligence is a unified entity, then certainly separateness is the greatest mystery of creation. The number of this Arcanum is II because Virgo thinks of everything in terms of dualities, the most common one probably being perfect versus imperfect.

What's highly important are the standards that Virgo adopts to determine what perfection is. If we define perfection as modifying anything in such a way that it furthers our spiritual evolution, then we're on the right track and in harmony with the patterns and forces of Creative Intelligence. Virgo, though, can get into trouble when any lesser standards are believed in, such as those that mainly serve the ego or that are embraced in an attempt to quell negative emotions such as fear or feeling worthless, or any attempt to escape feelings of guilt.

Arcanum II rules assimilation, meaning taking in and fully understanding information or ideas, or taking in and fully digesting food or nutrients. We've come into this life to assimilate our experiences, and since they are food for us as well, we want to assimilate whatever in them is nourishing and excrete or let go of the parts we don't need. This is why Virgo rules the lower digestive system, for the intestines are where physical assimilation happens.

Ultimately, the most important duality we deal with in life is the difference between outer and inner experience. Unfortunately, most of us are taught from birth that outer experience is all-important and inner experience is something to ignore when you can and cope with as best you can otherwise. One of the greatest secrets of metaphysics is that it is inner experience that creates outer experience, for we create our own reality through our beliefs. It is the hiddenness of this truth that is expressed by the goddess in this card wearing a veil. As we grow in consciousness we come to see through this veil more and more, for the veil symbolizes not only the truth just mentioned, but all illusions that we've generated through our beliefs.

The Egyptian goddess depicted here is Isis, the mother of Thoth. The connection between Isis and Thoth (the Egyptian equivalent of the Roman god Mercury and the Greek god Hermes) has been preserved in astrology by making Mercury, the planet corresponding to Arcanum I, the ruler of the sign Virgo.

It's an interesting coincidence that the transliteration of the Egyptian name of this goddess of duality, Isis, has come down to us in English in the form of the word *is* written twice—a double affirmation of the truth of being and of the nature of Arcanum II.

Aleister Crowley referred to her as the "Priestess of the Silver Star," since the Moon, which is usually shown on this card, corresponds to the metal silver. In earlier times all the planets were referred to as stars, including the Sun and the Moon. Because the Moon is depicted on this card, many writers have said that it is ruled by the Moon. Note that the numerological value of the Moon, which is Arcanum XX, The Sarcophagus/The Awakening, is 20, which reduces to 2 (2 + 0 = 2), so that Veiled Isis (numerological value 2) and The Sarcophagus (ruled by the Moon, numerological value 20), have a close affinity.

This card is the Virgin Mary in Christian symbology, she who was perfected such that she could give birth to the living God. Arcanum II also symbolizes the Tree of Life: the two columns on either side of Isis are the two sides of the Tree, and she herself symbolizes the stations on the Tree that form the middle column. (A detailed discussion of the Tree of Life is found in chapters 8 and 9).

A key word for this card is *assimilation,* which is the act of taking in or digesting something after it has been completely broken down. Assimilation is a facet of destruction, the numerological meaning here being that the only way the 1 can be attained is through the destruction of the 2. Assimilation is linked to the idea of feeding, because any pair of opposites are incomplete when separated; they need to feed off of each other for sustenance.

The flower essence corresponding to Arcanum II is centaury, which protects us from the desires others project onto us. It supports our ability to say no when we need to, and to not put ourself in a subservient role when it does not serve the higher good.

Arcanum II can signify the crossing of a threshold that separates the world of duality, otherwise known as "reality," from the more mysterious world of the coming adventure as signified by the rest of the cards. Though this threshold is described in a multitude of ways in various myths, it is always symbolic of a gate or threshold through which the person must pass.

This passing through a gate is quite often traumatic to the person, since it literally describes a separation from the secure and common experiential world that they're familiar with. To represent the traumatizing experience of crossing the threshold, the gate is usually guarded by a fearsome creature like a dragon, three-headed dog, or some such monster, who puts the person through a test or series of tests. The aspirant to the journey must prove their worthiness for undertaking the task by passing these tests, for only the most worthy should continue, and the land of this journey should never be entered by the fainthearted.

Outwardly, the meaning of Arcanum II is duality, and therefore it represents the outer world. Yet this card also can be defined as mystery, as it hides the path to perfection. For the aspirant to attain perfection they must first pass beyond the world of dualism. Interpreting this in terms of a biblical metaphor, ever since Adam and Eve were expelled from the Garden of Eden humanity has aspired to pass through the gate that guards that garden, which was and is still the symbol of perfection. (The snake, which is humanity's original undoing, is a symbol of the material world, and even its two-pronged forked tongue speaks of duality.) The gates of paradise, after the expulsion of Adam and Eve, were guarded by angels.

The figure pictured in Arcanum II is usually sitting between a black pillar and a white pillar, which represents the gate. In our deck is the Egyptian goddess Isis, and in the context of this card she is veiled. Through an obvious interpretation of her veil we can ascertain that something about her is hidden, and thus she represents the mysterious. However, we can look at her veil in another way, as if it were a disguise, and when we perceive it this way it's possible to see that she may appear to the aspirant in any mode she chooses: a fearsome dragon, a beautiful maiden, an old crone, or a beggar.

In *Alice in Wonderland,* Alice first falls through a hole in the ground and passes through a chamber where everything seemed to be in a state of disorientation; then she comes to a small door through which she cannot pass because of its smallness in relation to her largeness (the size issue being a dualistic concept). Even though there is no visible guardian at this gate or door, Alice has to undergo several tests and is given instructions from several sources.

In the Greek stories of the soul's journey to the underworld, the gate is guarded by the three-headed dog Cerberus, its three heads representing the realms of earth, air, and water, while the fourth realm or element is represented by the underworld itself, since Hades burns with eternal fire.

Another story about a gate involves the Symplegades, which in Greek mythology are a pair of huge rocks located at the Bosphorus Strait. Voyagers were discouraged from traveling in those waters for these rocks would unexpectedly clash together, crushing everything that tried to pass between them. These stones are indicative of the world of opposites and present an effective gateway, since quite often humans are crushed between the coincidence of opposites. In other words, the mysterious garden, a land or sea of perfection, is always difficult to enter because one must first go beyond the dualistic nature of the material world.

One of the more intriguing gates described in mythology is the trope of being swallowed by some strange or bizarre animal. These myths run the gamut, from Jonah and the whale, to the misfortunes of Pinocchio. An interesting parallel between this tarot card and "the gate that swallows" can be seen in the metaphor of the jaws of the whale being the two pillars of the gate. This agrees with the letter correspondence of Arcanum II, *B,* since, of course, in the Weilgart Language of Space (aUI) this letter means "together" (see chapter 18, "The Language of Space (aUI)"). In this way we are reminded not only of the jaws of the whale coming together, but also the clashing of the Symplegades together.

The metaphor pertaining to this particular card continues, because Arcanum II is ruled by Virgo, which anatomically governs the intestines. In this manner, we can understand the passing through the gate as the process of being actually digested or assimilated by mystery.

ARCANUM III: THE QUEEN MOTHER (ISIS UNVEILED)

Alternate name: The Empress
Number: 3
Sign: Libra
Anatomy: kidneys, lower back
English letter: G
Flower: scleranthus
Angel: Jophiel
Color: green

This card is a combination of the first two arcana. The idea of 1 (Arcanum I) becomes a mediator for the polarity of 2 (Arcanum II). These two cards together find a third point of common relationship, and activity is born. All activity is based on the triad of active, medial, and passive. Forces must act on something, and to do this there has to be a point of contact, which is the mediator. We can see this principle at work in the human body. On the physical level, muscles are the activators; they move the bones, which are passive. The medial points of contact are the tendons, which connect the bones and the muscles.

In astrology, Libra, ruler of this card, is the sign of relationship. Two things find a common ground, and the bond between them creates a third principle. Whereas the evenness of the number 2 alludes to a static quality, the number 3 is uneven and therefore moving. The idea of the number 1 is also in evidence.

Isis the Virgin (Arcanum II) here becomes Isis the Mother, and as such is a symbol of nature, which is always moving toward greater and greater refinement. Balance is not a goal that is ever completely attained here; it's an ongoing process that tends toward greater and greater subtlety. The idea of unity becomes a vortex for duality. The two polarities whirl around this center and create all movement.

The triangle, symbolic of the number 3, is the most stable form in all nature. It's also the simplest means of enclosing space with straight lines, hence the attribution of this card in the Language of Space to the letter *G,* the sound made deepest inside the throat, which corresponds to the concept of "inside."

In many decks the picture of Isis on this card is shown holding an eagle, the bird of awareness and the symbol of Arcanum IV. This signifies that hopefully the activity of number 3 will lead to the expansion of consciousness and awareness signified by the number 4.

When any two things are put together they will relate simply by the fact that they share a common boundary—they touch each other somewhere. But what makes any relationship come alive and evolve is when there's an energy exchange between the two entities such that they learn and grow from each other, and by doing so achieve the transformation signified by Arcanum IV.

This card encourages us to act with momentum, that is, to keep moving, even if we're not sure of what we're doing or where we're going, for movement in any direction is an effective way of drawing out our creativity. A lack of confidence or fear of being wrong or ineffective can cause us to hesitate, to draw back, to stop, but if we allow ourself to keep going and keep our attention on what we're doing as we go, it will eventually draw out what's inside us and thereby grow our awareness.

Activity is born from a center, from an inside, and its movement is always away from that center toward the outside. Our inside comes to know itself through the fruits of its activity. Our *doing* then becomes a mirror in which we're allowed to see the reflection of our inner self.

Isis Unveiled, the mistress of this card, is often shown holding the eagle, which is Horus, the Egyptian hawk god and the son of Isis. The number 3 symbolizes the three major substances of alchemy: salt, sulfur, and mercury. Salt is the material or earthly world (salt crystals are cubical in form and so relate to the stone cube spoken of in this chapter in the Arcanum I description). Since sulfur burns so easily, it's associated with the fiery realm (fire = creativity and spirituality), and mercury is that flexible go-between that links the first two together and thereby generates activity. An even clearer way of understanding salt, mercury, and sulphur is that salt links earth with water, mercury links water with air, and sulphur links air with fire.

The knowledge of the 1 manifesting in and through the 3 is quite old and is found in the Christian religion (God = Father, Son, and Holy Ghost) as well as the Vedic religion (Brahma = the creator, Vishnu = the preserver, and Shiva = the destroyer/transformer).

The flower essence corresponding to Arcanum III is scleranthus, which helps us to go ahead and choose so that we don't get caught up in wavering and wasting energy, needlessly changing our viewpoint back and forth.

Once the traveler has successfully crossed the threshold, she is ready to begin the journey in earnest. But where is she, or rather, where has she found herself? It will certainly be unlike where she has formerly been. In the movie *The Wizard of Oz,* the director, through a then-new photographic technique, emphasized the total difference between the two places where Dorothy finds herself. When she is in Kansas, and throughout the cyclone sequence (which certainly simulated the traumatizing effect of passing across a threshold), the movie is filmed in black and white, which effectively portrayed the mundane world of black-and-white duality; and then quite suddenly, as she steps through the door of her dislocated house, the film switches to color, a shock and amazement to people back in 1939.

At this point Dorothy finds herself in the land of Oz, and to her astonishment is greeted by the sight of flora and fauna in colors beyond the scope of her ordinary imagination. The land beyond the gate is quite often described as a miraculous garden that surpasses a person's wildest dreams.

Not long ago we were conducting a class in meditation on the tarot cards, and a student selected Arcanum III as a focus for her experience. Through her meditation she was taken to a beautiful garden, which she claimed to have difficulty describing because she could not find the proper words to express such perfection. Her guide for this experience was the woman pictured on this card, and the student said that the guide's countenance was warmer and more beautiful than any person she had ever encountered in her life.

The goddess on the other side of the gate in this garden of perfection is, of course, Isis, and yet she is quite different from the way she appears in Arcanum II. Her veil or disguise has been removed. The goddess in this context is often thought to be pregnant. She carries within her the perfection, and after the gestation period of the journey she will deliver this incarnation of perfection to the world.

However, even though this world of mystery appears so perfect and beautiful, the life voyager has not, merely by crossing through the gate, arrived at their final destination, for they have only just begun their journey. Since this mysterious world is so strange to the person they will find it difficult at first to maintain their equilibrium.

Arcanum III is ruled by Libra, whose symbol is the balance scale, which suggests a need to continually seek balance and harmony within every situation. Another interesting fact about Libra in the context of the journey metaphor is that astrologers frequently say a person born with the sign Libra as their rising sign (the sign on the horizon at the time of birth) will have a tendency to be physically handsome or beautiful.

As we have seen previously, this card signifies activity and fecundity. Once the threshold has been crossed, the initiate must now set forth on an active and productive search.

ARCANUM IV: THE COMMANDER (THE SOVEREIGN)

Alternate name: The Emperor
Number: 4
Sign: Scorpio
Anatomy: genitals
English letter: D
Flower: chicory
Angel: Jeremiel
Color: blue-green

Activity, as represented by Arcanum III, leads to the building of form, which is Arcanum IV. This card represents the four tangible and interlocking elements of fire, earth, air, and water, which all need one another. These are the forms of matter. If energy is held back from entering or emanating from a form, the form disintegrates—it ceases to exist. Forms are made powerful and definite by the regular and balanced flow of energy through them. Too little energy entering and the form withers, just as a plant will die from lack of water or sunshine. Too much energy trapped within the form and the form destroys itself, as in cancerous growths and repressed emotions.

The genitals are ruled by this arcanum because the sperm and ovum are the forms that determine the structure of life. We think of forms as being material, and yet science tells us that matter is built by regularizing energy patterns. Forms are rhythmic patterns of energy rather than something apart from or opposed to energy.

Where do these patterns come from? What generates them? The answer is consciousness, a keyword for Arcanum IV. Consciousness is made visible, or one might say tangible, through form. And desire, by nature, is form-producing. Desire is the key to evolution, because it is through the intensification and effective directing of wanting that we attain higher levels of consciousness.

Just as Arcanum II symbolizes the primary dichotomy of inner and outer, Arcanum IV also takes into account the dichotomy of higher and lower. It is these four principles—inner, outer, higher, and lower—that make up the world of forms. They are sometimes referred to as self (inner), not-self (outer), spirit or mind (higher), and matter or tangibility (lower). The self is a focus of change, the not-self a focus of opportunity, the higher is associated with goals or ultimate meaning, and the lower provides a focus or foundation for all manifestation.

The eagle symbolizes Scorpio's higher nature, and the serpent its earthly and physical being. The eagle soars above the earth. It's a creature of the earth and yet is capable of seeing it from a detached viewpoint. The serpent is a spine clinging to the ground. It can't stand upright. It's the latent raw power of one's awareness that can hold this form while simultaneously mutating into the eagle.

I don't like referring to the serpent as low, for it smacks of some religions' rejection of sex. Low strikes a bad note, but low things can be quite nice, like oceans and valleys and beds.

Awareness is inherent in all forms. Kabbalists tell us that even rocks and tables have it, and that we can purify vibrations anywhere with thoughts and acts of love and kindness directed toward physical objects, which includes your body. Even the stars receive and return your love, and it doesn't take them light years to do it—it's instantaneous.

The world of forms is sometimes a great prison that tests the serpent's power. It's the stone pierced by the sword of awareness. If this sounds sexual it's because it is. This penetration can only take place when the four qualities of the two dichotomies are brought together—made whole and balanced. Then the sovereign "I," the love-suffused ego, can take its rightful place on the throne of being and reign supreme.

To effect this harmony we proceed to Arcanum V, The Pentagram/The Hierophant, maker of music from substance's quaternity.

In the Egyptian deck a cat is depicted on the stone cube on which The Commander of Arcanum IV sits. Cats are symbols of consciousness and awareness and were sacred to the Egyptians. The eagle associated with this card is often white, to show purity of consciousness. Since the number here is 4, this card is represented by a square, a rudimentary building block.

The mythic serpent is known in Vedic science and religion as the kundalini force, the physical power of the body and sexual magnetism, which can be transmuted into spiritual energy. The Egyptians often used this serpent symbol in the form of the uraeus, a snake coming out of the middle of a person's forehead. The middle of the forehead is where the pineal gland is located. This is the gland of psychic awareness, sometimes known as the third eye. Some decks depict The Sovereign with this uraeus.

Arcanum IV is also associated with ritual, since ritual may stimulate heightened awareness and can be a vehicle for creativity. Ritual is seen in even the lowest animals during the process of mating, and in fact mating rituals, even in insects, can attain a high degree of complexity. The masculine element in ritual is provided by the person carrying out the ritual, whereas the feminine element is provided by the structure of the ritual itself as well as any inspiration that comes to the person engaging in the ritual to spontaneously add to or change it.

The flower essence for Arcanum IV is chicory, that alluring weed with sky-blue blossoms that the ancients knew as *Solis sponsa,* "bride of the Sun." It's for people who have trouble owning their own needs, and hence difficulty being direct in expressing them. Chicory helps us find power in vulnerability.

Scorpio, ruler of this arcanum, is the lord of the eighth house in the horoscopic wheel. The eighth house bestows on us the gift of regeneration and change, which is highly significant here since the life voyager achieves metamorphosis through their spiritual journey. This change, however, is primal, as opposed to complex, in that it is not the total transformation of Arcanum XIII, The Reaper, nor is it the cataclysmic, fatalistic change of Arcanum X, The Wheel. It's a natural change of form, as the number 4 signifies nature and its four elements. The world of form is regenerated through the psyche plunging into another place—the realm of the subconscious and subliminality, the realm of sleep and dreams, myth and magic. This new realm is not the same as the world of normally acknowledged reality, and yet it should not be considered unreal, but rather perceived as a parallel reality, with its own forms and denizens governed by its own laws. The tangible world of "reality" that we generally experience is governed by physical laws, while this other reality is governed by the astral, poetic laws of ethereality.

Arcanum IV is called The Emperor in some decks; he is the sovereign lord of this realm who is called on by the journeyer. This sovereign guide is fully skilled in navigating the terrain of this mysterious land; he can be of wondrous assistance to the traveler. In every journey, those of us who are predominately accustomed to a physical reality and answerable to physical laws need direction from an entity such as The Emperor, who can penetrate the veils of this mysterious astral/ethereal plane.

This arcanum signifies primal creativity, which is the magical stuff from which all true art arises.

CHAPTER TWO

Synchronicity and Major Arcana V–VIII

The tarot is a psychic tool, a wand of the sixth chakra carved from a fallen branch of the Tree of Life, which is forever shedding and re-growing its wisdom.

Irnad the Wise
(character in the Azoth novels)

Synchronicity is the simultaneous occurrence of events that appear significantly related but have no discernible causal connection. It is what most people refer to as coincidence. When you keep seeing the same word or number over and over, or when you are thinking of someone and then moments later they call you, these are synchronistic occurrences. These events can be relatively simple, like the ones just mentioned, or there may be ones that are far less likely to occur and because of that, they make a deeper impression on our minds.

I'll give you an example of a rare one that happened to me: a friend of mine and I were talking on the phone one day and it so happened that we discovered we were both traveling to Chicago at the same time. That in itself is a synchronistic occurrence. She was going to visit a friend, and so was I. This is also synchronistic.

When I got to Chicago I stayed with my friend in his apartment. He did rug restoration at home for a living and told me that a woman who lived on the first floor of his building was now working for him because his business was expanding. She came up to his apartment that evening and I was introduced to her, and she told me that tomorrow a friend of hers was coming from Kansas City (where I live) to visit her. It turned out that that friend was my friend, the one who was going to visit Chicago at the same time I was. Given the number of apartment buildings in Chicago, the chances of this happening are obviously extremely small. It blew my mind.

This occurrence gave me a great feeling when it happened, and even now when I think about it I enjoy the memory. Many mystics say that these synchronistic happenings are one of the ways that nonphysical beings communicate with us, for often an occurrence of this sort contains a message for you to discover. Sometimes the message is quite obvious, but at other times you may have to look more deeply into the occurrence to determine its meaning. I feel that the message for me in the example I just gave is that there are forces watching over me and guiding me whenever they can. So the message is, "We are here," which is often the message within synchronistic occurrences. These events then become a way spirits can remind us of their presence. Sometimes the message is as simple as that. I feel that at other times we may sense there is more to the message but may not be able to figure it out, and that can be because we're meant to absorb the message on a level other than the conscious one. In other words, we're meant to absorb its vibrations while bypassing our rational mind.

A beneficial practice for you to try is to keep a notebook in which you record all synchronistic occurrences that happen to you. You don't necessarily have to write a great deal about them unless of course you want to—if you write a few words about such occurrences and note when they happen, that's enough. The purpose of this exercise is that the more you watch for these events, the more they tend to make themselves visible. Keeping a notebook like this can be a means of aligning yourself more clearly with the harmony of the universe and can put you on a wavelength of resonance with cosmic forces.

Also, if you desire to understand any of these synchronistic events more fully, you can always ask what one of them means and then pull a tarot card to answer your question.

It's important to realize that when you do a tarot reading for anyone you are setting up a synchronistic occurrence; that is, there is a coincidence between the question asked and the cards that you draw from the deck. In a much broader context we can say that everything that happens to us carries a message, and so any and all events we experience are synchronistic. Of course we don't have to go through life interpreting every little thing that happens, but when problems do arise or there's something we want to know more about, we can, for instance, open the dictionary at random and place a finger on a page and see what word we are touching. We can then consider this as a message concerning whatever it is we wish to know more about. And, of course, remember that the tarot is a cosmic dictionary with moveable pages, for that's exactly what it is. When you own that book, all wisdom is potentially yours.

ARCANUM V: THE PENTAGRAM (THE HIEROPHANT)

Alternate name: The Pope
Number: 5
Planet: Jupiter
Anatomy: anterior pituitary
English letter: E
Flower: catalpa, peony
Angel: Zadkiel
Color: yellow

This card is, in effect, the big bang of the universe, forever expanding from a center—an explosion that from our viewpoint in time is so slowed down as to be imperceptible. It represents the life force spiraling out in ever-widening circles to animate all potentials completely and fully. The quintessence is channeled here through a supreme spiritual ruler who is the emissary of Creative Intelligence.

The Sanskrit word for both *teacher* and *Jupiter,* the planetary ruler of this card, is *guru.* Jupiter is the teacher and transmitter of wisdom (and the highest spiritual leader should be first and foremost a teacher, not just an instructor rattling off factual information). This card tells us that living and learning are synonymous, that death is the completion of a particular course of study, which is followed immediately by reviewing whatever karmic grade we've earned. This is what Swedish scientist, theologian, and mystic Emanuel Swedenborg means when he says that right after death the angels read our body back to us.

The only material forms based on the geometry of the number 5 (the pentagram, the pentagon, and so forth) are biological forms. The number 5 is rarely found in crystalline structures. From this we may infer that the number 5 is an engram (imprint) of life itself.

More specifically, the number 5 is significantly human—we have five fingers, five toes, and five appendages (two arms, two legs, and a head). The number 5 is a microcosm, a closed system capable of vibration with, and response to, everything outside itself. Humans are a receiving station for the macrocosm, capable of picking up every cosmic channel clearly. Humans are mediators between mind and matter. Our goal is to bring every channel of the full spectrum of the macrocosm into perfect harmony with all the others.

The mystery of this card is the way it resolves the seemingly opposite ideas of (1) eternal expansion and (2) complete fullness having already been achieved at any one point in time. Psychologically, this card is divine optimism, which knows the present as both a triumphant culmination of the past as well as the perfect beginning of a future replete with potential.

In its most negative aspect Jupiter is the planet of excess, and hence this is the greatest danger of this card. And yet to the initiate, excess is one of the least insidious pitfalls.

The poet William Blake was very much on the wavelength of Arcanum V when he wrote "The road of excess leads to the palace of wisdom" and "You never know what is enough unless you know what is more than enough."

The spiritual student involved in the great work is first admonished, through Arcanum III, to *do*. Naturally, this imperative to keep busy can lead to overdoing. Yet it is better to overshoot the mark than to have never aimed and fired. True teaching always involves plunging the student into a direct experience that he or she can participate in. The danger of underparticipating is always much greater than the danger of overparticipating.

The crowning secret of this card is the truth that no true teacher teaches only one thing, or even one thing at a time. Everything is always taught simultaneously, and every lesson is complete, a world in itself, a hologram of the whole.

Here the Higher Self emerges. Usually this card shows The Hierophant above two other figures on either side of the card; sometimes one is black and the other white. They kneel before him in obedience. These two figures represent all the dichotomies of lower being—for example, masculine/feminine, good/evil, objective/subjective. These polarities interact/dance/fight with each other until The Hierophant reveals himself, at which point their attention turns from each other to him. He is their harmonizer.

Learning and teaching are the same. If you want to learn something, teach it to others. The Hierophant is not necessarily an adept, for the same reason that a minister, psychologist, or any mentor or advisor does not have to have reached enlightenment to be able to help others evolve. The teacher grows *with* the student. This card expresses the positive aspects of parenthood—never critical or unnecessarily limiting, but always positively reinforcing.

The Hierophant (5) often wears a triple crown to signify the elevation of activity as a means of learning. We might say that this card rules the activity of myth-making, since myth tends to draw many forces together into a harmonious whole.

Jupiter, the ruling planet of this arcanum, is luck and good fortune—blessings showering down from higher powers. In a reading, this card signifies the need to take a fuller, more all-encompassing approach to life, as well as the need to strengthen and build on the multifarious connections that tie all of life together.

Catalpa flower essence corresponds to this arcanum. It's said to be a deep heart healer of current or past wounds and feelings of being unloved. This is because Arcanum V signifies wealth and prosperity, and the feeling of being unloved is a kind of spiritual poverty.

Peony flower is another Arcanum V essence. It magnifies the feeling of abundance and embracing all manifestations of life.

The guide who appears in the preceding arcanum, Arcanum IV (The Commander), is not the highest ruler of this realm, even though at times he might wish to play that part. In truth he's an elemental, a spirit who's closely linked to the person experiencing the journey and the one who assists travelers in attuning to their own personal power.

The true ruler of this realm and the ultimate guide for the querent (even though the person may not be cognizant of this) is The Hierophant, the guru, who is lord of the spiritual plane.

Whereas the elemental guide of Arcanum IV can be vitally helpful to the voyager, the journey must follow along a divine path, and only an angel of the higher spiritual planes can direct such a journey. Arcanum V, The Hierophant, is the path of higher learning that the seeker must travel in order to grow into their highest potential.

The journey is happening on multiple levels. There are inner and outer levels, which are the mental and physical bodies of humanity; and further, there are the higher and lower planes, which represent the spiritual and emotional bodies. One of the most common mistakes the voyager can make is to separate these levels into false categories of good and evil, for negation of either the physical or mental bodies constitutes a denial of life and God.

The guru of Arcanum V teaches love and acceptance of everything. It is the magic of this spiritual generosity that helps us to continually synthesize rather than divide, to accept rather than reject.

And what's especially important to know is that even if the guru, the symbol of this card, does not come to us in physical form, the guru will always sense our needs and will come to us on the inner planes to assist us in our learning. To attune to the guru's wisdom, all it takes is to enter into silence and allow him to speak to us.

ARCANUM VI: THE CROSSROADS (THE TWO PATHS)

Alternate name: The Lovers
Number: 6
Planet: Venus
Anatomy: parathyroid gland
English letters: U, V, W
Flower: rose, violet
Angels: Michael and Raphael
Color: all colors

Arcanum VI, The Crossroads/The Two Paths, is the macrocosm, the totality of all worlds. It is God, and because God is love, it is love. Love is magnetic and dualistic in its activity.

The Kabbalah says that divine love descends into matter through creation and is then liberated from matter through evolution. In human terms, the descent into matter is the release of sexual energy through outer objects, and the liberation from matter involves the transmutation of sexual energy to feed the higher mind. These are the "two paths" that energy takes, and it is through the movement of these two energies that the macrocosm exists.

This card is often symbolized by the Star of David: two interlocking triangles, one pointing up and one pointing down. In all there are six points to this figure. Mind and matter are locked together and pull in different directions. They signify the two themes of all art, literature, and thought: love and death. What we usually think of as physical love is actually death—the desire to lose one's identity to the object of one's desire, to drown, so to speak, in sensual passion. On the other hand, true spiritual work is actually the highest form of love, although on the outside it can mask itself in all the terrors and uncertainty of dying.

Of the two paths we're always tempted to choose the one that seems the easiest, or that sparkles the brightest. As Mae West famously said,

"When I have to choose between two evils, I always like to pick the one I haven't tried yet."

This card can be a temptress. The pull of entropy—the descending triangle—is far too alluring for most people to overcome. Potent currents of sensuality wrap the mind in iridescent smoke, and we're drawn deeper and deeper into the comatose, deathlike sleep of matter as our boat heads for the waterfall. The body's a machine, and the more we allow it to rule us, the more our consciousness mirrors it, becoming more and more machinelike.

Why is it this way? This is easy to answer: without having choices and without being pulled strongly in two different directions, we'd never be able to exercise and eventually perfect our free will. Creative Intelligence is free and made humanity in its own image, so therefore we're likewise free. Creative Intelligence made us as a fetus and placed both the him and her of ourself in Eden's womb.

But humans chose growth, so they ate the fruit of the Tree of Knowledge. The expulsion from the Garden is the fully developed fetus being expelled from the womb. By telling humans the Tree of Knowledge exists, Creative Intelligence conferred on human beings the power to choose.

Christ visited hell before going to heaven. We cannot be a perfect microcosm until we can relate to all aspects of the macrocosm, hell, sin, and death included. We would be denying these realities if we chose instead to swim forever in the warm amniotic fluid of innocence, that safe little sea of intrauterine existence. Consciousness cannot and will not transcend the realms of illusion until it has the capacity to achieve maturity, and maturity means embracing the full rainbow of experience.

Let us now speak of what the number 6, the number of this arcanum, means:

The Hebrew people of old found that the six-pointed star was the sign of their God and their faith, because 6 is a perfect number; the three numbers that divide into it evenly are 1, 2, and 3, which add up to the number itself, 6. These perfect numbers are very rare—there is only one between 1 and 10 (6); one between 10 and 100 (the number 28); one between 100 and 1,000 (the number 496); and one between 1,000 and 10,000 (the number 8,128); and so on. And 6 has the immense honor of being the first of all of them. You can find many more of these rare numbers on the internet.

The number 6 signifies perfection. This is why it rules love, for God is love, and we love the idea of perfection. If the universe is part of God, how could it not be perfect? Whatever we love we see as perfect, or at least we see the potential perfection in it, its spiritual possibility. Love gives us X-ray vision, allowing us to see beyond flaws, and it sometimes can cause flaws to become completely invisible to us, which is why they sometimes say love is blind and that Cupid wears a blindfold. Of course love can also see flaws sometimes as exquisite adornments or unique beauties—like the little artificial moles that the women of the French court kept in gold boxes and glued on their faces.

It's not easy for a perfect number like 6 to exist in this earthly realm of darkness and conflict. Everyone wants it; we want love and perfection, but so often when we feel we've captured even a small piece of it we often misuse it, abuse it, take it for granted, try to buy or sell it, or grow bored with it and discard it.

Kabbalists tell us that everything is already perfect the way it is. Hard to believe, isn't it? This just shows the power of illusions! The universe is already in a state of perfection. What's imperfect is our ability to see the truth of this. We can only see the perfection of the universe when our own perception is perfected.

This card helps us learn more and more how to love where we're at, how to love each step of the journey, and how to see the value in everything. The journey to paradise is paradise itself. We're all of us continually choosing. This card encourages us to become more and more conscious of the choices we're making so that we can come into a deeper understanding of why we're making them. If we keep doing this we'll come into finer and finer attunement with the perfection of 6, until eventually we'll see everything clearly for what it is. And then how could we not love all of it?

Flowerwise, we have rose for this arcanum, and one of the best rose flower essences to use is *Rosa macrophylla* from Tibet. Rose is also ascribed to Arcanum XXI, The Lord of the Dance. It goes with both, and this shows the great power of this blossom. Rose is a panacea, soothing the nerves, empowering the immune system, and softening and harmonizing wherever it goes. Rose petals make a wonderful tea.

Violet is another flower of Arcanum VI and has been called a flower of Venus since antiquity. It helps one attune to the innocence that one can never completely lose, although in most adults it's become misplaced. It's said to promote self-acceptance, which is akin to innocence since in that state self-rejection never crosses one's mind.

Even though we are describing these major arcana as sequences in a journey, it's important to keep in mind that on a deeper level their energies are all happening simultaneously. And so they have a temporal and narrative aspect, as well as an eternal and simultaneous one. Or, as American sci-fi writer Ray Cummings puts it, "Time is God's way of keeping everything from happening at once," the joke being that time creates the illusion of choice, and that in fact everything *is* happening at once!

Arcanum VI, The Crossroads, rules choices and the various types of pulls that different choices exert on us. Maharishi has stated that evolution is the strongest force in the universe, and I say that the second strongest is homeostasis, the urge to keep everything just as it is, in the same relative balance it's in, even if that balance is partial, pathological, and dysfunctional. Another way of saying this is that we all like to keep what's up and running, up and running, and because of this, the force of evolution is often felt as a gigantic inconvenience, which is why we resist it. Inertia is a perfect manifestation of homeostasis.

These two forces are the two paths of Arcanum VI manifesting in their purest form. There's always a test here, for we are being tested constantly. The forces of homeostasis often present juicy, tantalizing possibilities to us, but if we choose those possibilities over and over again, then there is a gradual and inevitable building up of frustration within us, for what our souls most want is to evolve, which means to choose the way of growth, even though that may involve temporary pain and fear. Just ask Dorian Gray.

If the traveler fails at this point—if they choose the lower, easier, more fun, seemingly brighter, more immediately gratifying path, with no worries, the choice will be presented again and again, over and over, in as many forms and lifetimes as it takes.

Remember, the trials of Arcanum VI are forever eased and alleviated by the supreme love and generosity of the one that came just before it, Arcanum V, the Hierophant.

Kabbalists tell us there are two paths: Choose one and all that you are suffers. Choose the other and only the ego suffers.

ARCANUM VII: THE VICTORY (THE CONQUEROR)

Alternate name: The Chariot
Number: 7
Sign: Sagittarius
Anatomy: liver
English letter: Z
Flower: agrimony
Angel: Raguel
Color: blue

This is the arcanum of transcendence. It signifies rising above the realm of matter. The number 7 reveals the seven forces of the cosmos that are mirrored in the seven visible planets of astrology. This card resolves the polar opposites of active engagement and detachment. More and more as we evolve we find that we can be actively engaged and completely detached at the same time. This is why Maharishi calls enlightenment a dualistic state of being. The process of evolution causes humans to be at once more and more effective in the physical realm, and yet increasingly unattached to it. You can and will have your cake and eat it too. All you need to do is order two pieces.

Sagittarius is the sign of the higher mind. It loves such things as religion, philosophy, and anything conceptual and metaphysical. Yet the animal symbolized by this sign is a centaur, whose upper half is human and lower half is horse. This combines muscular vitality with intellect. This sign is also typically interested in games, sports, and all athletics where there are two sides competing. Sagittarius is certainly fun-loving. It's the friendliest of the signs.

The key word for this card is *administration,* which signifies centralization of control. This arcanum is often symbolized by the six-pointed Star of David, as represented in Arcanum VI, The Crossroads, except now it also has a seventh element: a dot in the star's middle. This dot is an administrating point, a place where mind and matter merge to birth a seed.

The parting of the two forces that takes place in this arcanum is a key step in all unfolding. The great work cannot begin until the forces within a person are divided, taken apart, and broken down. If this doesn't happen, there is no way anything new can be built.

The great work does not destroy any of the elements or materials of creation, but only the patterns and forms they take. The reflex actions of the human robot are broken down and then reassembled on a higher and more truly alive level.

Evolution is a dance that involves both creation and destruction. We tend to see creation as a beautiful concept and destruction as fearsome. But if we look at nature we see that destruction is an integral and vital part of everything beautiful. A baby must lose its first set of teeth before gaining its second set. Autumn and winter must precede spring. If we cannot learn the art of destruction, we'll never be effective creators, because we will never be able to complete cycles.

Fear of destruction is one of the most insidious forms of materialism. It prevents one from acting for fear that something will be done wrong. People "save" their feelings and ideas out of a fear that if they are used and spent they will not be renewed, that is, recreated. Hence people slow the growth of their consciousness because they do not use the consciousness they already have. Both body and mind are destroyed through activity and use and are recreated through the quintessence, the akasha. Speeding up this process is the great work of alchemy.

This card rules concepts and all theoretical knowledge and speculation. It rules both philosophy and sports. But then isn't philosophy a kind of convoluted, wordy sport? The Conqueror is brandishing a bright crystalline sword that pierces with its illumination the darkness of ignorance. It must be made of obsidian, as are all the best modern surgical tools.

This card is also called The Chariot, a vehicle in which The Conqueror rides. His chariot is made from the same stone cube that appears in some tarot decks, but now it's hollowed out. And although The Conqueror stands on it, half his body extends above it. In this way he gets an overview of materiality while being able at the same time to be immersed in it. This is why this card rules concepts, for they're abstractions based on our perceptions of the material world.

Some tarot decks show the chariot being pulled by two sphinxes, one black and one white. This signifies the passage of time, the white sphinx being positive, harmonious circumstances, and the black one adverse or negative ones. That both sphinxes pull the chariot means that victory is ours when we deal with whatever we've called on karma to dish out, the blacks, the whites, and all the grays as well.

Usually the chariot has a canopy spangled with stars over it. These heavenly lights are higher powers, and the canopy symbolizes protection coming from celestial sources. It's interesting how the canopy shades the charioteer from the light of the sun—the harsh brightness of the conscious mind—so that the soft intuitive glow of the stars can be more clearly perceived and the possibility of connecting to the protective influences of angels is thereby heightened. The Conqueror enlists them to help free the self from the illusions and deceptions of materiality.

Plane geometry tells us that straight lines are segments of circles that have an infinite radius, therefore straight lines only *seem* to be straight because we cannot see them in infinite extension. Sagittarius delights in imagining the infinite extensions of anything and everything, which helps it to see with cosmic vision beyond the straight lines of our earthly, cubical realm.

This Conquerer is the widener of horizons that can open up multiple expanded viewpoints and hence a fuller, richer vision of existence. We might call this card "Star Trek consciousness."

Sagittarius loves all exotic, faraway, foreign things, for these influences from beyond feed and enhance the colors of its world. Contact with remote outposts give it greater and greater perspective, the commodity it most loves.

The flower essence of this card is agrimony, one of the universal remedies, for it helps one overcome denial and avoidance, the detachment we move into when we're trying to insulate ourself. Taking agrimony helps us see what we really need to see so that our Sagittarian cheerfulness becomes full, real, and light-infused, rather than just a mask of smiles we wear to hide the dark parts of ourself.

This arcanum represents the higher philosophical nature of humans and their journey as they transcend the tests of the material world. Through its resonance with Sagittarius it denotes the journey itself in that Sagittarius governs the widening of horizons and all travel, whether that travel be literal or metaphysical.

Sometimes the widening of horizons requires a battle, and then life becomes a battleground. In line with this contextual point of view, Arcanum VII, The Victory, represents the hero of the journey as a warrior ready for conflict. He is St. George who slew the dragon of materialism in the eleventh canto of book one of Edmund Spenser's epic poem *The Faerie Queene.*

The other name for this card, The Chariot, is likewise significant in that at this stage of the journey the hero must find a vehicle fit for battle in which he might travel with greater speed.

In astrology, Sagittarius is the ruler of the ninth house of the horoscope, and the ninth house governs understanding and higher learning. Indeed, as people experience the journey, they must strive for an ever more complete understanding of themselves and their purpose.

ARCANUM VIII: THE BALANCE (JUSTICE)

Alternate name: Justice
Number: 8
Sign: Capricorn
Anatomy: skeletal structure
English letters: H, Ch
Flower: mimulus
Angel: Azreal
Color: blue-violet

This card embodies Isaac Newton's third law of motion: for every action, there is an equal and opposite reaction.

This card has to do with questions. Questioning is asking, and asking is desiring. Questions always produce answers, and desires are always fulfilled in one way or another, though often in ways we might never have thought of, and at times we weren't expecting.

It seems that many questions are never answered, and that many people have desires that are never satisfied. Actually, all the answers are there, and as soon as one truly wants a desire to be satisfied it will be. The problem is that we fool ourselves into thinking we want something, or we talk ourselves into thinking we want some piece of knowledge. This conscious part of us really does ask and want, but we're constantly being overridden by the power of our ingrained and unconscious habit patterns, which are asking and desiring other things.

Because these unconscious desires are stronger, they're the ones that get fulfilled. This is one of the secrets of making magic work—focusing the conscious mind so intensely that it overrides the patterns of the subconscious, though a better way to work is to bring forth the beliefs held in our unconscious so that we can understand our hidden desires that cause self-imposed limits.

The biggest danger in magical workings is not being totally aware of all the different effects we're having on a karmic chain. We might use magic to get what we want and then find out later that what we thought we wanted is not *really* what we wanted, or maybe that other undesired things come along with what we get.

If we fully accept the fact that we have, right now, all that we most strongly want, we are then in a much better position to change those things that we keep telling ourself we do not consciously want. We must first ask the question, "Why have I drawn this part of my life to myself?" If the question is asked strongly and sincerely enough, the answer will eventually make itself known.

"Ask and it shall be given to you, seek and ye shall find." It all seems so easy. So why don't most people just go ahead and do it? Because they don't know how to detach themselves from the potential terror and ugliness the answers might reveal. It seems easier just to drone on through life and hope, weakly, for the best.

Many occult and metaphysical dilettantes use the concept of karma to explain away every difficulty and occurrence. This is utterly platitudinous. Karma explains nothing. It simply is. We wait around for our good karma, and the effect of this nonaction is that it simply waits around for us! This is why Aleister Crowley said, "Do what thou wilt shall be the whole of the law." *The first step is to do!* We cannot accrue any good effects until we generate good causes.

The ultimate danger of this card is complete stagnation, even in the midst of seeming action. The more unevolved Capricorn blindly upholds the status quo. This path leads inevitably into deeper ruts. The ray of hope here is that the pain and suffering that ruts represent to the creative genius of the human psyche will eventually force it to climb back out of its self-dug hole and move on at last to better things.

This card depicts the Egyptian goddess Ma'at, deity of justice. She's a key participant in the rite of the soul's underworld judgment that takes place in the Egyptian Book of the Dead. The soul is led to the underworld and its heart is placed on a balance scale. On the other side of the scale Ma'at places a feather, and unless the soul's heart is lighter than a feather, its work is not yet done.

The heart here signifies a person's spiritual life and love nature, both of these being the same thing. Some ancient religions believed that a human being's spirit enters the body through the top of the head and finds its dwelling place in the heart. If the heart is heavy it means that the person's love nature is still too immersed in the dark veils of matter, which generate egoic selfishness, and so the process of evolution is not yet complete. As the heart's veils are progressively removed in coming incarnations it will be greatly lightened until it passes the test.

If we can think of Arcanum XV, The Black Magician, as structure, then Arcanum VIII, Justice, is that which creates it. The figure on Arcanum VIII is female because she's the passive counterpart to the active law.

The balance scale in her hand corresponds to Libra and to Arcanum III, The Queen Mother, to signify that karma is predicated on action and activity—it's all about relationships. That action produces reaction and vice versa is the law that keeps everything in perpetual movement.

The sword in her other hand echoes all the thoughtforms evoked by the suit of Swords in the minor arcana: practicality, physicality, challenges, conflicts, etc. The blindfold she wears is reminiscent of the blind Fool of Arcanum XXII.

In human psychology this card means the power of discrimination, the ability to discern the differences between things and to make sound and realistic judgments based on that knowledge—in other words, what's important and why it's important, and what its importance is relative to. This height of practicality ultimately spells spirituality once the darkness of illusions and rainbows of delusions are washed from it. Nearly always multiple cleansings are needed.

Mimulus is the Bach Flower Remedy for this card, a strange and obscure one that has to do with worrying about lots of little things—discrimination run amuck—and so taking it helps one see what's really important on a soul level and find ways of manifesting that gold in physical reality.

This arcanum signifies the laws of Creative Intelligence. When we think about it in this context it can help us become more aware of the true nature of karma.

It often happens that when negative energy comes back to us we can't remember what we did to generate it, and this is often because whatever it was might have happened in a past life. It's possible we might be able to psychically tap into whatever the event was, but the truth is we don't need to know the details. As Maharishi says, "You don't need to know what's in the trash bag to carry it to the curb." Maharishi was a Capricorn.

Capricorn is the sign of shortcuts. It loves to come up with ways to conserve energy and make things easier. In karmic terms this means stopping negative reactions whenever possible—ceasing to meet negativity with negativity. The best way to pay off negative karma is to generate positive karma, which brings us back to the basis of all reality: love. For love always moves us into a higher vibration, and the more we embrace and become it, the more karmic debts are cleared.

CHAPTER THREE

The Threshold to Magic and Major Arcana IX–XII

Now that you're studying the tarot, you've crossed the threshold into the realm of magic and have begun the inward journey through the mysterious powers inherent in symbols. Symbols reside deep within the unconscious and promise a vast treasure to the successful traveler.

The journey itself is a symbol reflected throughout mythology. The quest for spiritual truth has always been conceived of as a journey, as in, for example, the search for the Holy Grail, or Odysseus's search for home. The treasure at the end of the journey may differ in appearance but always symbolizes a spiritual gift bestowed on the seeker. The Golden Fleece, the pot of gold, the golden nectar of life, and the princess with the golden hair are all symbolic of attaining the legendary philosopher's stone, which alchemists understood as the missing coefficient in the equation for transmuting lead—that is, the material self—into the pure spirit of gold.

Major Arcanum I, ruled by Mercury, the messenger of the gods, signifies the introduction to the journey. This personage, as The Magus, is privy to the interior world from whence all symbols emerge. The messenger arrives on the scene to announce the journey and point out the path. Alice before her trip to Wonderland was awakened by a rabbit, whom she followed down a hole.

The Veiled Isis card, Arcanum II, guards the threshold of magic. Mysteriously veiled, she sits before the gate or door or river. She permits the passage of only those aspirants who can pass her tests. The aspirant sees her variously guised or veiled as a beautiful woman, an old crone, a ferryman, or even a fearsome dragon.

Once the journey commences, multiple tests of initiation and attainment loom before the aspirant, who must perceive and interpret the archetypal symbols she confronts. These are the images of dreams that are at once alien yet familiar. Such manifestations are connected to physical reality through a psychic labyrinth. To penetrate to the core of the symbol and thus pass the test, the pilgrim must demonstrate great perseverance and innate purity.

Once the core of a symbol is penetrated and the elixir is discovered, the traveler returns to the conscious world, carrying with her the magical potion. She may now use this newfound power to transmute the leaden world into spirit.

The tarot provides the symbols for the journey, the tests in need of penetration, and the pure gold of spirit, and thus can be a focus for the psychic power of the one who masters it.

ARCANUM IX: THE SEEKER (THE SAGE)

Alternate name: The Hermit
Number: 9
Sign: Aquarius
Anatomy: nervous system, ankles, lower legs
English letter: Th
Flower: water violet
Angel: Uriel
Color: violet

The number 9 is the highest number that can be written with a single digit, therefore it symbolizes the end of a numerical cycle. This is not to be confused with the zodiacal cycle of 12, or the planet/sound/color vibration cycle of 7. Any number evenly divisible by 9, no matter how large, always has digits that add up to 9. The number 9 permeates all being and existence. It represents wisdom learned through experience. This doesn't mean that for every experience we have there is just one lesson to learn. It means that as we review our past experiences again and again, there is more and more that we can learn from them, for our past is like a literary masterpiece—it has many levels and bears constant rereading.

Arcanum IX, The Seeker, is a card of initiation. The term *initiation* has been used to describe the process of testing by which a person is allowed into an inner circle of knowledge and secrets that are guarded by elders or superiors. This is one aspect of the word, but there is another that hides a deeper truth: all true initiation is self-initiation. The elders do not guard the door, they wait for us to open it.

It's been the practice of many occult teachers to give their students information that is replete with discrepancies. As long as the student accepts these discrepancies without question, he is avoiding the door. Opening the door means seeing these discrepancies and resolving them internally within the self. The teacher is (or should be) always willing to explain, but only when the question arises in the student's mind. Before that point the answers would be nothing more than rote explanations and so would lack deep meaning for the student.

Arcanum IX tells us that what's important is not so much *what* we know as *how* we know it. For instance, it does not take so much time and energy to know the meaning of the twenty-two cards of the major arcana, and yet we could well spend a lifetime searching the vast labyrinth of their deeper meanings and interconnections. As our mind returns again and again to the knowledge we already have, that knowledge can grow richer and more resonant within our being. It's like knowing a landscape not through just seeing a picture of it, but through living in it, roaming it for many years and experiencing it during different seasons and different times of day.

Arcanum IX also rules the process of contemplation, which can give us new perspectives and views of everything.

The Seeker asks us to enter into new experiences without judging them, for judgments tend to limit and filter our experiences. A wait-and-see attitude is needed so that our biases and basic assumptions do not get in the way of pure experiencing. The Sage has left society to go on a search, and even though he may be looking for specific things, he also knows that he might find other valuable things as well. It's the joyous activity of searching that's important more than the satisfaction of having found something. Every moment reveals a discovery in itself, and so it's best to see all experiences as equally valuable in terms of potential, rather than being frustrated because we can't have the experiences we think would be better for us. Learning from whatever's at hand is the ultimate triumph of resourcefulness and the key to making life effective. The Seeker is the card of open-mindedness, though as I've often told astrology students, the wrong type of open-mindedness can cause your brains to fall out!

Just as the sword of Arcanum VIII, Balance, represents the suit of Swords, the staff of The Sage represents the suit of Wands. The Sage carries a lamp to light his way, and obviously this lamp was lit from a fire that he has previously encountered, hence the idea of illumination gained in the past and then used to light the way into the future.

The Seeker card proclaims the uniformity of experience, that is, it tells us that no one experience is better or richer than another. All experiences depend on how we enter them and how we read them. We are the richness that we bring to our experiences.

The Sage is apart from society; indeed, he is sometimes called The Hermit. This means that all experience is ultimately personal.

Numerologically, the letter combination of *Th* yields *T* (22) and *h* (8) (see chapter 15, "Numerology," for how to calculate the numerology of letters). These signify an intensification (22) of karma (8). The numbers 22 and 8 add up to 30, which is 3 times 10, or a blending of activity (3) and inspiration (10). The spiritual teacher and mystic George Gurdjieff said, "When you do anything, go whole hog." Another spiritual teacher, astrologer Ellias Lonsdale, says, "Angels love extremism."

These precepts are the gold that can be mined from this card. What Gurdjieff meant by what he said is that the best way to learn is to plunge into experience in a completely intense and committed way. Since we always get back what we put out, if we put out weak or half-committed acts, the universe will tend to react to us in a shallow and lukewarm manner. On the other hand, if we approach all situations with exuberance and a willingness to enter completely into them, we'll be more likely to get wholehearted and clear support back.

A keyword for this card is *loyalty,* meaning the ability to reach out to life in a confident and sure way, which expresses loyalty to who we really are. It also signifies the power to carry on with something long enough to glean its gold, which is loyalty to your own intent, and ultimately to your own evolution.

The flower essence associated with this arcanum is water violet, which encourages a person to be more connected to friends, groups, and people in general as a means of giving and receiving positive, supportive energy. It also helps us care less about what others think of us and helps us let up on judging ourselves. It supports greater connectedness with all beings, be they in physical bodies or those who live in the spirit realms.

We all look for supportive influences with which to connect, for we wish to align with those things that enhance our power and that offer us protection. The problem is that the supports we seek can actually inhibit our growth, for people often pick as friends and supporters those who enable their worst traits and who overtly or covertly encourage them to avoid self-exploration.

The Hermit is often a person who isolates herself from society as a means of protecting her soul from forces that might inhibit her evolution. In her aloneness she sometimes makes different sorts of supportive connections. She befriends nature or maybe makes friends with the spirits of plants and animals, as well as other nonphysical entities, such as those who have passed away from the physical plane, as well as spirit guides and angels, all of which can be a wonderful support for personal evolution.

At its highest level, this card is about making friends with yourself, about learning how to support your own being.

This card is pictured in some traditional decks as an elderly man walking a path with a staff in one of his hands and a lantern in the other. Like Diogenes, he searches for truth. His staff is the magic wand he uses to support himself as he goes—the staff of life and its experiences—while the lantern is an outer manifestation of his own inner light, which he uses to illuminate his way as he searches the dark byways of physicality. This stage of the journey denotes the pilgrim traveling along life's path, who through their own experiences can bring illumination to the dim world of obscurities.

This is the arcanum of initiation, which means entering a new level of understanding. In the mystery schools of old, formal initiation was a rite during which new secrets were revealed to the aspirant. In a broader and more eternal sense, initiations are those mystic epiphanies during which the soul sees the same thing, but in a new and unexpected way; they describe a time when yet another veil of darkness is removed to reveal what was always already there, but in a clearer light.

An ancient saying of alchemy is "Always choose quality over quantity" (*Qualitas super quantitas*). This means that it isn't how much you know that matters, but rather how deeply you know it. Since knowledge is holographic, you only need one small piece of it to see the whole of it. The truth is that it doesn't matter what you do as much as it matters how you do it, for any act that comes from the light of your center will always be supportive of life.

Magic can be discovered in the simplest and most mundane of activities. What reveals it is the luminous shining within ourselves.

ARCANUM X: THE CYCLE (THE WHEEL)

Alternate name: The Wheel of Fortune
Number: 10
Planet: Uranus
Anatomy: sex glands
English letters: I, J, Y
Flower: pawpaw
Angel: Raziel
Color: white

This card marks the beginning of a second cycle, since the number here is 10, and 1 plus 0 equals 1. It is a 1 of the second level, since this is the second time we have encountered the number 1.

This is a card of pure creativity, hence the rulership of the sex glands. It is not creativity solely as talent, ability, and proficiency, but creativity as divine inspiration. This is why Uranus is said to rule genius. The effects of this planet are sudden, accidental, and unexpected. It is through events of this nature that Creative Intelligence tries to get us to pay attention.

The Wheel is a closed system with eight spokes, which shows that its structure is based on karma (see also Arcanum VIII, Balance). This card governs situational morality, which believes that nothing in and of itself is either good or bad, but rather depends solely on the time, place, and circumstance in which it is found.

An interesting exercise is to try to think of good things and then imagine them in situations where their effects would be negative, and then do the opposite: think of bad things and look for situations where their effect would be good. This can help to free your mind of thinking of good versus evil and right versus wrong as unchanging notions. The idea here is that living by dogmatic formulas may be easy, but it's not real living. Uranus is the planet of freedom and independence; its effects help a person cultivate complete and perfect self-sufficiency. This finally comes about as the person allows the light of Creative Intelligence shining within them to suffuse their whole being.

The mystery of this card is that it resolves the dualism of order and freedom. Order often sets up rules that establish limitations. This card symbolizes order, which is kinetic, mutable, and unlimited—order that is surprising and catches one off-guard; order that startles and fascinates. Order on this vast scale may seem like chaos, but this is because our vision may be too limited to get a look at the whole structure—unless, of course, we view it through the eyes of our cosmic vision.

For instance, we may take a close-up snapshot of a painting, and when we later look at the image we see just cracks, blotches, and streaks. This photo may be just one square millimeter of the painting. The photo looks abstract and uncomposed, and yet were we to see the painting as a whole it might have a beautiful and harmonious composition. Reality operates on this same principle. Divine order is in the mind of Creative Intelligence, and if we can make our individual mind one with that big mind, our life then lights up with all sorts of meanings, many of which are surprises. We can then see reason and purpose for even the smallest detail. From this viewpoint, all things speak to us, and their voices sing in cosmic harmony. This is the breakthrough of divine inspiration.

The Wheel says that even though we may see similarities between things, the beauty of the universe lies in the fact that no two things are ever completely alike. Sixth-century Greek philosopher Heraclitus said you can't step into the same stream twice. The masks that God wears are endless and ever-changing, and even though we may try to categorize and define these masks, each one has its own expression and is imbued with many elusive subtleties. Life is a costume party. On a physical level, becoming one with the universe does not mean being like everything or everyone else so much as it means playing your own unique role in the cosmic plan, which is easy to do if you can get out of your own way. When the wand of your consciousness touches your inner light, a magic channel opens up through which a wealth of luminous and healing energies can flow forth into the world. Such great power dwarfs the miniscule ego.

This card sings of the beauty of uncontrollability and of all the forces at work beyond the horizon of our perception. These forces constantly flash into human experience, causing upsets, accidents, seeming disasters both great and small, and flocks of unforeseen exigencies. This is what keeps life from degenerating into somnambulistic predictability and hence stagnation. The Wheel is the magic potion awakening us from boredom.

Humans appreciate handmade things for their mistakes or flaws, which lend interest to them as well as the distinctive imprint of the person who made them. Balance is a universal principle, but it manifests in an infinite number of ways; this card describes the unique factor in any balanced scheme or situation, which often manifests as unseen balance.

This card, from its domain on the planet Uranus, rules accidents. In a very real sense when accidents hurl themselves into our lives, some or many kinds of fractures open up through which spiritual light has the power to stream. Due to the upsetting nature of change, though, and particularly change brought about by external forces, we usually feel these types of events to be negative in nature; however, this is because we're often only seeing the effects of the moment rather than the broader spiritual pattern.

Accidents are messages from Creative Intelligence. Much of life is spent in a dimmed-down state, not fully conscious, and yet not able to deeply rest or be at peace either. Accidents occur to wake us up; in a dramatic way they break or force us out of habit patterns. For instance, tripping and falling down may mean that Creative Intelligence is trying to tell you to slow down, while a bump on the head might be telling you you're hardheaded, or that you need to think more before you act.

I have a deep theoretical love of Uranus. I say theoretical, for often when it strikes I react with fear. To get Uranus to be gentler and gentler with us all we have to do is wake up more and more. As I do, I find my theoretical love growing more and more actual every day.

An Arcanum X flower essence is pawpaw, which helps you feel okay about being different so that you can be more comfortable with being who you are and not be burdened with the expectations that others place on your identity.

This arcanum also opens the possibility of theoretical or imaginal flowers, like the black dandelion or blue sunflower, which don't exist in nature, but whose energy might be projected into a matrix of water and then used to heal any and all sorts of maladies. Use the inspiration flowing from this arcanum to tap into such mysteries.

Concerning the journey as a whole, there appear to be two major modes of travel along the path. The first one is walking or riding, the traveling experience itself. This is the mode of the pilgrim who sets out on their journey and experiences each and every stone on the way, every turn and fork in the road. This pilgrim encounters entities who share the path or entities who have been placed along the path for the personal edification and enlightenment of the voyager.

At times the direction in which the pilgrim is traveling is clear, more or less, and the pilgrim is able to make decisions regarding the ongoing course of events, while at other times there appear to be aimless happenings or lack of direction. No matter what the events of the journey are, the voyager is still being guided nonetheless.

There's a second mode, though, that's quite unlike the first, and this is represented by Arcanum X, The Wheel.

At times one can almost believe that fate or God or mystery itself has intervened in order to alter the journey's fabric. The pilgrim who has been quietly seeking their path is suddenly lifted up and hurled forward or backward, upward or downward, through time and space. An apt metaphor for this experience could be that the course of the pilgrim's life has changed so dramatically that it's as if they've been struck by lightning.

Jonah, who did not choose to go to Nineva as God had directed him, was then swallowed by the whale. Dorothy, who'd become disenchanted with her home and family, was suddenly picked up by a cyclone and transported over the rainbow.

I've spoken of this arcanum earlier as divine inspiration, and indeed it is. If, as we journey along life's path, we are not moving fast enough, sometimes Creative Intelligence intervenes, and often in stunning ways. The path has been created and we are shown the way, and yet it is the nature of humans to dawdle along, to savor their homeostasis, to invent all sorts of excuses both elaborate and simple for themselves, and to generally procrastinate as Rip Van Winkle did with a nap.

Most of us cannot, by our normal human nature alone, follow the path to a swift attainment of the ultimate destination, so through divine intervention we're inspired.

Often in my classes when we've done guided imagery meditations, we've found ourselves loathe to go to a deep enough level of consciousness, only to find that suddenly we are transported through some trick or accidental observation into an entirely new and deeper level.

The Wheel rules the imp of the accidental, and yet we know on a metaphysical level that even accidents that occur to us physically always have a deeper meaning and reason. The truth is that there are no accidents, only disruptions to expectations, only shakings to loosen patterns and allow in a little more light and air.

A student of ours, a chiropractor by profession, has often discussed with us how in her experience she has encountered many miraculous cures that have been instigated as a result of severe accidents or upsets. The general pattern in these occurrences seems to be that the person will have a severe problem that began early in life, and even after repeated chiropractic treatment only a small improvement has been made. Her patient then undergoes a sudden and dramatic accident—for instance, an automobile crash or a fall down the stairs—and when the person then goes back to the chiropractor's office, an adjustment can be effected with far-reaching results. The accident in this case has shaken up some very old pathological pattern, and at the moment of imbalance the chiropractor is then able to help the body find a deeper, more profound balance that it hasn't known for years.

This sort of pattern also occurs on planes other than the physical. How often have we seen a person with deep-seated emotional problems, who, after experiencing a traumatic event, finds that they are suddenly in a more harmonious emotional place. Likewise, the spiritual life of a person can sometimes achieve a higher and clearer balance on the other side of trauma.

ARCANUM XI: THE MAIDEN (THE ENCHANTRESS)

Alternate name: Strength
Number: 11
Planet: Neptune
Anatomy: pineal gland
English letters: C, K
Flower: water lily
Angel: Tzaphkiel
Color: iridescent gray

This is a card of pure raw power. It usually shows a young, ethereal woman gently holding a lion's mouth shut. She's stronger than he is because her power is of her psyche and is generated by the subtle force of her pure being, whereas the lion's is mere physical strength. The lion is a symbol of personality, the voracious creature in all of us that yearns to be tamed and refined, but who can rage out of control if we let him since it's his nature to reflect all our stress. To tame him one must use intuitive craft and cunning. The power of the physical level is always obvious, but greater power is discovered at levels subtler than the physical.

When we have completed our cycle of the major arcana we will see that the astrological sign ascribed the lowest number is Virgo, and the sign ascribed the highest number is Leo. In this card the two forces meet, the lion and the virgin. The Sphinx, who has a lion's body and a woman's head, is also symbolic of this linking of these two energies.

These two entities have much to gain from each other. The lion knows the virgin as his master, and he in turn can be her protector. She in turn can offer careful direction to his powerful energy. The great work of alchemy can be defined in many ways, one of which is the perfection of one's individuality, which is typified by this card.

In astrology, Neptune is often thought of as a scary and destructive force. This is because its power can upset structure, usually in an undermining fashion that melts it away, dissolves it, takes away its edges. If one's individuality is limited, if the person has made herself little and petty, the inner power is locked into the being like steam in a pressure cooker.

If this pure, raw power is repressed too much, it gains even more negative potential until it finally bursts its container. Insanity results. Grow or die is the law of the universe. Neptune infuses a being with power, and if the personality is stiff and cramped, then this influx of energy will tend to tear the person down and dissolve biases, narrow thinking, and limitations.

Neptune is also the planet of idealism, because ideals are the most powerful thoughts a mind can embrace. If we link our being to high ideals, then when we experience any form of personality breakdown we know that it's only a prelude to the restructuring of the personality on a more harmonious and life-supporting level. Fear of insanity and of identity loss can actually cause those things that are feared. If we turn our thoughts from fear to idealism, we then have a focus that helps us withstand these sometimes terrifying periods of transformation.

Because of antiwar sentiments in our society, many people might object to the metaphor of life as a battle. This metaphor, though, does not necessarily imply any sort of violence. Being a good warrior is not just about grabbing a gun and running up to enemy lines screaming and yelling. A great many wars were not won primarily by brute strength, but rather by cunning and planning. Violence is mostly a waste of energy.

In this card we see a master warrior, who is not a man, but rather a woman. She has gained ascendency over one of nature's most powerful creatures, and she has accomplished this through the actualization of her psychic power, as well as through her love. It is important to realize that even though this card depicts the lion as something outside of her, the force she has harnessed is within her. Since the inner and outer worlds mirror each other when we've accomplished this feat, we naturally find that the outer world has lost its power to subjugate us.

We associate speed with Arcanum X, The Wheel, because it is duality attempting to reunify itself. This attempt creates a whirling motion whose friction generates sparks of inspiration, since inspiration is so fast as to be almost instantaneous. From these seeds of inspiration, refinement blooms, refinement being a delicate, ethereal manifestation of Arcanum XI, The Maiden. Psychic speed births strength.

We may see this at work in shafts of straw a tornado drives into a tree. The straw's too flexible to be driven unless it's done with great swiftness. Then that frail blade has a knife's power. The psychic power of The Enchantress vibrates at a much higher rate than the lion, whose mouth she holds shut in her delicate hands. It's because she reacts swiftly to her own psychic impressions that she can perform this feat. This card always calls for a firm yet gentle handling of the surrounding reality. It often calls for taking the indirect path that sometimes indicates deceit and deception.

The energy here melts and dissolves barriers rather than crashing through them. Sometimes a gentle kiss can work as well as a key to unlock a gate. A fine discipline associated with this card is tai chi.

The flower essence associated with this card is aspen, which helps one overcome fears, especially when they are of a vague or undefined nature. The way aspen trees send out runners underground to reproduce themselves is like the hiddenness associated with this card.

I'm tempted to say that another flower associated with this card is the waterspout, an evanescent, whirling "bloom" that's actually an oceanic tornado made of saltwater. It would be beneficial to gather the mists from these waterspouts and concoct a homeopathic remedy out of them, as an elixir of such water makes an excellent eyewash for the third eye.

This is the arcanum of psychic power. The spirit inhabiting this card is elusive, hidden. The aspirant discovers it through inner knowing. Uncertainty can darken and cloud its source, nature, and location, and so to discover it the aspirant must let go of all attempts to comprehend it logically, all attachments to rationality. The key to becoming one with this power is to entrain to it, to resonate with it, and as this resonance becomes clearer and clearer, the aspirant realizes that there is no limit to the power of this marvelous treasure.

The lion on this card links it to the sign Leo, ruled by Arcanum XIX, The Sun. Leo is the sign of the ego, that dominating aspect of oneself that clings to the myth of our separateness. Ego grows the mask of personality, and personality cannot exist without boundaries. In this arcanum, though, boundaries are nowhere to be found. This is not completely true, for there *are* boundaries here, but they shimmer, shift, and change; they expand and shrink; they are playful, confusing, deceptive. Entering Arcanum XI with one's ego intact always means that it will be experienced as a land of confusion, but the more the ego is let go of, the more one is able to both see and see through these beautiful phantasms, and we can thereby enjoy them without being duped by them.

In myth, Arcanum XI signifies all deceits and deceptions practiced by the spirit realm. The purpose of these is always to throw aspirants back on themselves over and over, until at last they enter the light of their inner knowing and can be guided by it.

ARCANUM XII: THE DEVOTEE (THE MARTYR)

Alternate name: The Hanged Man
Number: 12
Sign: Pisces
Anatomy: feet, bloodstream
English letter: L
Flower: rock rose
Angel: Sandalphon
Color: red-violet, magenta

Arcanum XII, The Devotee, is ruled by Pisces, the last sign of the zodiac. It signifies giving up, giving in, and letting go.

"Not my will, but thy will," said Jesus. The card is named The Devotee because this is what a devoted person does—she gives up something or lets go of activities and involvements so that she can devote herself to something else, hopefully something that helps others in need, something that furthers their evolution. Devotion is what most fulfills Pisces, and if they don't have it in their life they can feel adrift and directionless. It's why Pisces rules addiction, for addiction is a pathological devotion to something. This need for a spiritual purpose is why Pisces often can't seem to find a goal they want to work toward, because any goal they attempt to choose they lose interest in if they feel it is not spiritual. Actually, Pisces might be fulfilled by any goal as long as they can bring the love and light of spirituality to it. This is one reason why Venus is exalted in Pisces.

As the last sign of the zodiac, Pisces is the sum of all that's gone before, which makes it one of the two most cosmic signs, Sagittarius (corresponding to Arcanum VII, The Victory) being the other one. But whereas Sagittarius has the power to soar above earthly concerns, it's Pisces's inclination to become immersed in everything physical, and for that matter, in everything mental, emotional, and spiritual as well, as it is the most universal and immersive of the signs. This receptivity to everything is why it can have problems with focusing. Its uncertainty was aptly expressed by one astrologer who said, "Pinning down a Pisces is like trying to nail jello to a wall."

The person on this card hangs upside down because the highest part of him, symbolized by his head, is merging with the lowest part, the ground, while the lowest part of him, his feet, is raised up to the highest part, the sky. This means that spirit is here merged with earth in an effort to bring love and light into the physical realm and to raise skyward all that is lowly, symbolized by the feet, to merge with the highest spiritual energy.

The Devotee signifies sensitivity to everything, and hence a tendency to be acutely vulnerable. When this card comes up in a reading it's encouraging you to protect yourself and to keep your attention focused on goodness, love, and the realities of the spiritual realm, for herein lies your ultimate protection.

One of the biggest pitfalls of this card is guilt, which is always an unnecessary burden and leads to stagnation. Guilt arises from judging oneself, which should never be done, for it dissipates energy that could be used for helping and loving other people.

This card also encourages you to follow your inner guidance—your intuition—even when it seems to go against common sense and what others think you should do.

The letting-go this card is asking of you is beautiful and relaxing, and when you do it you make yourself more receptive to the soft and delicate voices of angels, who speak in the silence. Swedenborg tells us that the voices of angels are faint and ethereal, whereas the voices of demons tend to be rough, gross, and dominating. When you allow yourself to enter the all-pervasive silence of the universe, you are able to hear angels and receive their messages, which can come in any form—words, pictures, inklings, impulses, and even things that happen to you.

The number 12 is the first number falling under the category of *abundant numbers,* in this case referring to the mathematical meaning that when you add together all the numbers that evenly divide into it—1, 2, 3, 4, and 6—you get a sum that's more than the original number. Since 12 is the first and lowest of these abundant numbers, it's their queen. I say "queen" because it's an even number, and all even numbers are of the feminine gender.

Pisces, ruler of this arcanum, is the last sign of the zodiac. It thus contains all the other signs, and so in a sense it has no personality of its own. Another way to say this is that it has a personality made up of all the other personalities—a universal identity.

This card is commonly called The Hanged Man. He waits, suspended. He has not been harmed. He seems to be at peace. Pisces can feel directionless, as if it has no place to go or could go anyplace but can't decide which direction to take. The "roads" that fish travel in the sea are hard to predict and forever changing. When we're held in such suspension, when our freedom of outer movement is taken away, then our focus naturally turns inward, which is why Pisces can be one of the most spiritual of the signs and why it has always been called the sign of the poet, that alchemist of words who invents in the gigantic laboratory of the imagination.

One of the biggest issues in our world is winning and what that means, for this is the card of giving up, letting go, and submitting to outer forces. Winning is most often about striving against something, but this arcanum wins by quitting the race before it's over. What ultimately matters is what we think is important. Pisces craves to be a part of all realities, to be in sympathetic vibration with the superabundance of the universe. And so for Pisces, letting go and giving up is a way of discovering one's true self and winning in the highest cosmic sense. When you give up your identity and don't know who you are, you make it possible to become whatever you need to become.

The Martyr is often shown dropping coins on the ground. These coins symbolize that which they've earned. Negatively, the coins symbolize a wasting of life energy, and positively they mean that The Martyr is leaving treasures behind on earth so that others who come later can find them and use them.

The flower essence associated with this card is rock rose, which helps one overcome shock. I've found that it helps not only with obvious and gross shock, but also with what I call microshocks—all the jangling and discord of city living and stuff that's like sandpaper to a refined sensibility. And in a larger sense it is all those PTSD echoes that are still retained in our psyche from past lives. Rock rose flower essence can also wake up and make more sensitive those who think they aren't sensitive. I think everyone probably needs rock rose.

Of course, the tree from which The Devotee hangs is the Tree of Life. The inactivity permeating this card reveals it as having to do with waiting. But for what does the waiter wait?

The answer is simple: this aspirant is the *fruit* of the Tree, and what they are waiting for is about to ripen, at which time it will fall to the ground to then be consumed as nourishment by either an animal or the ground itself. In either case whatever eats it will be enriched by its flesh. Arcanum XII is the card of sacrifice, hence the name The Martyr. This card is Jesus, who gave himself to be "eaten" in the sacrament of Communion.

Even though this captive is found in a state in which she can seemingly do nothing outwardly, there is every possibility here of exploring the inner realms, of leading a rich inner life while she appears to wait.

And this inner exploring has the power to positively enrich the aspirant's outer world.

To embrace the energy of this card we must give up, let go, and know that in doing so we are not failing or losing, we're *allowing* ourself to be completely taken over by natural processes, which, if we faithfully track them in our consciousness, can carry us to enlightenment.

Some say that that priceless commodity sought by the alchemists, the philosopher's stone, is actually awareness, pure and simple. Through our awareness we feed whatever we're aware of. Deepak Chopra tells us that we become whatever we focus on. When outer activity ceases, which has happened in this card, awareness is then nourished and magnified so that it can complete the work of ripening our divine potential.

In myth, this card has to do with all failures and blockages encountered along the way, all illusions of energy wasted, for all such losses are always at a deeper level course corrections that need to happen as the force of evolution carries us toward our goal.

CHAPTER FOUR

Flowers and Major Arcana XIII–XVI

THE THERAPEUTIC USE OF FLOWERS

You will find throughout these writings on the major arcana that flowers are mentioned as corresponding to every one of them. If you wish to purchase any of these flowers in the form of essences that can be used for healing, you can go online and find them. Often a single essence will be sold by a number of different companies. You can also put a few drops of them in a spray bottle full of water and then spray them in your aura or in a room. This can be an excellent way of tuning in more deeply to each arcana.

Every flower corresponds to one or more of the major arcana. It would be wonderful to have a large dictionary that would tell the rulership of a great many of them. This is perhaps a study that someone will someday wish to undertake. In the meantime, you can figure out for yourself which arcana or arcanum a flower corresponds to by reading about the plant's growth habits or the kinds of things the plant is used for as an herb. And, of course, you may also use your own intuition.

An example is scurvy weed, which is one of my favorites. Its leaves are rich in vitamin C and were consumed in past times for their healing effects, which is how the flower got its common name. Its renewing and anti-inflammatory effects cause me to associate it with the sign Aries, and hence Arcanum XIII, The Rainbow, which you're going to read about next.

Other people might disagree with this rulership ascription, thinking perhaps that Sagittarius and Arcanum VII, The Victory, would be more appropriate, given the flower's intense blue color—blue corresponding to Sagittarius. I certainly think the energy of Arcanum VII is present in the plant but feel intuitively that the association with Arcanum XIII is even stronger. The fact that scurvy weed grows fast and is shallow-rooted, and also the bright blue color of its flowers, speak to me of newness and freshness—and Aries is the first sign of spring.

Perhaps if you were to tune in to the scurvy weed spirit you would feel that it has affinities to arcana other than the two I've mentioned. The best way to find out these rulerships is through direct experience of the life energy of the plant and exploring how that matches up with your growing experience with the cards. Tuning in to plant spirits can be a wonderful way of delving even deeper into the tarot.

ARCANUM XIII: THE RAINBOW (THE REAPER)

Alternate name: Death
Number: 13
Sign: Aries
Anatomy: head
English letter: M
Flower: impatiens
Angel: Ariel
Color: red, pink

This arcanum is often referred to as the death card, and in many decks it is called Death. Many unfamiliar with the tarot are frightened by its appearance and are horrified if it appears in a reading. Psychologists say that the fear of death has been a primary motivating factor in human behavior throughout history. To further confound those who are superstitious, this card is assigned the supposedly unlucky number 13.

However, this card in no way signifies a horrible omen of impending doom. Quite the contrary, its mystery embodies rebirth, rejuvenation, and regeneration. If you believe death is final, that is, that there is nothing beyond it, certainly the scythe of the rainbow that's always depicted in this card would ominously hang over your head throughout your life. Nevertheless, the metaphysical truth depicted here tells us that after death there's always a new beginning, a resurgence of life. Inherent in this concept is the further idea that when a particular manifestation of form has reached the completion of an evolutionary cycle, it must be reformed in order to continue to grow.

To realize this transformation, a dying to the old is imperative. Throughout our lifetime we experience many deaths. Once we've completed a cycle of growth we move on to new cycles of potential or else we hold back and basically stagnate until we're ready for the new cycle. Death is always a dying to old circumstances and patterns in order to birth a new and finer self on a higher plane of consciousness.

To die a horrible death, on the other hand, would be to permit our potential to stagnate too long in ruts of the past. The superstitious aren't really afraid of death itself, but fear, rather, the painful possibility of growth. Not dying, but *living* is the source of their fear.

Arcanum XIII, which in our deck is called The Rainbow, is ruled by the sign Aries. Aries denotes the pioneer who dies to their secure life patterns and advances into unknown and unexplored frontiers. The pioneer is made vulnerable in this manner. She stands alone, over an abyss. This is the way in which horizons are expanded. Pioneers blaze a trail so that others may follow with greater ease than they had. They aspire to the heights of mountains and lands beyond.

As a note to the superstitious: it's easy to get caught up in the security of past glories, to experience the comfort of a circle of friends who never challenge you to go beyond that which you have already accomplished. This is a kind of death, though you continue moving and breathing. The speech of these dead folks is hollow, containing little power, and their breath is a purely mechanical process.

If a tree, once grand with foliage, becomes diseased, the gardener must prune the dead branches that are sapping the tree's strength. In this way the tree can once again grow toward grandeur. The more we come to understand death, the more we greet it with open arms as it continues to come to us daily, both in its lesser and greater manifestations, for death is the magic wand that clears our path, opening a way forward.

The figure of death that appears in this card often carries a scythe and is harvesting in a field where human heads, hands, and feet are lying. These body parts are a human being's extremities. The meaning here is that the extremities or extremes have been cut away so that new growth has room to manifest. Hence the card may be thought of as a return to one's vital spiritual core. This core carries the life force and can symbolically regenerate new extensions—new "limbs"—in the coming new cycle. With each rebirth we extend ourself in new ways.

This card signifies crisis and the threat that crisis presents to that homeostatic illusion of stability we call life. The personage represented here is a skeleton, because although this card is ruled by Aries, it's the sign Capricorn that rules the skeleton, and Capricorn signifies karma. This means that the primary thing that is carried over into new cycles is karma, the unfinished dramas and lingering attachments of the former cycle—all the stuck places. We might also use the words *purgation* and *catharsis* to describe this card.

It's traditional to have a rainbow depicted in the background of this arcanum. The rainbow was first seen when Noah stepped out of the Ark. It represents God's promise to humans that the world will never again be destroyed by water. Destruction by water symbolizes becoming overwhelmed by subconscious, astral, and emotional forces. Once this happens and the psyche finally emerges and finds dry land, it achieves new awareness that can never be lost. In metaphysical terms, God's promise to humans signifies that once anything has truly been worked through it will never have to be dealt with again—unless of course we just thought we'd worked it through but it wasn't fully resolved and assimilated before.

When we're born we die at least in part to the spirit world. How much we die to it depends on our level of evolution. And when we die on the earth plane we're again born into the realm of spirit. The moment these changes take place constitutes a high point in awareness. The ancients tell us that most people who are ready to reach enlightenment do so during the process of dying.

It's interesting that the number 13 has strong associations with the

Moon. This is because there can sometimes be thirteen New Moons in a year. For the Moon to make a complete trip around the zodiac it takes about 27.3 days, and 27.3 × 13 = 355.29—about ten days less than a year. And so the Moon is also associated in a sense with new beginnings, as its energy has a flowing and unstable feel to it. We need the moistening quality of this instability to bring change into our lives. So whereas Aries, the ruler of this card, marks the time of the year when the Sun begins a new cycle, the Moon, at the rate of nearly thirteen times a year, is also bringing in faster and more frequent cycles of renewal.

One of the most important flower remedies that is associated with this card is impatiens. This remedy slows you down in the most positive of ways and so puts you in clearer and more harmonious sync with the movements of the universe. For this reason it can help dissolve and wash away frustration and the illusion that the only way to get ahead is to be pushing all the time. It reminds me of the Red Queen in *Alice in Wonderland,* who told Alice that she always had to keep running just to stay in the same place. She needed impatiens flower essence. Note too that people who live on this hurried wavelength are often not aware of it, so they might think they don't need this remedy, although they would greatly benefit from it. You might have to slip it in their drink when they aren't looking! Red impatiens is the most potent on a physical level, while white impatiens is for those who stressfully hurry toward spiritual development, and pink impatiens helps you slow down and take in more love, to savor everything more fully. Any and all three of these will often help a person who has problems sleeping.

Funny how the brightest part of us is the whites of our eyes and our bones, whose whiteness is not fully revealed until we've been dead awhile. The happy skeleton of Arcanum XIII isn't prone as it should be, but instead stands upright in the landscape and is busily at work, its clean bones shining beneath the rainbow. When I think of it I often imagine that illustration from the *Rubaiyat of Omar Khayyam,* in which a skeleton is dancing, garlanded in roses, while its flesh has been replaced with the flowers of love.

Some might think it strange that this figure of death would fall under the rulership of Aries, the sign of spring and rebirth. But it is in the season of renewal that we are most haunted by the ghosts of the past, for almost always there's something in our former life, some cyst or calculus or knot, that has not yet fully dissolved. As T. S. Eliot says, "April is the cruellest month, breeding / Lilacs out of the dead land." It's interesting that lilac flower essence is used to strengthen the spine, the skeletal core. And then of course there's those remains that persist longer through time: the bones.

One of the ways of looking at this arcanum is that it signifies whatever we drag along with us as we attempt new beginnings. Can we flesh out these old bones with new meat, or must they too be discarded so that we can completely start over anew?

The severed feet, hands, and heads of the card are the extensions lopped off in the process of renewal—where we have traveled (feet), all we've given and taken (hands), and all we've thought (heads). The memories of these must be at least temporarily pushed aside to make way for new experiences. It's why most of us don't remember our past lives—to do so would be too distracting (let alone embarrassing or demeaning) and could divert us from what's happening in the present. Later, when we're ready, these memories of the past can be summoned if we need them, or maybe if our curiosity persists. I say "can be" summoned, but believe me, in one way or another, like infections in the body, they will eventually make their way to the surface of the skin to be pushed out.

ARCANUM XIV: THE ALCHEMIST (TEMPERANCE)

Alternate name: Art (alchemy is sometimes referred to as the *ars regia,* meaning "royal art" or "the art of kings")
Number: 14
Sign: Taurus
Anatomy: neck and throat
English letter: N
Flower: gentian
Angel: Chamuel
Color: red-orange

The number 14 has been called by Russian occultist Helena Blavatsky (1831–1891) the most vital and important number connected with processes. There are seven basic activities in the universe, and these activities are symbolized by the seven main planets of our solar system. Each activity can be either form-building or form-destroying. Energy, by Einstein's equation, is either changing into matter (form-building) or is in the process of being liberated from matter (form-destroying). So each of the seven major energies are double, and it is this truth that multiplies the seven forces by 2 and thereby generates the number 14.

The Alchemist must learn and then use fourteen different procedures in her work. (And by the way, it's been said by a number of traditional authorities that women are better at alchemy than men!) If all fourteen procedures are not used, the work will fail. The challenge of The Alchemist is to integrate these energies in the proper manner. They are all positive when they are placed in correct relationship to one another. Taurus expresses the idea of "I have," and it is this completeness of having all the energies at one's disposal that amounts to true possession.

The Alchemist pictured in this card holds two cups, one of gold and one of silver. She pours liquid from one cup to the other. This symbolizes the fluid mind-energy flowing between the subconscious (silver = Moon = feelings) and the conscious (gold = Sun = willpower). The flow of vital energy between the cups is a closed system. This sense of closure sometimes appears in the Taurean nature as dogmatism, stubbornness, and hardheadedness, some of Taurus's worst characteristics, though Taurus people often say they're their best ones!

It goes without saying that all fourteen energies are always present in each and every person, but usually not quite in the proper amounts. Due to one's particular personality, some of the forces are weaker in some than in others, and some of the forces either collect more readily or are more easily dissipated. This card reveals the secret that the great work of alchemy is never so much a matter of actually changing oneself as it is changing one's focus. A chain is only as strong as its weakest link. What gives Taurus such great power is its ability to perceive weak links and then to reinforce them.

Taurus is the opposite sign of Scorpio. These two signs are complementary. The Scorpio vision pierces through the veils of matter, whereas the Taurus nature tends to work to realign and adjust the veils so that they can be seen through more and more.

The Taurean nature is slow and paced, like the tortoise in "The Tortoise and Hare" story of Aesop. (The hare, by the way, is a Gemini.) The driving patience of Taurus, which is unflagging, always gets the job done. The negative side of this is inflexibility, which, as we have seen, always spells weakness. The best that can be said for the slow, plodding work of The Alchemist is that work done in this manner is rarely inaccurate or capable of being undone. Rapid progress is always in danger of drawing rapid setbacks to itself. The Taurean nature, on the other hand, is far too immoveable to ever be compelled to relinquish one inch of territory once it's been conquered.

Even though life for Taurus may be constant toil up a steep incline, its footing is absolutely sure. The Great Pyramid of Giza, a symbol of the enduring work of humankind, was built near the end of the Taurean Age. This simple yet incredibly monumental structure shows what kinds of feats can be accomplished through effort that is steady and paced.

The water poured between the two vessels in this card is the water of attention. In tarot iconography, any flowing water such as streams and rivers represent the life force moving through space and time, the fluid point of awareness.

Here the fluid point is moving between inner life (the silver cup) and outer life (the golden cup). Art is messages sent from the inner life to the outer life, hence this card rules art as a function. Note that Arcanum VI, The Crossroads, rules artistic energy, or one might say the *process* of art, whereas Arcanum XIV, The Alchemist, rules art as *product.*

The sign Taurus has an enduring love of materiality because of all the comforts it can bring. Mind and spirituality have ascendancy over matter, yet the truly spiritual person does not despise the material world, but rather has great respect for its potential uses as a vehicle of learning—a kind of textbook. Art is the most sacred use to which it can be put. The sacred life is the artful life, full of spiritual beauty.

By art we mean true art, which is the same as the Native American idea of medicine. True art is inspiring, educational, and above all, healing. Hence the highest use of matter is to use it to heal the spirit.

The fourteen energies I speak of here are the seven lower and manifest energies of the Tree of Life, considered in terms of both their active and passive natures ($2 \times 7 = 14$). Each one of these energies may act, and also be acted on, hence the number 14.

We might title this card Stamina, for this is what integration calls for. Stamina is built on proper timing and has the patience to wait for that time.

Gentian flower essence is the healer of this card, as it helps one overcome the feeling of being let down after a failure or setback. It gives you the determination to keep moving forward and to keep trying.

The Alchemist is a cook, a combiner of ingredients who seeks the recipe for the ultimate food: the philosopher's stone. Were the universe a machine, The Alchemist's task would be much simpler, for then, by mechanical trial and error, various formulae could be tested until the right one was found. But machines don't create art.

Reality is not so dependably precise as that. The philosopher's stone can indeed be cooked up, but some of the ingredients, rather than being of a solely physical nature, are such intangible things as quantum forces and spiritual essences—inspirations that have an exceedingly brief shelf life. As well, so much depends not only on what the alchemist adds to the brew, but far more on the intent in concocting it and the psychic forces stirred therein.

Many alchemists would love to be able to depend on formulae, but even though these can be helpful in carrying on the work, what will bring it to ultimate success is the quality of one's consciousness. This is why when some people use a formula it never works, whereas when others employ it it's always successful.

The astrological ruler of this arcanum, Taurus, is the sign of *having*. Through exploring this arcanum, the aspirant comes to see more and more clearly what they *do* possess: some treasures and maybe some things the traveler probably wishes they didn't have and so must figure out how to get rid of.

Of course, we must always begin by recognizing our most obvious assets, but then as we grow more aware of our inner self, we discover the rich mines found everywhere within, all those many places where the precious ingredients of great value are hidden and stored away.

ARCANUM XV: THE MUSICIAN (THE BLACK MAGICIAN)

Alternate name: The Devil
Number: 15
Planet: Saturn
Anatomy: posterior pituitary
English letter: X
Flower: chrysanthemum, night-blooming cereus, black hellebore
Angel: Chamuel
Color: blue, black, gray

This is the arcanum of structure, and therefore, limitation. Structure inhibits and contains energy. It also organizes it so that it becomes more powerful. Structure is a tool, but unfortunately it can also be a weapon. As Marshall MacLuhan says, we shape our tools, and then our tools shape us. We structure our consciousness, and then the structure of our consciousness limits, inhibits, and contains the energy that pours forth from our Higher Self. Structure is necessary, but unfortunately it's something we're not usually as fully aware of as we need to be. Our lack of awareness of structure means that we tend to think the limits we work within are facts of life—unchangeable, something we cannot question or overcome.

We blind ourselves to the fact that structure can be broken down and then built up again in a broader and more expanded context.

Structure is fate, and fate is fact. The secret, though, is that we're free to choose our structure and hence our fate. Everyone and everything has a destiny, but this destiny is not forced on us. It's a matter of choice.

As long as we're living here on Earth, we are, of course, limited in certain ways. The true self knows no bounds and is therefore unlimited and free. It has chosen, though, to come down into the physical world and take on limitations, and so has arrived on this planet and put on a physical body. Its limitless quality has condensed itself into form. The soul in this manner has chosen to express itself within the structure of the first three dimensions of space and the dimension of time.

Limitation always implies power. We may think that limitation is weakness, and yet when divine energy struggles to overcome the limitations of structure it gains greatly in its ability to manifest.

For instance, if we do not limit our interests, we may get involved in a lot of different activities, and because we already have the limitations of time and physical energy imposed on us we may do these many things, but maybe do none of them very well. If, on the other hand, we consciously impose more limitations on ourself, such as taking on only one or two things to work at, we'll find we can go far in these pursuits.

We must always keep in mind that all limitations are ultimately artificial, and therefore unreal. We think of the devil—His Majesty Necessary Evil—as being a thing in and of itself, an equal and opposite force to God. But who created the devil? Why God, of course! Master Satan is simply a tool of God. While we are here and alive, we cannot escape the necessary "evil" inherent in bodily existence. And so instead of letting its limitations control and use us, we must learn to use such limitations for our highest good. In this way our divine spark gains powerful momentum, and the devil has done the work that God put him here to do in the first place.

Humans have always feared the energy of this card, which is why in many of the older tarot decks they give it the name The Devil. The only way to effectively use the energy of this arcanum is to make conscious decisions concerning how one is going to use one's time and energy, and where one is going to direct one's attention—to be proactive rather than solely reactive, for reactivity just generates the same old karma.

Arcanum XV corresponds to the Greek god Pan, the god of all of nature. The early Christians thought him a personification of evil because they were against anything pertaining to physical nature. They exalted the spiritual and renounced the physical. This renunciation has tainted Western civilization up to the present, and nature has consequently rebelled, causing massive ecological upsets. This is the price to be paid for not respecting the great cloven-hoofed god.

The Musician, a far brighter and more beautiful name for this card, corresponds to the planet Saturn, whose rings speak of limitations. Indeed, Saturn is the planet farthest from Earth that is still visible to the naked eye, so Saturn is a symbol of the visible limits of our solar system.

The alchemists made much of the difference between art and nature. What nature takes a long time to do, art can accomplish far more swiftly. Nature can make gold, but it took millions of years to do it; the alchemist (or artist), though, can make gold in a short while using the proper artistry and recipes. So Saturn, nature, and time are all associated with this arcanum. Note that the concept here is not time in the general sense, but time as the pacemaker of all cycles—time as Father Time, the reaper and harvester, who harvests the crops of circumstance planted by actions.

A fine flower essence to use to magnify the positive aspects of this card is night-blooming cereus, which sounds the depths of profundity, helping one overcome fears and limitations as you get in touch with your real gifts. Black hellebore flower essence, also sacred to this arcanum, will help you retrieve the lost parts of yourself, making you feel fuller and more complete. Chrysanthemum helps one to overcome the fear of aging and move gracefully into maturity.

Arcanum XV, The Musician, tells us that we must deal with our limitations—in fact, they make us do so. This seems like such a simple truth, yet so many people in so many ways fail to realize this or do everything they can to ignore this. Limitations are what creates the music of the universe.

Limitations, according to kabbalists, are the best things that ever happened to us; they are our ultimate teachers, and each person's specific limits are tailor-made to teach that person exactly what they need to learn, harsh as that often turns out to be. It's of great interest to me how some people feel relieved when they realize this truth and are thankful for it, whereas others find it terrifying.

As Seth, the disembodied teacher who spoke through channel Jane Roberts, told us, "You create your own reality through your beliefs." This means that all the stuff that's happening to us is the result of our own creations. Can you believe it? How wonderful to know this! For when we realize this we can then ask *why* we're doing what we're doing, and what we expect to derive from whatever it is we've set up for ourselves. Of course, we may not receive immediate answers to such questions, but while we wait for them to arise we can honor the fact that the Higher Self has cooked up something to put us through and always has perfect reasons for doing so.

Pan wears many guises and masks. One of them is the voodoo orisha Baron Samedi, who recently has been coming to me on a regular basis. He appears as an elderly black man in a top hat and waistcoat, and carries a black gold-tipped cane. The black hat most likely covers his horns. (He laughs at that one!) He tells me that we all get what we deserve, which is exactly the same as what we put out. It all comes back.

How easy it is, then, to control your world. All you must do is put out whatever you want to come back to you. That's what makes the music of this card.

ARCANUM XVI: THE PYRAMID (THE POWER)

Alternate name: The Tower
Number: 16
Planet: Mars
Anatomy: adrenal glands
English letter: O
Flower: holly, kudzu
Angel: Haniel
Color: orange

Arcanum XVI, The Pyramid, is usually depicted as a tower, a stone building, or a pyramid toppling down, struck by a devastating bolt of lightning. Very often people are shown falling from the edifice. In the story of the Tower of Babel, people were seeking to reach farther and farther into the sky, but then their tower fell, and through this the people learned a little more about their limits.

This is a card of destruction. Be careful of the foundations on which you build. The people who erected the Tower of Babel hoped to climb to heaven, so God sent them a lightning bolt to teach them that there was other work to be done down on the ground.

Positively, the energy of Mars can be directed toward construction. Mars initiated the building of the pyramid on this card; it is through the persistence of Mars that it reached completion. If there's a flaw in the premise on which it's built, this flaw will eventually manifest as a weakness, and Mars will bring about the destruction of this edifice as it did in the year 1303 AD, when an earthquake cracked the white limestone casing stones of the Great Pyramid, after which people started taking away these stones to use for other constructions.

Mars represents the masculine or active force in the universe. In Roman mythology, Mars is the god of war, however, more primitive interpretations of this mythic figure depict him as the god of fertility. In this vein we may perceive him as the active sexual function, the procreator. He's the initiator of life. He implants his energy, transmuting it into the life force.

The aggressive energy of Mars, which reproduces and constructs a civilization of humans, can also turn against itself and destroy that civilization. Humans beget humans, and humans kill humans. This dichotomy is the mystery of Arcanum XVI, and it must be resolved within the heart of each person.

Why do people needlessly destroy what they've created?

All of humanity's creations contain the essence of humankind, therefore when humans destroy their own creations we are ultimately destroying ourselves.

This aggressive force needs to be controlled. When it's properly harnessed and directed, it's capable of producing a golden age for humanity. Like the atom, once split releasing its power, this force of Mars can be used for either destruction or construction. Each person must decide the ways in which their energy will be directed and then take the initiative to see that their energy is directed toward the construction necessary to house the Higher Self here on the earth plane.

Construction is necessary in the process of evolution, but when anything is built on a flawed foundation, it may generate forces that work against evolution.

Once we've discovered the flaw in any foundation, it might then be necessary to turn this Mars force on our pyramid to destroy all or part of it, maybe even leveling it so that we can once again address the work of construction.

Both in conscious and unconscious ways we are constantly directing our energy toward the building of inner and outer patterns and structures. As these patterns eventually become obsolete, no longer serving our needs, we need to destroy them. In this way we clear away the needless debris from the field of our life so that new forms can take shape.

Some occultists link this card to the fall of the walls of Jericho. Physicist Kurt Mendelssohn (1906–1980), in his book *The Riddle of the Pyramids,* discovered that one of the pyramids of Egypt fell down during construction. It's possible that the original tarot card for this arcanum alluded to this event. At any rate the pyramid seems to me to be a more appropriate symbol than a tower, since in the pyramid structure there are sixteen radiations of lines (four radiations at the top and three at each corner), and 16 is the number of this card.

The two people depicted in some decks as falling from the top of the edifice symbolize the high position (one is a king) and the lowly position (one is a peasant). This shows that destruction comes equally to all, irrespective of authority or temporal power.

Sometimes The Pyramid is shown with a crown on its top to symbolize the first station of the Tree of Life, which is often referred to as the crown.

A good flower remedy for this card is holly, which helps one get to the source of one's anger and find more fulfilling ways of directing that energy into creative endeavors. Another good flower essence associated with this card is kudzu, which encourages persistence in times of emotional setback and helps one overcome destructive self-criticism.

The Pyramid (or Tower) depicted on this card signifies authorities and all authoritarian institutions, and not only the outer ones, but also those we've set up in our psyche. That means everything we take for granted and everything we accept as right and true. The lightning strikes this great edifice to bring it down, either partially or fully, if that's what it needs. Through this destruction, anything that has grown useless or burdensome is cleared away so that new inspirations can revitalize our being.

A young magician recently reminded me that in some old tarot decks this card is called The House of God. I think of this as signifying any "temple" of dogma that needs a good, swift kick in the butt to bring it down so that fresh new light can come in.

In Japan, they tear down the Ise Grand Shrine every twenty years and build a new one on a plot adjacent to the old one, as a means of renewing the energy of the place. This arcanum, The Pyramid, signifies the same sort of renewal process. We do the same thing with our bodies—dying every so often so we can build a new vehicle for ourselves as a means of refreshing our energies. We go to the gym to destroy muscle tissue so that it'll build back even stronger, which is a perfect metaphor for this card, since Mars rules muscles.

All manifestations of anger, the negative emotion of Mars, come from repressing the urge to tear down and rebuild, repressing what this card wants to do. The reason the tearing-down part is what's depicted on the card rather than the building-up phase is because destruction of what we've depended on in the past always tends to be the scary part. Unless we tear down, there's no room to build. We must first make a space within ourself, a space in which to express our creative energies, just as Creative Intelligence did when it created the universe.

CHAPTER FIVE

The Hebrew Alphabet and Major Arcana XVII–XX

The twenty-two cards of the major arcana correspond to the twenty-two letters of the Hebrew alphabet. In Hebrew, just as in aUI (see chapter 18, "The Language of Space (aUI)"), each letter is an actual word in and of itself.

Since earliest time, scholars of the Kabbalah have studied holy scriptures by adding up the numerical values of the letters in a word to find hidden meanings in that word, a practice known as *gematria* (see chapter 16, "Gematria," for a more detailed explanation of this numerology system). Words that add up to the same number value have similar vibrations and therefore are thought of as having similar meanings. Kabbalists see their holy writings as complex formulae, a vibratory web that can be studied to reveal the secrets of the universe.

A Kabbalah scholar once said that if a child were to be removed from society at birth and allowed to grow up in a forest, it would naturally grow up speaking Hebrew on its own. So far I don't think any feral children have been found who spoke to their discoverers in Hebrew.

Many occultists feel that classical Hebrew is a pure language, untainted by foreign pollutions or invasions of words from other languages. It was believed that the sacred texts of the Israelites were channeled directly from God, who had the wisdom and power to place this plethora of numerical meanings into the words.

Speaking of another culture, we find as well that many scholars of Vedic literature claim that the same purity and perfection associated with the Hebrew language is found in Sanskrit. These scholars say that every sound in Sanskrit is imbued with meaning, and that a person of highly developed consciousness can feel these meanings when they hear them without even needing to consciously know what the words mean.

All these claims are partial illusions, I feel. The fact is that all reality is filled with meaning. Maybe everything is a spiritual text. It's not possible to say that any one language is more pure in terms of its expressive power than another. Language is a tool, and the power of a tool depends on how skillfully it's used.

Many like to defer to antiquity when they make quality judgments, because humans in general like to think the older something is, the better it must be. Hebrew and Sanskrit are two of our oldest languages, so they hold great mystique for much of humanity. Since we're not really sure exactly how old these languages are or where they came from, we cannot even be sure they are "pure" in terms of their origin. What does "pure" mean, anyway?

In this book we've chosen aUI (see chapter 18) as the basis for interpreting the sounds of the major arcana cards, because since aUI is a synthetic (made-up) language, we can be certain that it is, in fact, pure, its source being one person. That's of course if you believe Dr. Weilgart did indeed make it up. I personally believe what he says about its origin: that he received it from extraterrestrials, and if in fact he did, there's no telling how old it really is until the ETs who gave it to him eventually let us know, which I feel they will, eventually.

Rather than devoutly adhering to tradition, or on the other hand ignoring tradition altogether and instead allowing ourself to be inspired solely by our own intuition (which in most of us is still evolving), I feel it's best to constantly compare information coming from many different sources, both inner and outer. In this manner we can grow in our minds rich and vivid pictures of reality with its many layers, and can accumulate in our imaginations in-depth and meaningfully connected visions of what we're studying.

An interesting therapeutic technique that kabbalists use to uplift and refine one's consciousness is to visually scan spiritual texts. This is frequently done with the Zohar,* the most important foundational text of Kabbalah, which is written in Aramaic. You scan the words at about the same speed you would read them if you could. If you would like to try this you can find the Zohar online. You don't have to know what the words mean; visually taking in their forms and shapes in the sequence in which they are found will be enough to bring spiritual forces into your energy field.

ARCANUM XVII: THE LIGHT (THE STAR)

Alternate name: The Star
Number: 17
Sign: Gemini
Anatomy: hands, lungs
English letters: F, P, Ph
Flower: cerato
Angel: Zadkiel
Color: orange

This card pictures a nude woman who pours water on both land and sea. She's an angel of truth, hope, and faith.

In Asian culture she's called Quan Yin. In the sky of this card there are often eight stars depicted, seven small ones and one large one that has eight points. In the card pictured here the large star is shown with eight points as a means of emphasizing its importance. The seven small stars are the seven visible planets in astrology, as well as the seven primary forces in nature (Sun = synthesizing, enlivening; Moon = nurturing, feeling, perceiving; Mercury = adjusting, commu-

*In addition to online sources of the Zohar, I recommend the complete Aramaic text of the Zohar edited by Rabbi Michael Berg, as well as his companion volume, *The Secret History of the Zohar*.

nicating; Venus = loving, appreciating; Mars = initiating, asserting; Jupiter = expanding, harmonizing; Saturn = organizing, limiting), which correspond to such things as the seven colors of the rainbow.

The eighth star is an eighth force, which ultimately outshines the others—it's our own personal star, radiant in our inner "sky" rather than the outer sky.

This eighth star is the interior light that illuminates our spirit. The number of this card, 17, has an affinity with the number 8 because the numerological value of 17 is 8 (1 + 7 = 8). The number 8 is the number of karma (see Arcanum VIII, The Balance, for details), which signifies action and reaction. It is this law of karma that gives humans the hope of overcoming any and all difficulties, challenges, and suffering. If you know that all aspects of your outer life are a mirror of your inner self, then you have the possibility of changing these outer circumstances through adjustments you can make on the inner plane.

The astrological sign Gemini has to do with clarification and vivification, which means "the activity of giving vitality and vigor to something." Clarification is always a process of comparing the inner to the outer. If someone asks us to clarify something they are asking us to explain what we mean—to adjust the words we speak so that they more clearly mirror what we have in mind to communicate. This is why evolutionary thinking is always a process of clarification between the inner and the outer.

Thinking is a dualistic process, and Gemini is the most dualistic sign in the zodiac. Thoughts move in two basic ways: outward, toward contemplating and arranging particulars; and inward, toward greater refinement and subtlety and the realization of universals. It's necessary to keep these two movements in balance. Most people let their thinking drift too much toward what is external—something they have learned from our society. An example of this is the materialistic scientist who doesn't have any spiritual beliefs and who's only interested in the so-called facts of nature.

On the other hand, there are people who concern themselves with universal principles and yet can't apply them effectively to their outer lives. Yet we clarify our knowledge of universal principles by experimenting with their application. It's this process that stimulates the growth of our inner sun, that star of eight points that shines in the sky of this card. When this wondrous light finally rises, revealing itself, it never sets. The visible star we call the Sun is only a shadow by comparison.

The sign Gemini is ruled by Mercury, which also rules Virgo. As you'll recall, Virgo corresponds to Arcanum II, Veiled Isis. She represents the hidden secrets of nature. In Arcanum XVII, not only her veil, but all the rest of her clothes have been removed. The secrets of nature are now no longer hidden. The woman pictured on this card, Isis disrobed, is now able to divide her energies, as symbolized by the two cups out of which she pours the waters of consciousness. One stream she returns back to its source—the sea of being. The other stream is poured down to water the parched earth that represents the cold practicalities of visible outer life that thirst for her magical moistening.

It's traditional to have a tree in the landscape of this card. The tree on our card is at the bottom left and has ten circles on it to show that it's the Tree of Life.

Destruction can reveal the indestructible, which is the Higher Self. As such, this card, The Light, is a return to core and source, the refreshing act of reattuning oneself to one's inner light in the act of meditation.

Gemini is directly opposite the sign of Sagittarius in the zodiac. This means that philosophy (Sagittarius) and direct experience of one's inner spirit (Gemini) are polar opposites that tend to reinforce and enhance each other.

This card represents awakening from the dark night of the soul into the light of possibility. It has the power to clear any residue of trauma from our being by reconnecting the pieces of ourself that broke off during the occurrence of traumatic events.

The Bach Flower Remedy that corresponds to this card is cerato, which is beneficial for people who are always asking for opinions from other people. This is often a sign of not trusting one's own inner light. Whether you do this or not, cerato clarifies and enhances your inner knowing.

So much seeking going on in the outer world, when the truth is that what is sought is within us. The alchemists sought to make gold because they knew that gold would then give them the potential to obtain all other material things. Gold was a commodity through which all other commodities might be possessed. But to what end? It always seems that no matter how much gold anyone obtains, it's never enough—it never fulfills that ever-present need that keeps us striving for something we can't clearly define. That something is enlightenment, and the unfulfillable striving for everything else is addiction.

Arcanum XVII, The Light, reveals that what we truly seek is the light inside us, the inner light hidden by the distractions of the outer light. Gemini, negatively speaking, is the sign of distractions, the restless, nervous flitting from thing to thing in a constant search . . . for what? Gemini is the sign of liveliness, and the restlessness of this sign indicates the misuse of that liveliness as a kind of lit-up, kinetic, frenetic chaos that scrambles everywhere and goes nowhere.

The greatest positive power of Gemini is its ability to turn inward and become attuned to the source of liveliness, this source being its own inner light: the imagination. The imagination has within it the power to transform and heal our outer reality. The star that shines in the sky of Arcanum XVII is our imagination, the creator of all positive and negative karma, the living philosopher's stone, the eternal gold that has the power to heal all suffering.

Arcanum XVII is where we become aware of the existence and nature of this gold. The next five arcana following this one tell the story of how we can become one with it. Even though these arcana follow one another, in a higher sense they're simultaneous. Always remember that time is nature's way of keeping everything from happening at once.

Every single one of the major arcana might be the beginning or end of any journey. The tarot is ultimately holographic: each and every card is found in every other one, just as the seven smaller stars in Arcanum XVII are synthesized in the eighth star, which is the biggest. This is one of the most important secrets of The Star.

ARCANUM XVIII: THE NIGHT (THE MOON)

Alternate name: The Two Towers
Number: 18
Sign: Cancer
Anatomy: breasts, stomach
English letters: Sh, Ts, Tz
Flower: clematis
Angel: Gabriel
Color: yellow-orange

Arcanum XVIII, The Night, represents the womb. The womb provides nourishment and sustenance. The unborn child is given shelter and security. Never again will the child be so physically close to its mother, surrounded and sustained by the very source of life itself.

"How terrible, I think, must be the loneliness of infants," says the poet Edna St. Vincent Millay, describing the painful separation of the just-born child from the mother's womb. The newborn is expelled from the warm darkness of the womb, which has enveloped them for so long, and emerges into the cold, harsh glare of reality. Arcanum XVIII is our link to the womb, to the mother source, to our first home, and to the desire for comfort and security.

Our time in the womb was one of rapid growth—never again will we develop so fast physically in such a short time. Arcanum XVIII is growth as a result of proper nurturing and care. Cancer rules the home and self-establishment, the mother principle. Self-establishment in this respect refers to the inner self. The adult creates a home that can sustain him or her. The inward journey leads the traveler home, to the core of their true self. Dorothy in *The Wizard of Oz* wished to go home to Kansas, where she could experience security and contentment. Home is where you can be comfortable and at peace with yourself. Ideally, home provides the best environment for growth. In alchemy, "home" is the laboratory in which the great work takes place.

The negative side of this card is that if we grow too defensive we can seal ourselves up in what we wish to be a place of protection, only to realize eventually that since we've prevented our free movement, what we've really constructed around ourselves is a prison.

These "homes" that Arcanum XVIII builds around itself are certainly not always of a physical nature, for they can also be made out of fantasies and anything else that might bring comfort and evoke a feeling of hominess. They can be certain foods that bring on nostalgia, or drugs that seem to bring peace and freedom from care. Arcanum XVIII clings to these things, and so this card can indicate difficulty in letting go of something, even if that something is obstructing our progress or even harmful.

For the sake of security, Arcanum XVIII shuts out whatever is threatening and shuts in whatever seems to be friendly or offer security. The problem is knowing which is which. As Arcanum XVIII figures this out more and more clearly, its positive qualities are progressively freed so that they can flourish to the fullest.

This is the only major arcanum card that doesn't have human or humanlike figures on it. This shows the impersonal nature of environment, a concept ruled by this card. Humans live in environments and are influenced by them, and although they have a strong inclination to identify with them, they're ultimately not a part of them. This card reminds us of that.

As each card is associated with a method of healing, this arcanum is associated with environmentalism—making sure that the influences of the environment are positive and conducive to the state of mind we desire to have. The Chinese call this feng shui. We are constantly feeding off our environment, ingesting vibrations from it. Therefore we must be careful to remove wastes and poisons from it.

And do not forget that our most potent environment is our past. There is often much pollution in that environment that can toxify chronically. But it also can be cleaned and made pure by changing our relationship to our past.

Positively, this card signifies protection and innocence, though too much protection can take away the vulnerability needed to learn from new experiences, and innocence clung to for too long can turn into a prison.

Cancer is noted for being an extremely tenacious sign, but when it does let go, its rejections can be thorough and complete.

The flower remedy associated with this card is clematis, which is indicated for an excess of dreaming or mind-wandering, for The Night always seeks forms of medication that will soften the harshness of the world and place barriers between the self and the coldness of reality.

Now that we've discovered the inner light of Arcanum XVII, The Light, we have here what we need to contend with, that is, the challenges of Arcanum XVIII, The Night.

Just as Arcanum XVII signifies the true light of our Higher Self, Arcanum XVIII might be said to signify the false light of the ego self, represented by the light of the Moon; indeed, The Moon is the name commonly given to this card in many tarot decks. The light of the moon is false because it's reflected. The Moon has no light of its own—it's a dead world.

We must be careful here with labels, for this card is no more positive or negative than any other. Once this false light is recognized for what it is, it no longer has the power to harm, confuse, or mislead us.

Cancer, the ruler of this arcanum, is the sign of home, that place we may always return to for security and protection. This card concerns the false light because so many things we seek out for protection and security are actually dangerous to us or have a deleterious effect on our being. People, places, and forces that seem to be our friends often turn out to be our enemies.

There's a contrast in this card between having a place to be, a home, and having to constantly travel a path, seeking, wandering, and being homeless. The beetle, scorpion, crab, or crustacean often depicted on this card has an exoskeleton, meaning that it carries its home with it. Our true home is our heart, the source of our love. It is there that we can always find security as we move through the deceptive lights and shadows of the outer world.

ARCANUM XIX: THE DANCE (THE SUN)

Alternate name: The Sun
Number: 19
Sign: Leo
Anatomy: heart, upper back
English letter: Q
Flower: vervain
Angel: Raziel
Color: yellow

Leo is the sign of self-expression. The question is, what aspects of itself can it and will it express? All people inherently have the urge to express their true selves, that is, their spiritual nature. But there are energies that can get in the way of this. When our ability to express ourself is darkened and muddied by fear, anger, sadness, or egotism, then the expression of our spiritual self is dimmed. This frustrates Leo, which then urges it to find ways to release these disturbing influences so that its true and clear light can shine forth just as brightly as it wants to.

Arcanum XIX often depicts a child riding a horse. This is to signify that clear self-expression wants to flow from our child self, that it ideally carries the innocence and spontaneity of a child. The horse the child rides signifies the power that comes from this naïve and unselfconscious approach to living and being, and how this innocence can carry it forward with great force.

The sign Leo is about the need for self-assurance and consequently has to do with all those emotions that can get in the way of that self-assurance, such as the fear of looking bad or being criticized, or maybe worst of all, being ignored.

One of the recurring themes of the tarot is the eternal conflict that goes on between the false light and the true light. By false light I mean all those alluring illusions at play in the physical world, those mirages that promise the fulfillment of our desires. False light tends to be obviously bright and is often flashy, for it wants to grab our attention.

True light, on the other hand, tends to be hidden, subtle, and elusive. We find it in silence, in going deep within ourselves. And whereas false light is unpredictable, tricky, full of shadows, and ultimately undependable, true light is eternal, the source of pure joy—it is who we really are and what ultimately fulfills us.

Leo's strongest desire is to reflect and express the true light, but as its desire for attention and adulation is strong it sometimes settles for an expression of the false light as a means of grabbing some attention so it can momentarily feel good about itself.

The negative side of Arcanum XIX is the building of facades that serve to hide the true personality. During the Venetian period of drama in Italy, the commedia dell'arte emerged, which was a form of theater comprised of an improvisational company who wore the grotesque masks of various stereotypes. When the actor donned one of these masks, he or she then began to repeat those speeches and gestures that were obviously expected of the caricature they represented. In this manner actors were quickly able to communicate with a minimum of effort to the audience who the character was. Likewise, humans are often led to playing out the mask that is expected of them within a situation and therefore are easily and superficially understood by all. But, of course, not really.

The two lions dancing on this card signify the great work of seeking true self-expression. Dance has been chosen as the artistic medium of this quest because it involves the whole body, and because people have always had the urge to spontaneously dance with one another as a means of joyous interaction.

Leo is about two things: the challenge of finding and holding a connection to the true light, and learning to see the false light for what it is. One of the ways of doing this is to keep expressing yourself, to keep letting out what's inside you and then witnessing it, looking at it, and learning from it. Each one of us is the sacred book of ourself. All the secrets of the universe can be learned from studying oneself.

This card is decisive. Even a wrong action, if carried out with decisiveness, may not be as potentially harmful as a right action put forth in a wavering, tentative way. Often this card is depicted with a child on it since children have a natural sense of self-assurance—until it's undermined by adults. Gertrude Stein said that it didn't matter whether or not words had meaning so much as it mattered that they had force, which I assume to mean expressiveness. This card puts expressiveness first—the dramatic gesture, the vivid pose or declamation.

We may also think of this card as acting out the dictates and commands of the heart, rather than the head. The heart is the seat of God, that place in the human body where spirit resides. The Egyptians thought the heart a more important organ than the head. The Chinese assumed the brain to be a minor organ. In hieroglyphics, the Egyptians depicted the heart as a jug to show that it held the life force energy like the way an earthenware vessel holds water.

A healing flower remedy associated with this card is vervain, used whenever anyone is trying too hard, often without even knowing they're doing so. For some people, trying too hard no matter what they're doing becomes a way of life. Always remember that environments are invisible.

The greatest joy is to reflect the spiritual light, and this is what Arcanum XIX does. The spiritual light reflected reflects back to us, proliferating joy, play, and enjoyment of both the phenomenal and eternal realms. This is what the sign Leo, which rules this card, most wants to do. Problems arise when this reflective mirror becomes dusty, muddied, cracked, marred, or distorted. The only thing that can cause these imperfections is the ego. Of course, the ego is a problem in every card, but here it takes center stage, the place where it most loves to be.

I'm sure most of you have noticed how good it feels to help and support other people. This is because such activity momentarily alleviates the pressures and burdens of the ego. We feel good about ourself when we give, and that good feeling may derive from one of two sources, or both of them: the fact that in giving we're expressing divine love; or that giving feeds our ego by making us feel we're generous and hence good. Kabbalists suggest that anonymous giving helps to prevent the second possibility.

Whatever you're doing, you're always giving, because you're emanating energy, which is affecting the whole environment—both the immediate one as well as the whole universe. Clean your mirror, for even though such work will inevitably be painful to the ego, it cannot help but magnify joy. Then you can dance with the whole of life.

ARCANUM XX: THE AWAKENING (THE SARCOPHAGUS)

Alternate names: Judgment, Resurrection
Number: 20
Planet: the Moon
Anatomy: pancreas
English letter: R
Flower: moon flower, rock water, aspen
Angel: Sandalphon
Color: white

This card rules the subconscious, all those energies and thoughtforms that we humans have denied or repressed, yet which carry a life of their own within our being. As a person expands their conscious awareness, they gradually bring aspects of their subconscious into the realm of conscious thought, illuminating a greater portion of their inner world.

The subconscious is the realm of memory, which includes bodily memories. Memory extends beyond the mind and brain, encompassing deeply ingrained habits and patterns within the physical self. Astrology tells us the Moon rules cycles, and because of this, habits. A habit is always a cyclic occurrence. A cycle is a rhythmic construct occurring at periodic intervals through time. Cycles and habits are powerful, though many of them work below the level of consciousness. Habit patterns condition our whole lives, and until we become aware of them we can't do anything to change them or to liberate ourselves from them.

Habits confine the spirit just as the body confines consciousness, or the way a sarcophagus contains and holds a body. This card symbolizes a reawakening from habits.

How do we grow into an understanding and awareness of our habits? First of all we must give attention to our immediate surroundings and circumstances. The journey of a thousand miles begins with a single step. We may have high-minded goals and plans, but unless we begin to actualize them in our immediate situation, we can never fulfill them.

The Moon also governs impressionability. The body, like the subconscious, is soft wax that takes on the imprint of whatever is around it and whatever it comes in contact with. The stresses and strains of outer life impinge on us, leaving marks. These marks strongly influence our being, to the point that we carry them with us and act on the basis of their specific design. This is what psychologists often speak of as "programming." The first thing we must do to overcome this programming is to be attentive to our own immediate reactions to life. This is not a process of thinking, but more of feeling: allowing ourselves to experience our own spontaneous emotional impulses. From this point on, the healing power of pure attention itself can naturally transmute these habits from binding chains to effective tools for living.

You might wonder why this confinement is necessary. The answer is simple. All growth involves pushing against something else. If a person did not have these overwhelming forces of outer life impinging on their consciousness they wouldn't be able to develop enough strength to overcome them. The light of spirit shines within, but it's hidden beneath the dense veils of material creation. Evolution is the process of intensification of this light until it pierces through all veils and shines forth in supreme splendor.

But this light is hidden before it is revealed. Creation is a game of hide and seek that Creative Intelligence plays with itself. Hindus have always believed this, but Western humanity has had trouble accepting this because the people of Western civilizations think there needs to be some more serious reason for life other than recreation. They've failed to realize that Creative Intelligence's joy and amusement is serious business.

The Moon's gravitational pull on the Earth symbolizes a transformative power that can draw hidden or latent thoughtforms from the depths of the subconscious. This drawing comes and goes in waves like the ocean tides and generates constant restless movement. But then again, is the ocean restless? Who are we to say if water needs to be calmed? If it wishes calm it can climb into a cloud and then go sit in a pool for a time. Water wants the Moon's guidance and follows a repeating system constructed by celestial rotation. Hence the association of this card with habits that are at root seemingly meaningless cyclic movements that the vegetative spirit within forms as self-medication.

This card also governs reincarnation and the past, that infinite time before the present that dreams the subconscious into being.

It also says that any negative action will inevitably be undone by a positive one, hence the idea of resurrection, another name given for this card. Negative actions set up negative echoes that don't die away until the psyche lets them go.

A therapeutic flower remedy to use with this card is aspen, especially when there is fear, for this card can signify vulnerability and impressionability, and aspen alleviates fears, especially when they are free-floating and seemingly unattached to anything. Another medicine for this card is the Bach Flower Remedy rock water, the only one of the Bach remedies that isn't a flower—it's a homeopathic preparation of water from ancient healing wells and springs found around the British Isles. It can help you flow with everything more smoothly.

The purpose of cycles is that they induce awakening. The whole universe is based on cycles, for the whole universe is in a state of perpetual awakening. Habits are cyclic behavior, and whether they be good habits or bad ones, they eventually will lead to some sort of awakening.

Awakening is a relative process, for there are many parts to ourself, many layers and levels, each one asleep or awake to varying degrees. Things keep coming back to us because we have more to learn from them, more to get out of them, because there are parts that we still need to let go of.

Cyclic returns can be demoralizing. When the return happens, we often think, "Gee, I thought I was through with that stuff. I thought I'd already worked through that one." But vampires will always continue to climb out of their coffins until their lair is discovered and they're dealt with.

How exhilarating it can be to perfect and refine habits, to reduce or expand them to bring greater harmony into our lives. This is what Arcanum XX, which is called Judgment in some decks, is all about. We might, however, prefer to call this card "The Most Recent Judgment," for it's only the last one until the next one comes around.

CHAPTER SIX

Tarot Odysseys and Major Arcana XXI and XXII

CLIMAX OF THE GREAT WORK AND TRANSFORMATION

If we think of the major arcana as a quest, or odyssey, then it has two endings. This is because it has two numbering systems: one being from 0 to 21, and the other being from 1 to 22. In other words, as I've said before, The Fool, or The Traveler (Arcanum XXII or 0), is both the beginning and end of the quest.

But the less traditional ending, 21, ruled by the Sun, contains a secret which I discovered myself—though it could well be that some other researchers of the past discovered it too, and I'm not aware of it. The secret has to do with the Sun's dual role. You see, the astrologers of old named Saturn "the greater malefic" and Mars "the lesser malefic." They thought that these two planets accounted for most of the misfortune we experience down here on Earth. Kabbalists, though, tell us that all human suffering derives from the ego, and as the Sun rules the ego I have given it the name of "grand malefic." What I mean by this is that when one is not in a state of enlightenment then the ego, as signified by the Sun, can be a terrible fire that wreaks all sorts of destruction, often in hidden and subtle as well as overt ways; but once enlightenment is reached then that same energy sheds its light in such a full and pure way that it allows us to see meaning and purpose everywhere, in all things. And so we could say that as we move on our path toward enlightenment, Arcanum XXI, The Lord of the Dance, can be our worst stumbling block, but once the goal is reached we find that the stumbling block is actually the goal, and that it has turned into that stone of the philosophers we have been seeking all along.

ARCANUM XXI: THE LORD OF THE DANCE (THE ADEPT)

Alternate names: The World, The Universe
Number: 21
Planet: Sun
Anatomy: thymus gland
English letter: S
Flower: sunflower
Angels: Michael and Raphael
Colors: yellow, gold

This card, The Lord of the Dance, represents the ultimate goal of the great work. It's the crowning glory of the major arcana and as such it signifies enlightenment and the fulfillment of the purpose of human life. It's often represented by a dancing figure to signify the balanced yet dynamic quality of life fully lived. The astrological ruler is the Sun, because this star is the center of our solar system. It radiates tremendous energy and ideally represents the perfect balance between the material and the spiritual realms.

Usually the four entities that represent the four fixed signs are also depicted in the corners of this card: a bull for Taurus, a lion for Leo, an eagle for Scorpio, and a man's head for Aquarius.

These four signs are sometimes called the four avataric gates, or the four doors of power. The man's head symbolizes *knowing,* the lion *daring,* the bull *willing,* and the eagle *keeping silent.* These are the four instruments of the occultist. The occultist must know through plumbing her own depths; she must have the courage and daring to follow through on her own convictions; she must strengthen her will and direct it toward being industrious and disciplined; and she must keep silent as a means of entering the realm of understanding. This keeping silent is not for the purpose of withholding secrets from others, but rather to learn how to consciously contain energy within the self for the purpose of growth. This does not mean that we shouldn't spend our energies freely for the benefit of other people, but rather that we should act without constantly objectifying what we're doing through words and objectifying thoughts.

Often when we tell others what we're thinking they disagree with us or unwittingly send other negative energies our way. The true occultist is ultimately an optimistic person, and when meeting the outside world with their optimism he or she often receives pessimistic feedback or is otherwise misunderstood. Occultism is at root experiential, and experiences are easily distorted through words. When we name an experience we limit it, and people often tend to use words to remove themselves from experience.

Whenever this card appears in a reading it signifies illumination, which points the way to the completion of our life purpose. It signifies the most unchanging part of our nature—that which lies beneath the mask of personality and which shines with brightness, even though clouds may obscure it temporarily. It is the true philosopher's stone sought by the alchemists. It is so pure that everything it touches partakes of its purity. In the words of T. S. Eliot, it is "the still point of the turning world" that provides a center around which all else revolves in harmony and beauty of movement.

Our purpose is to center ourself so that all the powers and forces of our being find a common source from which we can create music with one another.

This card represents the magnum opus, the great work of alchemy. The numerical correspondence for this term is the number 110, which reduces to 2 and is 11 × 10. This shows a merging of inspiration (10) and refinement (11), or, one might say, a refinement of inspiration. Note that the numbers 10 and 11 add up to 21, this card's number (see as well chapter 15, "Numerology").

The image on this arcanum reminds me of the beautiful Shivas cast in bronze that have come down to us from eighteenth-century India. They picture Shiva in his aspect as Nataraja, the Lord of the Dance. He has four arms—one of them is hidden in the picture on the card in the Azoth Deck, shown in this book—and stands with one foot on a demon, and he is surrounded by a ring of flames.

The Sun, astrological ruler of this card, is associated with the number 360 since it is how many degrees there are in a circle, the circle being the zodiac with its twelve signs of 30 degrees each. In terms of describing an actual year, this number is not perfectly even—actually it's 365 days plus a little less than six hours that make up the yearly cycle. Its number of days are not even because the universe doesn't operate on iron-clad rigidity. All numbers, figures, and forms are off somewhat to allow for creativity, surprise, and life. The number 365 reduces to 14 (3 + 6 + 5 = 14). This associates the alchemist or gold-maker with gold, the metal of the Sun that is associated with this card.

The ideal number, 360, breaks down into component parts of 2 ×2 × 2 × 3 × 3 × 5. Here we have three 2s and two 3s, as if the 2s and 3s were imbibing the nature of each other, with the vital and vibrant 5 being the result of the addition of the 2 and the 3 playing the part of justice of the peace, as his hierophantic nature so directs him.

Kabbalists have revealed to us another secret: there are seventy-two names of God. If we multiply the number 72 by 5, we obtain 360, to signify the names of God (72) becoming living (5) words.

Also note that the only sign that the Sun rules is Leo, corresponding to Arcanum XIX, The Sun, and the number 19 squared equals 361, just one digit more than the ideal, 360. This signifies the living names of God (the 360 as 72 × 5) giving birth to, or being the foundation of, the divine avatar (Arcanum XIX, The Sun), the God incarnate dwelling in the world of form (dwelling in the world of form because 19 is squared, squares being forms, patterns, and measurements).

Also note that 19 is the maximum number of years that comprise the cyclic pattern of solar eclipses. The number 11 represents the number of years that form the cyclic pattern for sunspots, and again we see here the number 11, that of the great work of alchemy.

Another deity associated with this card is Mithra, the Iranian god of the Sun, whose rites were adopted and modified by early Christians. The name Mithra adds up to 53, which is 8 on the level of 6, or 2 × 2 × 2 on the level of 3 × 2. (See as well chapter 15, "Numerology," and chapter 16, "Gematria.")

Another god of the Sun is Abraxas, who is credited among the gods of ancient Egypt, Persia, and Syria. He is depicted as a cock that has two serpents for legs and a lion for a head. The lion refers to Leo, the cock is the bird announcing the dawn, and the two serpents are the Sun's twin motions, once around Earth every day and once around the zodiac every year.

The name Abraxas is associated with the magical incantation *abracadabra,* which through gematria becomes the number 64, the number of the Chinese Book of Changes, or I Ching, which is the square of 8, or karma, manifesting in the world of form.

We also have here the symbology of the Great Central Sun. Everything revolves around something greater, and all revolves around the Great Central Sun.

Where is the Great Central Sun? Everywhere and nowhere. It's anywhere where there's consciousness and balance, and so it's the point of ultimate centering.

The flower essence corresponding to this arcanum must, of course, be the rose, which heals the feeling that life has no meaning and helps a person find a sense of direction. To take it you can use the Bach Flower Remedy known as wild rose, or you can use *Rosa macrophylla* flower essence whose bloom comes from Tibet, and which Guru Dass, one of the foremost teachers of kundalini yoga, says is an exceptionally powerful remedy.*

If we assume the number of The Fool, Arcanum XXII, is 0 rather than 22, then Arcanum XXI is the last card of our journey. This is the end, the finish line; we have reached the goal, which is to move from duality back to unity, hence the order of digits of the number 21, showing the 2 returning to 1.

---

*A good source for this remedy can be found online at Pegasus Products.

The astrological ruler of this arcanum is the Sun, which signifies goals and purpose. The light of the Sun shines everywhere. Most of it travels out into space in all directions for countless light years before it falls on anything, if it ever does. The part of it that falls here on us doesn't favor any one thing. It's just as content to fall on a desert as an ocean, on a saint as an evildoer.

I said earlier in this text that "the road to paradise is paradise," and that truth bears repeating. We have already arrived at the goal, though most of it don't know it yet. When I say "know it," I don't mean just with your mind, but with your whole consciousness. That's enlightenment—realizing you are paradise, and paradise is you.

ARCANUM XXII OR 0: THE TRAVELER (THE FOOL)

Alternate name: The Materialist
Number: 0 or 22
Planet: Pluto
Anatomy: crown chakra
English letter: T
Flowers: walnut, rock water
Angel: Metatron
Colors: indigo, black

The Traveler, Arcanum XXII or 0, is both the beginning and the end of our journey of transformation. In many tarot decks this figure is called The Fool, someone who naively believes in fantasies and illusions. Or maybe this personage is someone who is called foolish because they don't buy into the fantasies and illusions that everyone else believes in and sells.

Of course, this card rules beginnings because the number 0 precedes everything, but Arcanum XXII it is also the end. When this card appears in a reading, it isn't advising us to do anything different from what we're doing, but rather, to do what we're doing in a more intense, more extreme way, to not be afraid to go all-out. This is what will cause a transformation in the situation, transformation being the best word to describe this card.

The Traveler signifies intensification, which always generates power. It has to do with all the issues we have around power, such as the fear of it, the poverty of it, the desire for it, and the addiction to it. In the J. R. R. Tolkien fantasy *The Lord of the Rings,* power is represented as the ring and the way the ring causes its wearer to become drunk with power. The ring's power to create invisibility relates to the nothingness of its 0 attribution. The intense power of this card can generate tactics of coercion, threat, and pressuring. It rules such things as lawless gangs, the Mafia, terrorists, and all criminal organizations, all misusing the energy of this card.

The highest meaning of the traditional name for this card, The Fool, signifies one who could escape the bonds of matter and yet chooses to remain imprisoned in the material world so that he might aid the other prisoners—what Buddhists might call a bodhisattva. The Fool is innocence personified. He is beyond the narrow dictates of society, not because he has denounced them, but because for him they do not exist. In his mind they are no more important than a handful of leaves blown by the wind.

The Fool is often shown carrying a bag. This is because he is also the Magician of Arcanum I. Within the bag are his magical tools that are implements for healing and for the spreading and refining of knowledge. The bag is tied to a stick and is symbolic of male genitalia—the creative force. Now, though, the tools are concealed—internalized. This Fool is often depicted strolling past a fallen obelisk, a symbol of chaos, or walking unwittingly off a cliff, since physical existence means nothing to him. He is blind to its limitations. He cannot fall off the cliff—it's not his destiny, and even if it is he'll probably land on his feet. Negatively this card symbolizes those who are so bound up in materialism that they are blind to spirituality. Time and the force of evolution will eventually show them the way.

In a deck of playing cards The Fool of the tarot is the joker, and there's a nugget of gold to be gleaned from this, as spiritual teachers throughout history have used humor to express spiritual truths. The Sufis are especially known for this. Jokes have the power to express ironies and to reveal the often ridiculous ways of humanity. Jokes soften and lighten the spirit. Their fire magic can shine light into the darkness of the earthly realm. Their healing power is great, and they're born from this card.

It's quite unfortunate that the nineteenth-century occultists Papus* and his contemporary, the Polish mystic Mouni Sadhu,† have changed the ordering of the major arcana so that this card, The Traveler, falls between Arcanum XX and XXI. This goes against tradition. Maybe the rationale was that since the number 20 corresponds to the Moon and 21 to the Sun, that the card signifying the solar eclipse, The Traveler, should fall between these two since an eclipse is a meeting of the Moon and the Sun. This is faulty reasoning, though, because we have to have both the Moon and the Sun before an eclipse can happen.

The Fool, here designated in his role as The Traveler, is bound up with the idea of continuance—The Traveler moves on, even in the face of a destroyed civilization, represented by the fallen obelisk seen in some decks. The Traveler denotes continuance even beyond walking off a cliff. All must go on, and any stops along the way are only an illusion. Death is simply nature's way of telling you to slow down—but only for a while.

The Traveler and The Magician are essentially the same being. The objects in the Traveler's bag are the magical implements of Arcanum I, The Magician. Whereas The Alchemist, Arcanum XIV, is a symbol of art, The Traveler signifies artlessness, or one might say, the new innocence—not just as a current fad, but as an eternal one, the timeless Zen concept of no mind.

There is the initial innocence of youth, but there is a new innocence that comes after much experience. Ideally this is the innocence of old age. I'm not speaking of senility, but rather, an effortless wisdom—the wise person who knowingly laughs at the trials of other aspirants, not in a way that offends or makes fun of them, but with a sound that lightens

---

*The pseudonym of Gérard Encausse, a French physician, hypnotist, and populizer of tarot and the Kabbalah

†The pen name of Mieczyslaw Demetriusz Sudowski, a devotee of Ramana Maharshi, who wrote extensively on spiritualism and other esoteric subjects

their spirits and helps them gain cosmic distance from the pettiness and ridiculousness of earthly illusions, because she has been there before.

Humanity first became aware of the planet Pluto after its discovery in 1930. This was the time of the Great Depression in America. Nazism was on the rise, and much work was being done in atomic science. The Great Depression showed us how greed can kill, Nazism showed us that the way to world peace is certainly not through genocide, and atomic science showed us that leveling cities is definitely not going to do the job either.

Now that Pluto is on the scene, notably with the first Pluto return of the United States, occurring between 2022 and 2024, we can expect more and more awakenings of this nature. The tenor of these awakenings will be just as gruesome as we want them to be, since Pluto never decides the nature of the awakening, it only compels the awakening to happen. The more one meditates, the gentler these awakenings become.

Astrologer and occultist C. C. Zain has said that Arcanum XXII, when thought of as number 0 in the tarot, is positive and good; but when it is thought of as XXII it is evil and bad. I'm completely sure this is erroneous. The number 0 merely shows Pluto as the ever-present basis of reality, whereas 22 is its manifestation—the illusory overlay of nothingness.

The Bach Flower Remedy rock water is a good one to use for any problems associated with this card, as well as the last card of which we spoke, Arcanum XXI, The Lord of the Dance. Rock water softens without reducing power, and it helps you to be in the flow with whatever is going on so that all intensity can be met with more grace and ease.

Walnut is another flower remedy to use with this card, for it helps you through any and all kinds of transitions and makes you more impervious to outer influences.

Think of the twenty-two major arcana as a curving line that forms a circle, just as the ouroboros does. Arcanum XXII is the serpent's tail, and Arcanum 0 its mouth.

There is, in one sense, nothing here, or rather nothing that can be limited or defined by words. Arcanum XXII encourages us to keep doing what we're doing and to not be afraid to do it with greater obsessiveness. It affirms the truth that each arcanum is a door into all the others. It truly matters not what we do as long as we allow ourself to find and surrender to the love within us.

We call this card I Fool because in social terms he seems like nothing—unimportant, a free-floating denizen who has liberated himself from rules, norms, accepted social roles, and all other taken-for-granted biases. The more we can be like this Traveler, the easier it will be to progress, and the beauty of it is that we needn't necessarily forgo any social perks to do so, for if we so desire we can always play the game outwardly while inwardly enjoying our freedom—if we can maintain our detachment. What matters most here is taking a light, unattached approach to existence, and especially to not shy away from our own intensity, for it is those places of intensity within us that will unite us with our inner power and inevitably speed our evolution.

The Fool is the tarot's true monarch, though he'd rather spend his days roaming mountain slopes and forests and desolate wastes, and then find a cave in which to spend the night rather than be imprisoned in a palace and forced to sit on a throne, where he'd be saddled with servants, paperwork, passwords, and all the endless tasks of rulership.

If you like you can celebrate his birthday: it's April 1.

The Fool, the ambassador of all spiritual forces, sends you love and wishes you well!

☽ *Workshop One: Journaling with the Tarot*

Now you've been introduced to all twenty-two cards of the major arcana, which together reveal the processes of human evolution. They are magic transparencies through which we can evoke universal archetypal experiences from within the deep strata of our individual psyche. Each of these mysteries is a step in every person's life journey.

Turning a single card in response to a question concerning a given situation can shed light on the deeper meaning of it. In this manner we can gain clarity about the situation by gaining from the card some idea of what the real nature of the question is, and therefore how best to handle the situation.

I love doing one-card readings—it's a great way of focusing on the essence of a single card. And if after relating to the card you have picked in answer to your question—and by relating to it I mean that you have gotten some meaning from it that pertains to your question—then if any other specific questions come to mind about the answer you received or about anything else pertaining to your original question, you can always draw another card or cards to further clarify.

✦ Your Tarot Journal

An excellent method for intensifying our understanding of the cards is to compare our daily experiences to the cards we draw every day to help us work with them. A good way to do this is to start a tarot journal.

First, separate the twenty-two major arcana from the rest of the tarot deck. Then each morning shuffle these twenty-two cards and ask the question, "What are the vibrations surrounding this day for me?" or "What is there for me to learn today?" Then fan the cards out on a table in front of you face-down. Select at random a single card that will serve as an answer to your question. After recording the card you've drawn in your journal, read the essay from this book that pertains to the selected card.

At the end of the day it will be helpful to your study of the tarot to briefly write down those events that have occurred during the day, and if you can see how they relate to the card you drew, write down those insights as well.

If you want a quicker and simpler way of interpreting the cards, rather than going back and reading the whole essay for each one found in chapters 1 through 6, you can instead refer to the major arcana summary list you'll find in the next chapter.

Don't be discouraged if at first this seems difficult at times. If you've selected a card that doesn't immediately seem to fit the events of the day, it may be because there's some part of the card's meaning that applies to your day but that hasn't yet occurred to you.

It's best to never leave a journal page blank, but rather, to always record the card you drew and then recount the events that seemed most important during the day. By doing this, meanings that are not apparent to you at the time you drew the card may become clearer later as you work more with the cards.

Always remember that you learn more from what you don't understand than from what you do understand.

CHAPTER SEVEN

Ritual as Magic and a Summary of the Major Arcana

People invent all sorts of rituals to help them read the cards. Here are some you might find helpful:

- Some readers wrap their cards in a special cloth, such as a piece of black velvet. It's kind of like a blindfold for the cards to help them rest between use. Personally, I like purple velvet for this, or midnight blue. You can also wrap your cards in a psychically generated fabric of light that will clear them on a continual basis.
- Light a candle before reading the cards, and as you do, ask for spiritual light to fill the room and for your guiding spirits to be present during the consultation to help you see what you need to see in the cards that will come up. If you don't have a candle, you can imagine one and then imaginally light it.
- Ask out loud or silently that the psychic space between you and the person you are reading for be cleared of all extraneous energy, and that the vibrations of each of you be harmonized together so that communication is full and clear.

- On the table where you do the reading place a wand, a knife, a cup, and a coin, and ask these symbols to draw in the positive energies of the four elements. Asking The Magus of Arcanum I to be present at your reading is also helpful.
- Place your favorite crystal such as a quartz crystal on top of the deck before shuffling it, setting the intention that this crystal will help to bring focus and clarity to the reading.
- Place a glass of water on the table, asking it to absorb any negative, disturbing, or distracting vibrations during the reading. Then at the end of the reading always make sure to get rid of this water; do not drink it.
- Spray the room in which you are working with blessed water or water to which a fragrance has been added. The scent of roses is always a good choice. And if you don't have a spray bottle you can always dip your fingers in the glass and then flick them around the room.

Given these suggestions, I think you'll be able to come up with other rituals you can perform to assist you in reading the cards. The most important thing is that you're comfortable with whatever you do.

If you like to do lots of rituals, then do so—they're wonderful! If you wish to take a more casual and non-ritualized approach, it's fine to proceed this way also.

One of the great beauties of rituals is the way they slow down the energy around you and assist you in contemplating the spiritual realities you're tapping into. They give you a preparatory space in which to become calm and centered, a kind of psychic antechamber to pass through before entering your intuitive laboratory.

Kabbalists are very big on moving slowly—they recommend it highly. Too often we move with speed because the world is continually telling us to hurry up. Too much speed can cause us to overlook things, and many people use speediness as a means of avoiding things they don't want to deal with. So savoring the moments of rituals can help you to relax and sets the tone for a clear and meaningful reading.

NOTE ON KEYWORDS

A major mistake made by new students is a tendency to stick maybe too closely to the few keywords they learn in the beginning. The problem with this is that words never adequately or completely describe the nature of the forces at work in the tarot, and often there are many more words, phrases, and ways of saying things that will make the ideas these words are trying to express far more vivid to the reader.

We may take a picture of a tree and think that we have recorded how the tree looks, but we must realize that our picture only gives one view of the tree, and in one season. One hundred pictures all taken from different angles will give us a much better idea of what the tree actually looks like, and if we take hundreds of pictures in other seasons we get an even better idea. In the same manner, it's good to strive to see the cards of the tarot from more than one angle, because it is our refined and intimate knowledge of them that will serve to make the task of reading them deeper and more light-filled.

A SUMMARY OF THE MAJOR ARCANA

I. THE MESSENGER (The Magus)

Alternative names: The Juggler, The Magician
Planet: Mercury
Anatomy: thyroid
English Letter: A

Keywords: mind, communicating, flexibility, cleverness, unity in diversity, ingenuity, resourcefulness, attention, inquisitiveness, quickening, speeding up, the present as the point of power, dexterity, deftness, point of view, a shifting of attitude and outlook, finding a new perspective with which to look at things, deception (including self-deception, trickiness, con games, being duped, having your attention too easily diverted)

II. THE GUARDIAN OF THE GATE (Veiled Isis)

Alternate names: The High Priestess, The Papess, The Female Pope
Sign: Virgo
Anatomy: intestines
English letter: B

Keywords: assimilation (chewing on things thoroughly so as to fully digest them), perfection, the world of duality, analysis, mystery, purification, technical ability, problem solving, attention to the right details, service, responsibility, criticism (try to put it in a diplomatic way and use it for a good purpose), sustainment, responsibility, duty, purity, seeing the parts instead of the whole, differences, pettiness, lack of confidence, never good enough, overthinking, making too many things to do for oneself, self-criticism (which makes it difficult to develop confidence and self-assurance), attention to the wrong details

III. THE QUEEN MOTHER (Isis Unveiled)

Alternate name: The Empress
Sign: Libra
Anatomy: kidneys, lower back
English letter: G

Keywords: equivalence, activity, productivity, fecundity, equilibrium, relationships, connecting, opportunities, dynamic balance, poise, superficiality (often engaged in just to keep the peace), compromise, rationalization, finding the link between things or how they are the same, smoothness, sociability, beautification, extremism, ups and downs, a fear of relating causing the person to take a superficial approach to connecting, an inability to make up one's mind.

IV. THE COMMANDER (The Sovereign)

Alternate name: The Emperor
Sign: Scorpio
Anatomy: genitals
English letter: D

Keywords: creativity, transformation, making changes, sexual function, awareness, realization, keeping quiet about things, regeneration, penetration of matter, command, desire, wanting revenge, taking an indirect or secretive approach, the libido, sensuality, secretiveness as a means of gaining or holding power, awareness of hidden motives in others, potency, silence, hidden feelings, spiritual questing, resentment, jealousy, desire for revenge, at the mercy of one's own repressed passions

V. THE PENTAGRAM (The Hierophant)

Alternate name: The Pope
Planet: Jupiter
Anatomy: anterior pituitary
English letter: E

Keywords: enthusiasm, upbeat attitude, harmonization, expansion, excess, growth, evolution, religiosity, coordination, trying to do too many things at once, going too far, doing too much, paternalism, learning, teacher, guru, compensation, enabling, taking in more, verve, exuberance, livingness, generosity, outreach, optimism, too much, good luck (which you need to be careful to not waste)

VI. THE CROSSROADS (The Two Paths)

Alternate name: The Lovers
Planet: Venus
Anatomy: parathyroid
English letters: U, V, W

Keywords: appreciation, choice, attraction, aesthetics, art, magnetic force, values, love principle, path of least resistance, allurement, beautification, temptation, relaxation, rest, ease of flow, decisions, intimacy, centripetal force (drawing things toward oneself), eclecticism, laziness, selfishness, taking the easy way out, greediness

VII. THE VICTORY (The Conqueror)

Alternate name: The Chariot
Sign: Sagittarius

Anatomy: liver
English letter: Z

Keywords: administration, transcendence, cutting oneself free, mind over matter, philosophy, widening horizons, cosmic attitude, friendliness, rising above the material, rising above problems, overview, broad vision, religion, theory, abstraction, ethics, the exotic and far away, laziness, being unrealistic, not so good at dealing with details, being in denial

VIII. THE BALANCE

Alternate name: Justice
Sign: Capricorn
Anatomy: skeleton
English letters: H, Ch

Keywords: discrimination, evaluation, focus on the major points and avoiding side issues, reducing anything to its essentials, practicality, karma (action/reaction), social role, laws of God, backlash, objectivity, interaction, being impersonal, chain reaction, professionalism, conservatism, propriety, cautiousness, carefulness, trying to cover all bases, being judgmental, economizing

IX. THE SEEKER (The Sage)

Alternate name: The Hermit
Sign: Aquarius
Anatomy: nervous system
English letters: Th

Keywords: loyalty, wisdom through experience, collector of experience, seeker, card of initiation, knowledge, mental idealism, free-thinking, wild ideas, mindlessness, liberalism, group orientation, objectives, open-mindedness, the acceptance of differences, interpretation, focus on the future.

X. THE CYCLE (The Wheel)

Alternate name: The Wheel of Fortune
Planet: Uranus

Anatomy: sex glands
English letters: I, Y, J

Keywords: independence, individuality, uniqueness, change, accidents, unpredictable events, pure creativity, eccentricity, experiments, loneliness, isolation, antisocial, rebellious, revolutionary, misunderstood by people, alienated, avant garde, suddenness, surprise, strangeness, interruption of patterns, being different, one of a kind

XI. THE MAIDEN (The Enchantress)

Alternate name: Strength
Planet: Neptune
Anatomy: pineal gland
English letters: C, K

Keywords: obligation, giving to others, receptivity, refinement, raw power, psychic power, intuition, confusion, idealism, dissolving physical barriers, potential, intangibility, nuances, idealized love, tenuousness, illusions, delusions, misinterpretations, misunderstood, unclear or unformed, being subtle, magic

XII. THE DEVOTEE (The Martyr)

Alternate name: The Hanged Man
Sign: Pisces
Anatomy: feet, bloodstream
English letter: L

Keywords: sympathy, dedication, commitment, worry, justification, decision to let go of something (expend energy for a higher cause), resolve, empathy, addiction, guilt, regret, remorse for past actions, feeling trapped, hang-ups, claustrophobia, giving up, letting go, habituality, release, uncertainty, confusion, cosmic mind

XIII. THE RAINBOW (The Reaper)

Alternate name: Death
Sign: Aries

Anatomy: head
English letter: M

Keywords: aspiration, transformation, rebirth, dying to the old, rejuvenation, pioneering, crisis, brashness, headstrong, plunging ahead, pushing through boundaries, impatience, preemptiveness, precipitant action, getting it over with, impatience, being abrupt, avoiding what you need to address, confrontation

XIV. THE ALCHEMIST (Temperance)

Alternate name: Art
Sign: Taurus
Anatomy: neck, throat
English letter: N

Keywords: integration, proper combination of forces, life as art, dogmatism, stubbornness, eccentricity, virility, stamina, stability, seeking out creature comforts, ability to pace oneself, slow and steady use of energy, immovability, heaviness and dullness, getting it together, possessiveness

XV. THE MUSICIAN (The Black Magician)

Alternate name: The Devil
Planet: Saturn
Anatomy: posterior pituitary
English letter: X

Keywords: sensitivity, structure, order, focusing and defining, limitations, necessity, natural laws, self-questioning, concentration, ecology, narrowing, depression, melancholy, being exacting, shrewdness, touchiness, fears, need for patience, things happening slowly, frustration, blockages

XVI. THE PYRAMID (The Power)

Alternate name: The Tower
Planet: Mars

Anatomy: adrenal glands
English letter: O

Keywords: initiative, action, assertiveness, persistence, aggression, creation or construction and destruction, hostility, excitement, anger, self-motivation, dissatisfaction, pushiness, indomitability, centrifugal force, productivity, explosiveness, uncontrolled energy, hot-tempered, conflicts

XVII. THE LIGHT

Alternate name: The Star
Sign: Gemini
Anatomy: hands, lungs
English letters: F, P, Ph

Keywords: vivification, clarity, hope, truth, thoughts, the interior light that illuminates the spirit, perceptions, communication, ideas, bringing a sparkling quality to situations, facts, thinking, logic, glibness, visualization, scattered energy, jumping from thing to thing, seeing both sides of things, observations, distractions

XVIII. THE NIGHT (The Moon)

Alternate name: The Two Towers
Sign: Cancer
Anatomy: breasts, stomach
English letters: Sh, Ts, Tz

Keywords: expansion, security/insecurity, extension, deception and self-deception, mothering, nurturing, nostalgic, family-oriented, self-establishment, vehicles and mediums, symbols, tenacity, moodiness, feeding, home, innocence, sustenance, defensiveness, clinging to things

XIX. THE DANCE

Alternate name: The Sun
Sign: Leo

Anatomy: heart, upper back
English letter: Q

Keywords: assurance, personality, self-expression, self-completion, ego, drama, role-playing, overcompensation, emoting, histrionics, facades, daring, bravery, assertiveness, courage, being magnanimous, ego gratification, nobility, self-aggrandizement, touchiness, feeling slighted

XX. THE AWAKENING (The Sarcophagus)

Alternate names: Judgment, Resurrection
Planet: Moon
Anatomy: pancreas
English letter: R

Keywords: feelings, emotions, liberation from matter, cycles, habit patterns, immediate situations, subconscious or unconscious, everyday life, plainness, mundane and daily affairs, normality, raw substance, subjectivity, impressionability, instincts, animal nature, feeling vulnerable, need for protection

XXI. THE LORD OF THE DANCE (The Adept)

Alternate names: The World, The Universe
Planet: Sun
Anatomy: thymus gland
English letter: S

Keywords: will, self-actualization, higher consciousness, purpose, goal, fulfillment of the self, centering, mastery, balance, ability to see the relative value of different things, importance, worth, vitality, illumination, royalty, ultimates, glory, being conscious, authoritativeness, synthesis, egotism, selfishness, self-aggrandizement

XXII. THE TRAVELER (The Fool)

Alternate name: The Materialist
Planet: Pluto

Anatomy: crown chakra
English letter: T

Keywords: obsession, intensification, transmutation, influx of energy, universal welfare, material or spiritual blindness, extremes, foolishness, the unknown, complete failure, union with the force of evolution, obliviousness, pranic energy, pressures, power struggles

☽ *Workshop Two: The Three-Card Spread*

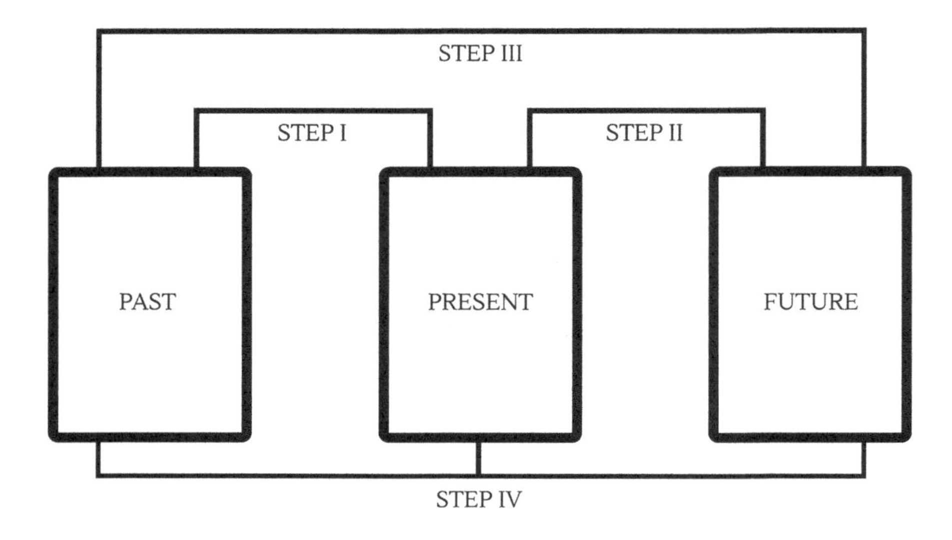

Now that you have learned the basic interpretations of the twenty-two major arcana cards, also known as the major mysteries of the tarot, you can now begin doing readings for yourself and others.

To review, the major arcana express the totality of the human experience. These twenty-two symbols illuminate the human journey. It's therefore quite valid to ask questions using only these twenty-two cards to gain the answer you seek in your reading. They represent the steps of the inner journey. In this respect they can be understood as processes that can be employed for navigating the forces of reality.

The three-card spread is an easy means of laying out the cards to answer your questions. This spread is quite versatile and is an excellent layout to use for problem-solving.

I think it's always good to have a question for the three-card spread, so the first step in this layout, as in most effective spreads, is to formulate that question.

✦ Formulating the Question

The biggest pitfall when it comes to posing a question to the tarot usually involves the desire to ask a question that could be answered with either a "yes" or a "no." There are no cards in the tarot that specifically say "no" or any that say "yes." Some readers have contrived ways to arrive at yes/no conclusions, but ultimately any of these are purely arbitrary. I feel the student reader is better off not dealing with yes/no questions. Questions like "Will I get married—yes or no?" reduce the free will of the querent to that of a leaf being blown this way and that by the whimsy of the wind. If this is your philosophy—that overpowering fate always trumps your unimportant free will—then you might as well be flipping coins to derive your yes/no answers. Replacing yes/no questions with metaphysically sound inquiries is an art, the art of discovering the real and meaningful question behind the question.

Here's an example of employing this art: let's take the question, "Will I get married?"

Well, has anyone asked you to marry them? If the answer to this is no, and you would like to get married, then perhaps the question should be: "What do I need to do to attract a romantic relationship to me that can result in marriage?"

If the answer to the question "Has anyone asked you to marry them?" is "no," but there is a person with whom you are having a romantic relationship, then perhaps the question should be: "What would the value be of me marrying this person?" or "What can I do to bring this relationship toward marriage?"

Other possible questions in this situation could be: "What do I have to learn from this relationship?" or "How can I best create a positive change in this relationship?" or "What are the vibrations surrounding a marriage for me?"

At its most powerful, the tarot can be a guiding light that illuminates the particular path of life you're on. But do not ask such things as "Should I take this particular path—yes or no?" Form instead a question about it in this way: "What is there for me to learn in taking this particular path?"

✦ Choosing the Card

Once the question has been formulated and asked aloud (to assure its clarity), then separate the twenty-two major arcana from the deck and shuffle them. Now, deal three cards from the top of the deck and lay them out face-down in front of you from left to right. You will read them as you read a book—from left to right. Card number 1 will be on your left; card number 2 will be in the center; card number 3 will be to your right.

You will read these cards one at a time therefore you need to turn the first card over, and only after fully interpreting it do you turn the second one over. Don't be in a hurry to turn over the next card, but rather give your full attention to the first card and allow its energy to speak to you.

✦ Card Number 1

The card appearing in this first position represents the past of the matter. In the interpretation of it you'll discover the tone of the events and circumstances that have conspired to bring the situation in question up to this present point. If these three cards were compared to a tree, this particular card would represent its roots.

Another analogy from plant life is to liken this card to a seed. The arcanum appearing in this position may provide insight into the variety of seed, whether it be an acorn, a flower, or perhaps a weed. One shouldn't bother describing the photographic details of the event, as in revealing the quality of the experience. For example, a young querent asks, "What value would there be for me in moving out of my parent's home?" The first card of the reading is Major Arcanum XVI, The Pyramid. The quality of this card may indicate the need to act and be aggressive in the environment. The reader may psychically pick up from this an argument or other aggressive or hostile act, and though this insight is valuable, ultimately it's important to convey to the querent only the quality inherent in the past of the matter. Once the reader has explained this quality, the querent can confirm the original psychic impressions received by the reader.

So for our example, let's say that the querent confirms a growing hostility within the home.

✦ Card Number 2

This second card stands at the pivot point of the reading. Its central position indicates the area where balance can be achieved. The card in the center represents the present energy of the matter, and therefore, due to its strategic position in the reading, points to that which is necessary to actualize the situation. This focus on the now is the key to the gate that opens the future.

Time is illusory; we live only in the present, and we act only in the present. The card appearing in this position of the reading alludes to the alchemical act of transmuting the events and circumstances of the past into the golden future that we will to be. This is the point of impinging consciousness, the energy radiating from one's inner Sun.

The answer to the question, as you can see, never comes from the outer world, but rather from within the person. If indeed something is needed from the outer world to complete the transmutation, the querent must attract that something. The reader need only reveal the quality of this energy without ever telling the person what he or she should do.

For example, turning once again to the querent who has asked about leaving home, Arcanum X appears in the center position of the spread. The quality of this arcanum refers to independence, a need to hold or establish the person's individuality, the exercise of free will, or maybe even rash or inspired behavior. The reader need only tell the querent that this is a time to affirm their individuality. It may well be that the querent can only do this by moving out, yet on the other hand, moving out at this time might be a rash step, and the resolution of the situation might come from the querent declaring independence within the existing environment.

Perhaps the querent has built up hostility (Arcanum XVI) toward those at home because they hold him or her too close, whereas in actuality they do this because the querent has never seemed to desire more freedom (Arcanum X).

It's good for the reader to explore with the querent the various and often dichotomous possibilities within the situation.

✦ Card Number 3

The card in the last position expresses the possible tone of the future. In the analogy of a tree, it represents the foliage, the blossoms, and the fruit. Through the first card the past has been revealed, and through the central card the present has been illuminated. Finally, through the last card, the future, the gateway to potential, is opened. For the person who understands the true power of free will, the future is full of possibilities.

Many people go to a tarot reader expecting them to reveal the past by describing its events in detail so that the psychic abilities of the reader can be validated. Likewise, these people often assume an attitude toward the future card that demands the telling of the outcome that fate has unalterably dealt them. The reader must be firm with these people, for much to their chagrin, their fate lies in their own hands, to be realized through their own actions.

As you peer through the gateway of the cards into the querent's future, don't limit yourself to a single perspective, but rather consider the possible paths that radiate from the situation in a multitude of directions. From this vantage point you're then free to advise the querent of their possible futures. Needless to say, the most positive possibilities should be emphasized, though never to the exclusion of obvious pitfalls or to the point of only telling the querent what they wish to hear.

For example, let's say that the future card in this reading for the querent requesting advice about leaving home is Arcanum XVIII, The Night. Should the querent's new sense of independence (Arcanum X, The Cycle) be actualized, it could bring to them comfort and the possibility of a new security (Arcanum XVIII). This implies the expansion of the inner self and shows a need to more firmly ground and establish that self. Arcanum XVIII rules the home and shows a need to lay a foundation for oneself. This card rules the home, and whether the querent decides to leave his parents' home or stay, he is being encouraged to find a source of inner sustenance. The hostility or aggression revealed by card number 1, Arcanum XVI, The Pyramid, does not necessarily come totally from without, so possibly the querent must first deal with his own hostility. Likewise, it's important that he realizes his own unique needs (card number 2), and proceeds to fulfill them. This card we are now working with (number 3) could indicate a deception, but not one that is necessarily perpetrated against the querent from the outside—it could allude to self-deception as well.

Security comes from inner tranquility and can never be achieved solely by changing the physical location of one's home. If we identify our security with those shells in which we live, then we will be forever insecure, since all shells are ephemeral. If the shells with which we so heavily identify do not provide us with sustenance, it's no wonder that we fester with hostility toward the harsh, external world (cards 1 and 3). True freedom is an art that relies on the pure creativity that flows from the inner self (cards 2 and 3). The quality of this entire reading emerges as a simple train of thought, which is this: aggression has accrued in regard to the current state of relationship to the environment, thus calling for a change or freeing-up (Arcanum X, The Cycle) of the person's sense of individuality, to thereby achieve an inner security (Arcanum XVIII, The Night), no matter where the person chooses to live.

So in answer to the querent's question, the value for him in moving away from his parents' home lies in the discovery of his own inner freedom, though the move is not necessary to this discovery. Once the quality of the event is revealed, any decision that remains true to that value is inherently positive.

Even though explaining this reading took some time and used the techniques of reasoning and logical synthesis, when it comes to interpreting the meaning of the cards, what is most important is your instincts, your *psychic impressions* concerning the situation and the meaning of the cards. In any particular situation you might come up with a completely different interpretation of them, and that's as it should be.

If you have any difficulties in getting in touch with your inner knowing, then considering the meanings of the cards can be a great support to you. As you cultivate your intuitive powers, I'm sure you'll find they will grow, and then most likely your use of the cards will become progressively more flowing and spontaneous.

✦ The Matter of Timing

The three-card spread is a highly versatile method of doing readings. The first card symbolizes the past and summarizes the quality of past events. These events of the past have brought the querent to the present. At any time during a reading we can question what has created the situation. We know from the placement of the cards in a three-card spread that the first card produces the second, while the product of the second card is the third.

Oftentimes people who seek the help of a card reader want to know when a particular event is going to happen. The cards don't indicate time, though the reader may intuitively perceive that some event may occur shortly or further away in time.

Although the three-card spread doesn't usually reveal the timing of an event, the card reader may consciously impose a time element on the reading. It's best to consult with the querent concerning this time factor, however, it's only necessary that the reader have the time factor well-established within his or her own mind. The reader, in order to impose a framework of time on the reading, needs to structure the question so as to include it.

For example, the querent may wish to know when a situation will be resolved. By consulting with the querent, the reader may decide to phrase the question in such a way as to include the time factor. Therefore, the reader might ask, "What are the vibrations surrounding the resolution of this situation within the next month?" In this fashion, the first card relates to the source or foundation of the situation, or whatever within the situation needs release. The second card implies the energy necessary for the resolution of the situation, and the final card will explore what the situation will look like by the end of the period of time being questioned.

Take care in phrasing the question so that you do not end up asking something like, "Will the situation be resolved by the end of the month?" If you do this, you've asked one of those pesky yes or no questions and you've thus further complicated the job of interpretation.

There are some time-based questions that don't fit directly into the three-card pattern, but which are still valid to ask. In these cases you can do a layout of cards that will suit the needs of this particular question.

For example, a woman in one of our classes told us she was being pressured at work to decide when she would take her vacation for the coming year. Not having considered where she wished to go or the type of vacation she would be taking, she felt she had no way to make a meaningful decision. As a classroom project she wanted to know if we could help her with this.

We began the reading with a three-card spread in order to analyze the quality to be derived from a vacation. The first card in the reading revealed what she needed to experience or learn from the year's vacation. The second card was seen as a means of finding the energy that would be called for in order to have a successful experience, and the last card described the potential for any higher value to be gained from it. Through this reading we were able to elevate the concept of a vacation, imbuing it with the potential for being a personal growth experience for her.

Four cards were then selected to represent the four seasons of the year. Each card was in its turn interpreted to evaluate the quality of a vacation taken during that particular season. The reader did not attempt to advise the querent as to which season would be positive or negative, since we know, metaphysically speaking, that each season would have both positive and negative possibilities. The reader then explored the quality of each different season as related by the cards and described those to the querent.

Once the querent decided which season to pick based on those descriptions, three additional cards were selected to represent the three months corresponding to that time of year. Again, the reader interpreted each card in turn, being especially careful that the querent understood clearly the quality inherent in each card.

An additional key of this interpretive session included a reiteration of the first reading concerning the overall quality being called for during this vacation time. In this way the overall quality of the vacation was constantly being related to each additional card being interpreted, and as we proceeded, the reader and querent imaginatively explored the potential connections of meaning between the cards.

After the querent had specified her selected month, four additional cards were drawn to represent the particular weeks of that month. Each card was once again interpreted until the querent felt that a positive pattern had been established, and her decision was apparent. Although this reading represents a unique situation that might never present itself to you as a reader, I've described it in order to show you how you can manipulate the structure of your readings so they can solve time problems posed to you.

✦ Pulling Additional Cards

Sometimes as you're doing a reading for a person they'll ask a second question tangential to the original one. It's fine at this point to draw an additional card to interpret the second question, or maybe even to lay out three more cards for it if you want to.

Also, at times a question might come to you, the reader, which could serve to clarify the original question, and it's fine to silently voice the question to yourself and then draw an additional card to answer it. These tools give you ways of amplifying your reading and gaining greater insight to share with your querent.

PART TWO

The Kabbalistic Tree of Life

CHAPTER EIGHT

The Stations of the Tree of Life

Trees are some of the oldest living things on Earth, which is probably why the ancients chose them to be the central symbol of Western occultism.

Trees are found in myths all over the world. Adam and Eve were expelled from the Garden of Eden because they ate the fruit from a forbidden tree. In Genesis 2:9, we read: "And out of the Ground the Lord made to grow every tree that is pleasant to the sight and good for food, the Tree of Life also in the midst of the garden, and the Tree of the Knowledge of Good and Evil."

When Moses went up the mountain to commune with God, the Lord appeared to him as a burning bush. When Jesus was crucified, his cross was made from the wood of a tree.

In Norse mythology we have the tree called Yggdrasil, the foundation of the whole world. In Joseph Campbell's multivolume book *Occidental Mythology,* we read: "The gods give judgment every day at the foot of the ash, Yggdrasil, the greatest of all trees and best; its limbs spread over all the world, and it stands upon three roots." The three roots of the tree correspond to the right side, the left side, and the middle of the diagram that you can see in the illustration of the Tree of Life in this chapter.

Campbell draws an analogy between Yggdrasil and the famously sacred Bodhi Tree that Siddhartha Gautama sat under for forty-nine days and nights to achieve enlightenment and become the Buddha. Campbell says that in Norse mythology, the father god Othin (or Odin, as he is frequently known) hung on Yggdrasil and was pierced by his own lance, a sacrifice to win the wisdom of the runes—those symbols drawn on wood or stone that are basically another version of the arcana of the tarot.

We know the Druids worshiped trees, and we have a Druid epic poem that's come down to us called *Cad Goddeu,* or "The Battle of the Trees." In this poem, twenty-two different kinds of trees do battle with one another. These trees are the twenty-two cards of the major arcana. At Stonehenge, that great prehistoric monument of Britain, there were twenty-two blue stones set in a circle, and a larger circle of fifty-six stones set into the ground around it, which are now missing. The chalk pits where these fifty-six stones were once placed are known as the Aubrey holes (named after the seventeenth-century antiquarian John Aubrey, who first wrote about them); they correspond to the fifty-six cards of the minor arcana.

Stonehenge was preceded by an earlier monument known as Woodhenge, which is similar to Stonehenge in construction except that it's made of standing wooden posts. There is significant evidence that the people who built Stonehenge were in contact with the peoples of the Mediterranean area, and very possibly the Egyptian culture. This reveals the link between the Druid culture and the tarot, since many occultists feel that the tarot was born in Egypt.

All the secrets of the universe are contained in the Tree of Life. The branching of a tree symbolizes the manner in which life diversifies—a single branch dividing and redividing, the one becoming the many.

THE TEN SEFIROT OF THE TREE OF LIFE

The Tree of Life, the central symbol of the tarot, is an ancient symbol that is found in many cultures and has been studied by many explorers of the occult. It is a representation of the structure of the macrocosm that describes every force at work in the universe.

The Tree is formed of circles and bands, as you can see in the illustration that follows. The circles, known as Sefirah, or stations, are the root centers of energy of the cosmos, and the bands that connect them, known as the paths, are energy channels through which these

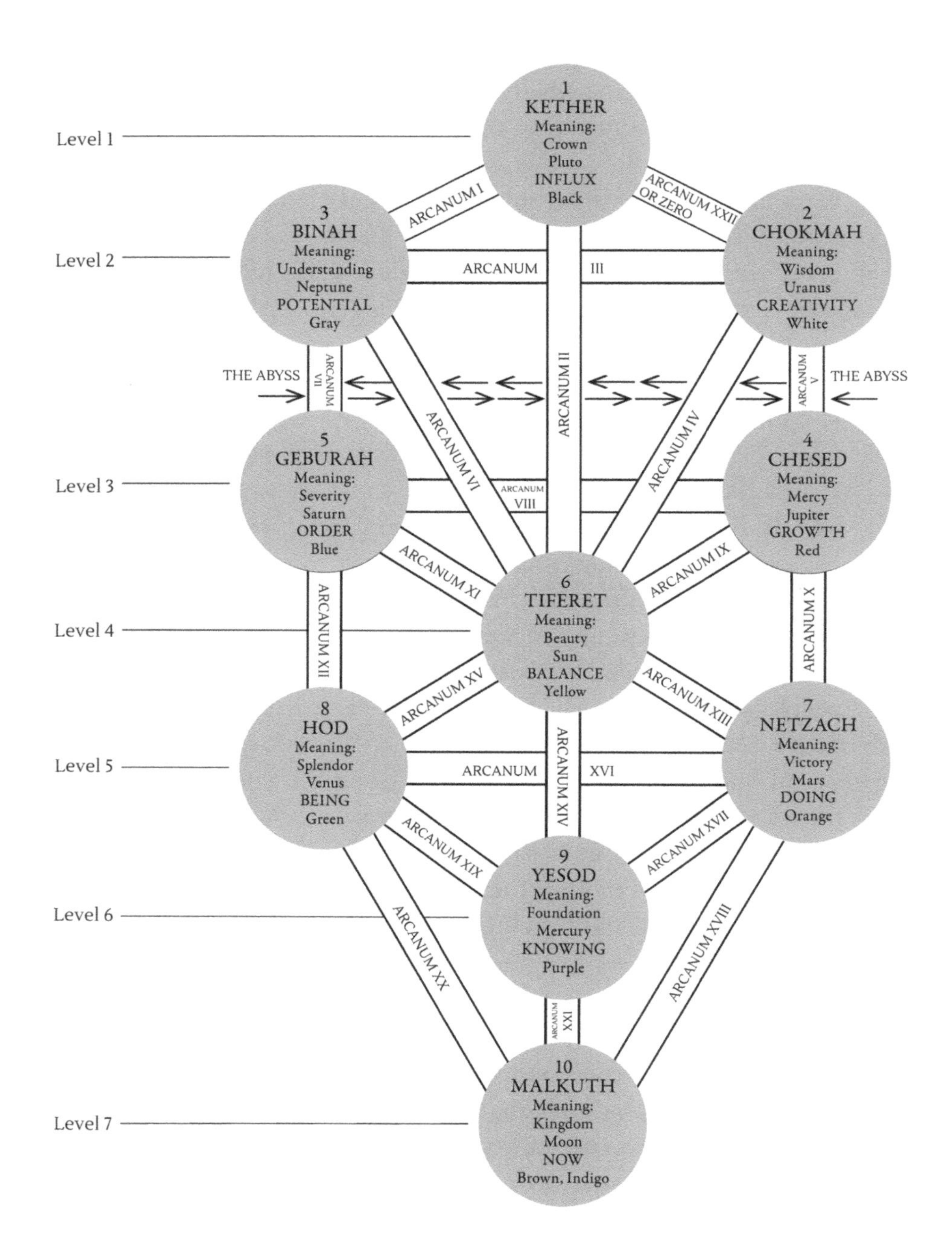

The Tree of Life

The ten circles represent the ten stations, or Sefirah, which are connected by the twenty-two major arcana. Each one of these stations is ruled by a planet and a color.

primary energies flow between one another. Note that there are ten circles and twenty-two bands, or paths. These twenty-two paths are ruled by the twenty-two cards of the major arcana.

Each energy center, or Sefirot, is associated with a planet and a color; as well, certain keywords signify the energy of a particular Sefirot. There are also certain sounds associated with each station that come from aUI, the Language of Space—a discussion we'll explore in greater depth in chapter 18. Each center has a Hebrew name, along with its English translation.

The highest part of the Tree symbolizes the realms most removed from the physical, whereas the lowest part of it symbolizes the material world. The right side of the Tree symbolizes masculine, or positive and active energy, whereas the left side of symbolizes feminine, or negative and receptive energy. The four circles going down the middle of the Tree symbolize neutral energies.

As you can see in the figure on the previous page, there are seven levels to the Tree. Some of these levels have two Sefirah on the right (masculine) side of the Tree and on the left (feminine) side, whereas some levels of the Tree have only one Sefirot, on the main pillar of the Tree. When a level has two Sefirah, the energies symbolized by these stations are polar opposites.

Sefirot six is at the center of the Tree because it's located halfway between the top and the bottom, that is, between the spiritual and the physical, and halfway between the right, or masculine side, and the left, or feminine side of the Tree.

Note that the colors ascribed to the first three circles are actually colorless, whereas the colors associated with the next three stations are primary colors. The next three circles following these are associated with the secondary colors, which are those hues made from mixing two of the primary colors together. The last station is associated with brown, a mixture of all the pigments. In its most exalted aspect, station ten is associated with the color indigo, which is a deep bluish purple that is not often seen in its pure form in nature.

The band formed by arrows and labeled "The Abyss" is a region that separates the higher spiritual realms from the visible and knowable world below it.

The Tree of Life is the key to understanding the minor arcana, which we are about to study, as well as the subtler and finer implications of the major arcana, which we will look at again in a new light as we analyze the workings of the Tree.

When we read the stations of the tree from bottom to top, we're moving from the realm of matter upward, toward the realm of spirit. This movement is often represented by a serpent who entwines the trunk of the Tree. The serpent has always been a sign of the raw psychic and physical force latent in humans. In Norse myths there's a great dragon, or serpent, called Nidhoggr, who gnaws at the roots of Yggdrasil.

Most of the information we have about the Tree comes from Hebrew mysticism, which has produced an immense number of occultists. In Kabbalah, the area above the Tree of Life is known as *Ain Soph Aur,* "the realm of limitless light." This primordial light is not the physical light we can see, but rather a reservoir of unbounded power without quality or form.

As Ain Soph Aur forms the first station on the Tree and then reflects downward, creating the other stations, it mutates and proliferates into all the various forces of reality. Ain Soph Aur is the limitless light of bliss consciousness. Its opposite are the *kelipot,* the shells, shades, or veils which are the darkness that serve the function of both concealing and limiting as well as protecting us from the intensity of Ain Soph Aur before we are ready to experience it completely.

The entire Tree is based on triangles. The first triangle is made up of the first three stations of the Tree.

Kether

The first, uppermost station splits into two equal and opposite forces that are symbolized by stations two and three, forming a triangle. Note that this first triangle is upward-pointing, and that the first station on the Tree sits at the apex of this triangle. This first station represents the **influx** of light from the realm of Ain Soph Aur and is known as **Kether.**

This is the point that represents the primary source of all energy. The power that flows through it is infinite and boundless. It is a well that can be drawn from but never emptied. It appears in fairy tales as the cup that is never drained. Its negative force is that it has the power to destroy structure because its energy is so potent that only the most stable and perfect of forms can contain and hold it. Otherwise it will explode any imperfect structure.

The second and third stations are, respectively, **creativity/Chokmah** and **potential/Binah**. Creativity is a positive masculine force and hence flows forth from station two on the right, the masculine side of the Tree. We cannot have the change that creativity brings, though, without having something for it to be born out of, and hence potential/Binah, station three, is the feminine counterpart of creativity/Chokmah, located on the left side of the Tree.

Stations four, five, and six form the next triangle, the apex of which points downward. Whereas the first triangle symbolizes the three faces of Creative Intelligence and points upward, this second triangle is Creative Intelligence's three-part reflection in the world of form, hence it points downward.

Station four is **growth/Chesed,** the direct progeny of station three, which is potential. Growth is on the right side of the Tree and hence is a positive or masculine force. Growth is also the visible and tangible manifestation of creativity, station two, which is the station directly above four. The secret here is that all creativity is ultimately growth. Even if the change in question is an upset or a seemingly negative situation, it provokes awareness, and hence a growth in consciousness.

The feminine counterpart of growth, on the left side of the Tree, is seen in station five, **order/Geburah.** Growth is always based on a structure or system, and hence station five governs all physical laws and the order they impose on reality. Station five is directly below station three, potential, which means that potential manifests itself in the physical world as order. Potential cannot manifest unless it has a vehicle by which to come through. Potential is only what *could* be—the realm of possibility—but order brings it down into the visible and tangible world.

Growth and order working together in harmony produce station six, **balance/Tiferet.** Station six sits at the apex of this second downward-pointing triangle, and because it is on the middle pole of the Tree, it represents a merging of masculine and feminine energies.

Because the physical and visible world is always dualistic, there are two downward-pointing triangles. The second one is formed by stations seven, eight, and nine, with nine at the apex of this reversed triangle.

Station seven, on the right of the Tree, symbolizes **doing/Netzach,** because as soon as balance, station six, is attained, it will be lost in the ongoing stream of time unless something is done. This signifies that balance isn't static; it's moving and dynamic and hence must be actively maintained. Because station seven is on the right side of the Tree, it is a masculine energy and has as its feminine counterpart station eight, **being/Hod.** Balance cannot be maintained just by doing, because an overabundance of activity and aggressiveness would make balance impossible. We have to know when to cease activity and just let things be. Station seven is directly under station four, growth, which means that on a lower level growth always manifests as doing. We cannot grow unless we take the initiative to grow.

Station eight, being, the feminine counterpart of doing, is directly under station five, order, signifying that being is always based on structural limitations imposed by order. We cannot be or exist unless we are defined and in some way ordered, structured, and hence limited. Only nonbeing is unlimited. Anything physical is less than infinite as long as it continues to manifest.

The interworkings of doing and being synthesize in station nine, which is **knowing/Yesod.** This comes about through a constant adjustment of doing and being, hence it's the power of flexibility, the ability to bend without breaking. It's the ability to adjust, which is true power. How can anything be destroyed that is fully capable of adjustment and flexibility? If a person does something and fails at it and then does the same thing again and fails at it again, and this happens over and over, they are a failure; but if they can be resourceful and take a new approach after failing, then they are flexible, and hence powerful.

The last station on the Tree, station ten, **Malkuth,** is the only one that is not part of a triangle. It's a point in and of itself. It symbolizes the **now,** the immediate time and space situation of any being that exists. Kabbalists have always stated that influx (Kether, station one) is in the now (Malkuth, station ten), and that the now is within influx. This means that influx always occurs in the now, and it is in the now and only in the now that the influx of energy can occur. As well, the now is where all energy is lost and hence is the only place where energy can be regained.

Kabbalists also make connections between stations three and ten. Both stations are symbolized by women. Station three is often referred to as the Divine Mother, since it is potential, which is the mother of everything. Station ten, which is the now, is the bride, and she is married to station six, balance. This means that the now should ideally be combined with balance. It's this marriage that births perfection.

If you look at the diagram of the Tree of Life you will see that station six is ruled by the Sun, whereas station ten is ruled by the Moon. These two planets symbolize the long-range goals (the Sun) of a person, and the immediate short-range limitations (the Moon) that keep the person from that goal and represent the challenges that have to be overcome. You will also see, if you look at the paths that connect the stations, that station six, balance, is connected with every other station except station ten, the now. This signifies that station ten is the energy to be redeemed in the great work of perfecting consciousness. Its primary message is "pay attention!" In other words, there's a need to always faithfully look to the immediacies of any situation in which you are involved. Don't get lost in the past (what has been) or the future (what could be). Find the golden focus of your consciousness in the now again and again, until at last it's found forever.

You might wonder how you can use the energy of Kether in a tarot reading. Well, first of all, Kether rules the intensification of anything—it's about anything becoming more and more of what it already is. This is what we're all doing. And Kether is about transformation as well—intensifying anything until it's pushed toward changing its form, which is what evolution is all about.

The scary thing about Kether is that it can upset any and all established balances, but the wondrous thing is that its perfect knowing always carries us toward the realization of our eternal self.

SEFIROT TEN: MALKUTH

Meaning: Kingdom
Planetary ruler: Moon
Color association: brown, indigo
Keyword: Now

Malkuth is the lowest station on the Tree of Life, the darkest region of life. The energies here are constantly seeking liberation. At worst, energy is dissipated here and eventually dries up completely until it's like the cratered surface of the Moon.

This is the region where we're held back, kept from realizing our full potential. This is the land of human refuse, all that's been wasted—the junkyard of the psyche. However, within this refuse, a treasure awaits discovery. Herein we encounter the collective unconscious, where the dark archetypes of humanity's primal past lurk. Malkuth is the land of vague, deep-seated fears with which people continually struggle. This is the realm of sleep and nightmare, wherein all cycles end and begin anew.

Cryptic symbols and strange hieroglyphs are the mode of communication in Malkuth. This is the kingdom of fallen humanity, and within the depths of this kingdom humans search and surely will find the seeds of their redemption.

Malkuth rules the immediate situations in which each new cycle begins. Humans seem to be perpetually lost within the now—so much so that they aren't able to see it. The mystery of Malkuth calls for them to pay attention to immediacies and thus to become conscious of the beginning of each new cycle.

Malkuth rules the repetition of these cycles, for humans are compelled to continue to play out the same cycles over and over until whatever they are supposed to learn is fully assimilated.

Never forget that Kether, station ten, is concealed within Malkuth. It is the philosopher's stone asleep in Malkuth's cave of darkness, which we are bound to eventually discover. Let us forever celebrate this event that we will each inevitably realize.

SEFIROT NINE: YESOD

Meaning: Foundation
Planetary ruler: Mercury
Color association: purple
Keyword: Knowing

Yesod is at the roots of the Tree of Life and is found directly above station ten on the middle pillar of the Tree. Yesod is Mercury, representing the knowing of the mind as both the phenomena of thinking and of feeling, for feelings are both deeper thoughts and the basis of all thoughts. With this understanding we see that the foundation of the Tree is mental in nature. Humans were created in God's image, and so the human mind serves as the roots of the Tree.

Since the Tree of Life represents the universe, Yesod, its foundation, is the *prima materia,* the material from which all else is made. Creative Intelligence thinks everything into existence, and so all you experience both within and without oneself is an elaborate thought process divided into myriad strands to weave the fabric of reality.

From this station of the Tree flows all phantasms of the human imagination, since through eidolons the multifarious forms of reality are born. To imagine anything is to create it, to bring it form and life.

Yesod, as knowing, is power manifesting through the creation of form, and in this process Yesod is consummately flexible and adaptable. The Tree must be flexible in order to cope with the constant agitations of change, so the foundation of the Tree as Yesod must have infinite flexing potential in order to withstand the endless storms of time and the vast illusions of space.

SEFIROT EIGHT: HOD

Meaning: Splendor
Planetary ruler: Venus
Color association: green
Keyword: Being

Hod is the lowest station on the feminine or passive side of the Tree of Life. It's the garden of earthly delights that contains within it the now-vacant Garden of Eden, but also countless other gardens of lesser purity. Venus, the empress of Hod, is magnetic—she attracts to herself all manner of things, the most beautiful as well as the most ugly, the purest and the most tainted, though sometimes we cannot tell the difference between the two—between spiritual and physical things, mental and emotional things, and every form of love and all types of pleasure. Her only criteria is that they reflect splendor and glory, either in their truth and essence, or in their deceptiveness and surface appearance.

In Hod, the art of *being* is practiced. Hod demands total submission to that which flows through the garden. The river that flows through Hod brings with it an abundance of life, and since Venus governs aesthetics, Hod permits and encourages a full appreciation of the splendors of life in all its forms. The universe does not provide meagerly for humans, and Hod describes *being* as the appreciation of that which has been provided.

However, there are snakes in this garden, poisonous ones, since the tempting passivity of Hod provides fertile ground for them to flourish. Hod invites temptation unto itself: every soul who enters Hod is confronted with a choice and will choose what he or she deems the most beautiful; the mirror that shows them whatever their eyes tell them is the finest picture.

Hod is the temple of dreams and wish-fulfillment. Yet for the person who does not possess crystalline sight, it becomes a labyrinth, a voracious digestive system wherein the unwary traveler loses their way. The mythological Greek goddess Circe is a case in point: she beckoned to humans from Hod's land, and once they'd entered her precincts, she turned them into wolves and pigs.

SEFIROT SEVEN: NETZACH

Meaning: Victory
Planetary ruler: Mars
Color association: orange
Keyword: Doing

Netzach implies creation, which means making things happen by *doing*. To create requires endurance and audacity as well as patience. We're creating all the time, meaning all the time we're making things happen, even if it's just in our minds. Creating can be a dangerous activity, for what we create will either reflect Creative Intelligence and so magnify the light of Spirit, or will generate some form of destructiveness, discord, or negativity. Because they fear the latter, many people repress their creative urges, but this is ultimately impossible, for even if a person refuses to take risks, they waste their creative potential, which is another, worse sort of risk. It's best to create and fail and learn from failing and to keep on keeping on, which is what the endurance of Netzach is about. Through this Sefirot we learn to work with our passion—how to direct it, focus it, and modulate it.

Being proactive is what's needed to make the best use of this energy. Proactivity is the opposite of reactivity. Reacting is an expression of one's karma, whereas proacting means taking the initiative to clear any and all negativity around and within us.

Nothing is accomplished without initiative and vital action, even if that action is something as passive and subtly engaging as meditation.

The proactiveness signified by Netzach calls forth our creative powers, which can be used for either creative or destructive purposes, for to make way for what we're building we must also clear away those nonessential and dead forms that obstruct our path, that take up the space we need for our creative projections.

Victory comes through *doing,* the keyword of this Sefirot, as expressed in the axiom "nothing ventured, nothing gained." Life's battle places humans in a vulnerable position, and yet it is through this vulnerability, this risking, that we attain our greatest victories.

Humans can and will achieve their highest potential when they enter this battle with their complete being; the *doing* of life craves to be a total encounter.

SEFIROT SIX: TIFERET

Meaning: Beauty
Planetary ruler: Sun

Color association: yellow
Keyword: Balance

Tiferet is the beauty of *balance.* It stands at the center pillar, the heart of the Tree of Life. This is the Tree's powerhouse of vitality, which flows constantly into the rest of the Tree, just the Sun's rays flow into our earthly realm.

Tiferet is the eye of impinging consciousness transcending matter. Consciousness feeds into and flows from this core to and from all directions. The diagram of the Tree of Life shows that station six is connected by the paths to all the other stations except for station ten. There's a constant, perpetual flow and exchange of the energy of Tiferet with the other Sefirah; it is the light of consciousness flowing between all the stations of the Tree.

As energy flows from all these stations (except number ten) and moves through Tiferet, this central station controls and *balances* those various energies. Through Tiferet, human consciousness establishes and maintains a vortex of universal purpose.

The human being's will centers here, perfectly and tenuously *balanced,* and is directed outward through long-range, higher goals.

After Creative Intelligence created the universe, it stepped back and surveyed the creation and affirmed that all was good. This good goes beyond a conventional sense of good and evil; it is the good that translates as beauty. It is good because love has perfected it. Creative Intelligence's creation is totally good and perfect in that it's exactly as it should be, down to the slightest detail. This creation is good since it's totally meaningful and utterly purposeful. It exemplifies the quality of beauty because all creation is in perfect balance. Each element of creation inherently expresses purpose and meaning, which links intrinsically with the purpose and meaning of all the other elements of creation. The beauty of Tiferet joyfully expresses itself through dynamic equilibrium.

Negatively, Tiferet represents the ego, the source of all forces that work against consciousness evolution. It is by losing one's attachment to the ego that the "shells of darkness" that kabbalists call the *kelipot* fall away, allowing Tiferet to shine forth in all its glory. The kelipot can also be conceived of as veils of shadow that wrap all around us, veils that have become so much a part of us that unless we have a highly refined awareness we don't even realize their presence. There are potentially many layers of these veils that have likely accumulated in not only this lifetime but in our other lifetimes as well. The higher we evolve the more these layers fall away, one by one. These kelipot are evil, but I hesitate to use that word to describe them, for the word has such an absolute feeling, whereas kelipot can be very subtle and can come in many different types and species, just as evil does, or just like the fauna of our biological realm. They are veils of ignorance and delusion, and were they all to suddenly fall away from a person when they are not ready for this to happen, then the spiritual light could overwhelm them—could even actually destroy their physical form. This is what makes gradual and steady spiritual progress so important. We all go at the pace at which we can stand; if that pace is too slow, then events will appear in our lives to help us to speed up somewhat.

SEFIROT FIVE: GEBURAH

Meaning: Severity
Planetary ruler: Saturn
Color association: blue
Keyword: Order

Geburah is the central station of the three stations on the feminine side of the Tree. Geburah represents Creative Intelligence in the role of Giver of Law, which is to say *order.* Geburah manifests the laws of nature, which are the laws of Creative Intelligence. All elements of creation find themselves limited by nature, and all elements of creation are subject to these laws. Creative Intelligence is infinite, but humans in their temporal and single incarnational form are finite, bound and limited by the laws governing physical forms.

Geburah constantly reminds humans of their limitations by imposing *order.* There is work to be done within the constraints of evolution, and consciousness craves to evolve within the structure of physical incarnation. The soul incarnates into the physical body, that is, physical reality imposes a set of definite limitations on itself so that it can carry out specific evolutionary tasks.

To humans who can't, won't, or don't intuitively tap into the vibration of divine purpose, these structures and limiting factors can seem harsh, unjust, and without reason. This is why Geburah is translated as "severity." Nevertheless, these are the very structures that Creative Intelligence has established in its infinite wisdom to set up the evolutionary field that can most help we creatures evolve.

Maybe the deepest secret of Geburah is that when we impose limits on ourself, then Creative Intelligence doesn't need to do it for us. When we restrict, focus, and concentrate our energies through such activities as meditation, helping others, creating art, spreading love throughout the world, letting go of our ego, and simply flowing with the Tree of Life, we free ourself of the difficult circumstances that Geburah can and will create to push us forward. Then they will no longer happen because they are no longer needed, because now we are pushing ourself forward.

The trick is to be steady and gentle in one's pushing.

SEFIROT FOUR: CHESED

Meaning: Mercy
Planetary ruler: Jupiter
Color association: red
Keyword: Growth

Chesed is the merciful parent found in the central position on the masculine side of the Tree of Life. Just as red is the most expansive color in the spectrum (it is difficult to contain red within a form, as it always appears to be expanding beyond its form), this station governs expansiveness and perpetual *growth.* Humans need to honor their limitations (Sefirot five, Geburah), and yet they should always remember that it is their task to constantly explore their highest potential. Human horizons are ever widening, as the soul's evolutionary potential is boundless.

Chesed is where the multiplicity of elements within creation can achieve harmonious relationships with one another. Though humans are finite, as they gain a harmonious relationship with the other elements of the universe their boundaries merge with those of others. Creative Intelligence in its infinite mercy grants the boon of higher evolution to the souls it has created. Chesed symbolizes enthusiasm for living, and when humans embrace this, then *growth* is spontaneous. In this manner, every moment of life can be realized to its fullest.

Chesed implies religion. Established and traditional religions, with their dogmas and creeds, are not necessarily ruled by Chesed; rather, this Sefirot rules the natural expression of sanctification for all elements of creation, the light of pure religion shining to a greater or lesser degree in all religions.

In Chesed, we perceive all life as sacred, as being replete with meaning and value, and therefore we savor every moment, every event we experience, and then radiate love to every living creature. Through this love we water a luxurious *growth* of wisdom and nourish our evolving souls.

SEFIROT THREE: BINAH

Meaning: Understanding
Planetary ruler: Neptune
Color association: gray
Keyword: Potential

Binah is the highest station on the feminine side of the Tree of Life. It signifies Creative Intelligence's creation. The light of Creative Intelligence permeates all of creation, creating an omnipresent, shimmering glow.

Binah births *potential.* It's the seed of all that's probable and possible, the mother of all alternative and parallel universes, all fantasies and realities. The shifting, shimmering light of Binah is glimpsed in flashes at first, then as the soul wakes up more and more, its illuminations brighten one's whole world, becoming steady and eternal once enlightenment dawns.

Just as we need structure and limits in certain contexts, in others we need ways to move beyond those boundaries. I sense that extraterrestrials have found those ways, and so for them communication can take on amazingly complicated patterns, such that thousands of people can receive messages of great diversity coming through dreams, synchronicities, subtle urgings, and other forms that merge with their own intuitive knowing, to the point that creature separateness melts away. This psychic merging is our way forward, our way to know and love one another far deeper than we thought was ever possible.

SEFIROT TWO: CHOKMAH

Meaning: Wisdom
Planetary ruler: Uranus
Color association: white
Keyword: Creativity

Chokmah is the highest station on the masculine side of the Tree of Life. It is Creative Intelligence as *Creator,* in contradistinction to Creative Intelligence as the *creation itself,* which is Binah, station three.

Uranus, the ruler of Chokmah, corresponds to pure *creativity,* reflected in humans as the highest divine force within them.

Chokmah is inspiration—unpredictable, fluid, and continually surprising in the new and unexpected forms that flow from it. It's the vibrant aliveness and expressiveness of the universe, which constantly changes and flows.

Chokmah is the channeling of spiritual energy, which can allow the wonders of the universe to come through the human form as long as the person remains open to inspiration by letting go of expectations, the fear of failure, and attachment to all those structures we try to maintain to keep everything predictable and recognizable.

When the psyche aligns with Chokmah, joy and ecstasy result. But when Chokmah is repressed due to the fear of its wonderous powers, it then devises many "accidents" and creates many diverse sorts of cracks and breakthroughs, through which its lightning energy can flash forth.

Chokmah is the individual genius of every person. One of humanity's greatest challenges is how to work with and express this brilliant power. Because Chokmah is founded in freedom, this challenge can only be met on an individual basis by each one of us. The more we meet its challenges, the more we spark others to wake up to its power.

SEFIROT ONE: KETHER

Meaning: Crown, Seed
Planetary ruler: Pluto
Color association: black
Keyword: Influx

Kether is the highest station on the Tree of Life. It sits at the crown and hovers in darkness and latency at the Tree's apex.

Kether is the mysterious, unknowable seed of all realities, the mother and father of consciousness and life, the *influx* of all energy, the Ain Soph Aur, the limitless light.

The spirit of Kether is the source of all beginnings, which is why it has also been given the name *seed.* Seeds have much to do with hiddenness: their DNA is invisible to the eye, and seeds will not grow unless hidden in the darkness of soil. Of course, the color of Kether has to be black, but it glimmers with indigo, that akashic hue.

A seed contains all the information to reproduce the plant that produced it, and Kether, as the seed of all possible universes, therefore contains an infinite amount of information, all which has been dropped into the soil of Malkuth. Kabbalists of the past always cautioned students about contemplating Kether, for they said that almost anything you might think or say about it limits it, and therefore would give you a wrong or distorted idea about its true nature. It can't be defined, for it's truly unknowable, even though, ironically, it's what we are. This tells us that our goal is not to know ourself—it's to *be* ourself! When we can fully be ourself, then all knowing is a natural and inevitable given.

CHAPTER NINE

The Paths on the Tree of Life

The writing in this chapter comes from a very mental rather than an intuitive place. For this reason it might seem dense, and because of that some people might find it challenging. If you have trouble keeping your attention on this part of the book you can come back to it later, once you've integrated the totality of what this book offers.

Another strategy is to read this chapter in a more intuitive way—don't try to "make sense" out of it, just listen to the sounds of the words and allow their meaning to penetrate your mind like rain falling on the ground.

I think it's important to see the relationship between the major arcana and the stations on the Tree, which relate to the minor arcana, because as you digest the thoughts given here it will help you get an even deeper understanding of the major arcana.

If there are some major arcana you want to know more about or tune into more deeply, you can place your hand on the section in this chapter that corresponds to that card and just let yourself perceive the information psychically. This can be a great way to read, whereby you can pull things out of a book that you might never have realized were there!

The paragraphs that follow contain some new keywords in relation to the major arcana and the stations, or Sefirah, of the Tree of Life. Often

I use alternate keywords to define a concept so that its force can be more accurately described.

Whenever we define a concept, we limit that concept. By using new keywords I hope to redefine and hence clarify a concept so that it can be perceived from a new perspective. In this way, alternative meanings and new implications for metaphysical truths can be continually discovered.

Path Number 1

Arcanum XXII or 0: The Traveler (The Fool)
Connects stations one and two

It is The Fool that connects influx (station one) with creativity (station two). *Change* could be another way to characterize station two, because the highest form of creativity is beyond physical law and always represents a true change from the created order of things. The way the influx of energy (station one) flows into creativity (station two) is through The Traveler, which is numbered either Arcanum XXII or 0. This arcanum symbolizes the highest form of spiritual energy. It's a spiritual energy that is oblivious to physical and tangible reality because it's beyond matter. One has to go beyond the physical before the endless *influx* of energy from Kether (station one) can flow into the creative center of Chokmah (station two).

Kether is ruled by Pluto, as is Arcanum XXII, The Traveler. This signifies that the path from station one to station two is the result of the direct influx of the boundless energy of Source into creativity.

Path Number 2

Arcanum I: The Messenger (The Magus)
Connects stations one and three

Influx (station one) and potential (station three) are connected through the mind as represented by Arcanum I, The Messenger. And what is mind if not an influx of potential? Whereas station one is represented by a single point or focus—a seed—station three is represented by an infinite number of points that scintillate with an ethereal irridescence. The one (station one) becomes the many (station three) through

Arcanum I, which is the symbol of unity in diversity, for no matter how diverse it all becomes it is still the one, because it's all God. Potential (station three) is the infinite number of possible manifestations of the influx of energy of station one, and this energy is potentiated through the divine mind, as represented by Arcanum I, The Magus.

Path Number 3

Arcanum II: The Guardian of the Gate (Veiled Isis)
Connects stations one and six

Arcanum II, The Guardian of the Gate, is the great mystery and enigma of reality. As station one produces an influx of its infinite energy into reality and into our being, how can the balance, which is the essence of station six, be maintained? That this can happen is the great mystery, and hence Arcanum II connects these two stations.

Arcanum II also represents the quality of perfection, meaning that we can only maintain our balance (station six) following an influx of energy (station one) when our centering energy (station six) is perfect (Arcanum II).

Path Number 4

Arcanum III: The Queen Mother (Isis Unveiled)
Connects stations two and three

Arcanum III, The Queen Mother, is movement, activity, and productivity. It brings together the polarity of creativity and potential. Since station two is ruled by Uranus, it symbolizes the divine nature inherent in the human being. From this is derived the idea of complete independence and liberation. Station three is ruled by Neptune, which symbolizes idealism and obligation. Since all movement is an attempt to maintain balance, the quality of movement, as represented by Arcanum III, is revealed as a constant balancing of complete independence (station two) with obligation (station three).

We can read this path as the productivity (Arcanum III) that results by connecting pure creativity (station two) with the infinite sea of potential (station three). Archetypally, stations two and three symbolize the great forces of yin and yang in Chinese cosmology. They are usually portrayed as two forces, one black and one white, whirling in a circle. The yin, feminine force (station three) and the yang, masculine force (station two) generate movement (Arcanum III) in and through each other.

Path Number 5

Arcanum IV: The Commander (The Sovereign)
Connects stations two and six

Arcanum IV, The Commander, is consciousness and awareness. This is the result of the union of creativity (station two) and balance (station six). Lack of awareness is the cause of all disease, and disease is imbalance. This implies that awareness can heal anything and everything—which is true. Awareness itself is the sole healing principle because it brings one's being back into a balance that is constantly recreated in every moment.

Awareness is also the inspiration (station two) that connects us to the beauty of everything and to everything interacting in dynamic balance (station six). The word *creativity* is often used to describe Arcanum IV. In this sense it is creativity within form, whereas the creativity of station two is unhampered by form—it's a free-floating creativity, which is Creative Intelligence. Creative Intelligence (station two), through creating in form (Arcanum IV), attains the balance that is pure beauty (station six).

Path Number 6

Arcanum V: The Pentagram (The Hierophant)
Connects stations two and four

Arcanum V, The Pentagram, is harmony, which is the growth (station four) of creativity (station two). Growth can be aimless and chaotic, but when growth is inspired, harmony is the result. Station two also expresses the idea of total independence, and Arcanum V, The Pentagram, expresses the idea of learning as an activity a person undertakes that brings about growth. We are all growing in our own way, and learning is only cut off when you attempt to become the sort of person whom society, friends, and the outside world wants you to be. Grow in your own way! Your inner teacher, your Higher Self, will guide you.

Learning is actually the freedom to grow rather than the assimilation of facts. If your learning doesn't inspire you to grow, then it's not true learning, but rather just a collection of facts.

Path Number 7
Arcanum VI: The Crossroads (The Two Paths)
Connects stations three and six

Arcanum VI is love, and love is shown here as a refinement (station three) of balance and consciousness (station six). Although the keyword I've been using for station three is potential, I use the word refinement here—another good word to describe station three. We could also say, though, that love (Arcanum VI) sees all the potential(s) (station three) that dwell in beauty (station six). Arcanum VI, The Crossroads, is also the arcanum of free will, showing that free will depends on being conscious (station six) of our potential (station three). How can we have free will if we are not conscious of all of our potential choices, and how can we become conscious of this if we do not know the true nature of potential itself? The will (station six) is only free (Arcanum VI) when it achieves total refinement (station three). We may also say that true love (Arcanum VI) is the fulfillment of conscious (station six) obligation (station three), and also that false love (Arcanum VI) is the ego (station six) suffering its delusions (station three). Here is either extreme weakness or extreme power—it all depends on how it's used and whether or not it's in alignment with our true self.

Path Number 8
Arcanum VII: The Victory (The Conquerer)
Connects stations three and five

Arcanum VII is the arcanum of transcendence—of mind over matter, elevating the soul as heaven pulls it upward. Station five represents the limitations of the material world, physical laws, and the structuring of being. Until the structure of being is refined (another keyword for station three), one cannot transcend. Before the material world is transcended, a means must be found by which one can transcend, and this means is the understanding (another keyword for station three) of physical law (station five) as seen in order. The connection between understanding, the new keyword I'm using for station three, and potential, its overall keyword, is that the deeper our understanding becomes the more potential we perceive in that which we are understanding.

Transcendence is brought about through a commitment (station three) to the natural order of the universe (station five), "natural order" meaning here all the physical and metaphysical laws that determine the limits and rules of interaction by which anything happens. One can also think of Arcanum VII as the force of evolution, the only irresistible force in the universe. It is the force of evolution that orders (station five) all potentials (station three). The crystallized and defined realm of station five is lifted into the great spiritual sea of station three through this force of evolution.

Path Number 9

Arcanum VIII: The Balance (Justice)
Connects stations four and five

Arcanum VIII symbolizes karma, and karma is the ordering (station five) of growth (station four). It is natural for growth, especially in its early stages, to be a fast process, whereas order tends to produce slowness. Karma is action and reaction, and for it to be positive it has to be paced—the proper rhythm between the speed of growth and the slowness of order. Karma is bound up with the concept of time. It is true that there is a world of timelessness, but karma is not a part of that world. Karma is of the realm of the past, present, and future. Karma is the limiting of growth so that growth may proceed in a surefooted manner. If growth were not limited in this manner, it would run away with itself and burn out.

Path Number 10

Arcanum IX: The Seeker (The Sage)
Connects stations four and six

Arcanum IX is an essay on wisdom. Wisdom lies buried deep within the soul, and experience unearths it, making it shine forth like a brilliant diamond. Wisdom, seen as a connecting path on the Tree of Life, is that which connects growth (station four) with balance and consciousness (station six). Wisdom (Arcanum IX, The Sage) is purposeful (station six) growth (station four). The Sage is one who combines the qualities of beauty (station six) with growth (station four). The Sage sees the beauty (station six) of charity (station four). This person is giving, because generosity is a quality of station four, and givingness is always imbued with meaning and purpose (station six).

Path Number 11

Arcanum X: The Cycle (The Wheel)
Connects stations four and seven

Arcanum X is an essay on the nature of cycles. In every aspect of reality, cycles are present. In the material world this is reflected in the circular motion of electrons around protons and neutrons and the whirling of galaxies. Think of all the circles going on in you right now. Emotional, mental, and creative energies also manifest in cycles. Cycles (Arcanum X) are growth (station four) activated (station seven). Station seven represents doing, and when growth (station four) is an actual and dynamic process (station seven), a cycle is the result.

The mystery contained in the placement of Arcanum X on the Tree of Life is that both growth/expansion (station four) and destruction/construction (station seven) are part of creation. Plants feed on soil enriched by countless seasons of dead leaves. Trees nourish themselves through the cycle of death, decay, and growth. Any growing entity must assimilate something, and that which is assimilated is that which must first be destroyed.

Path Number 12

Arcanum XI: The Maiden (The Enchantress)
Connects stations five and six

Arcanum XI, The Maiden, reminds us that the greatest power derives from subtlety. Subtlety and power synthesize the ideas of order (station five) and balance (station six). When order is brought into balance, power is the result. True power depends on becoming conscious (station six) of physical law (station five). One who is completely conscious of the order on which the universe and reality are based possesses complete power.

The young woman of Arcanum XI performs an act that seems supernatural or magical—closing the lion's mouth. She can do this because she is conscious (station six) of physical laws (station five)—completely conscious of them. Also, ordering (station five) the will (station six) implies discipline (Arcanum XI), which shows that power comes through discipline.

Path Number 13

Arcanum XII: The Devotee (The Martyr)
Connects stations five and eight

Arcanum XII symbolizes the human body with its twelve parts or organs. The human body is an organization (station five) of magnetic forces (station eight). We also associate Arcanum XII with the end of a cycle of physical manifestation. The human body is a material form made as a vehicle for consciousness. At the end of any cycle (Arcanum XII, which is ruled by Pisces and thus the end of the cycle of the zodiac or the cycle of time), we have the potential of appreciating (station eight) the structure (station five) that has created the cycle, so that when we go through the cycle again (such as when we reincarnate) we do it from a more informed perspective.

The human body is organized (station five) splendor (station eight). On another level this is commitment (Arcanum XII) born of deep (station five) love (station eight).

Path Number 14

Arcanum XIII: The Rainbow (The Reaper)
Connects stations six and seven

The beauty (station six) of the constructive/destructive force (station seven) comes from its ability to transform (Arcanum XIII, The Rainbow). Purposeful (station six) doing (station seven) gives meaning to death (Arcanum XIII, The Reaper). Death and birth are always the same thing. We cannot have the one without the other. Death and birth are high points in awareness. These high points are generated by conscious (station six) action (station seven). Awareness is the basis of thinking, thinking the basis of action, and action the basis of birth and death.

A high point in awareness is a timeless point that divides the past from the future. Once we have contacted this high point we are never the same, and the more we contact it the more we continue to change, which is what life is all about. This transformation (Arcanum XIII) initiated (station seven) by awareness (station six) is as inevitable as death, the bringer of the rainbow of potential.

Path Number 15

Arcanum XIV: The Alchemist (Temperance)
Connects stations six and nine

The mind (station nine) experiences multitudes of thoughts, and when these thoughts are brought into balance (station six) with one another, integration (Arcanum XIV, The Alchemist) is the result. All thoughts and ideas are true and valid, provided they are put in proper combination or context (and therefore proper perspective) with one another. Arcanum XIV has to do with this proper combining.

As Arcanum XIV is The Alchemist we can also say that alchemy is the magic of making the ego (station six) more and more flexible (station nine), until it is transformed into a vehicle for communicating divine light. We can also express this path by saying that alchemy (Arcanum XIV) is a synthesis (station six) of ideas (station nine).

Path Number 16

Arcanum XV: The Musician (The Black Magician)
Connects stations six and eight

Arcanum XV has to do with fate. Fate is real in that it is a direction in which something is moving, a trajectory. It is unreal, though, because the future does not exist. Fate (Arcanum XV) is a purposeful, meaningful balance (station six) of magnetic forces (station eight). This shows that fate is not some monstrous demon lying in wait for us. In truth it is simply a righting of the balance of magnetic forces in our being that are unbalanced. When these forces are in their proper balance, then Arcanum XV can be read as *sensitivity,* which is conscious (station six) love (station eight).

Path Number 17

Arcanum XVI: The Pyramid (Power)
Connects stations seven and eight

The proper balance of doing (station seven) and being (station eight) depends on initiative (Arcanum XVI, The Pyramid). This is one of the most mysterious paths. It reveals the secret that both doing and being require doing (initiative, Arcanum XVI), since both Arcanum XVI and station seven are ruled by Mars. This points to the fact that life is ultimately predicated on activity (Mars) and not passivity (Venus, the ruler of station eight). Initiative (Arcanum XVI) is required to start something (station seven), but it also takes initiative to know when to stop and rest (station eight).

Path Number 18

Arcanum XVII: The Light (The Star)
Connects stations seven and nine

Arcanum XVII, the interior light that illuminates the spirit, synthesizes the ideas of doing (station seven) and flexibility (station nine). It is the force of doing that penetrates the darkness of matter, and when this force of doing (station seven) is imbued with the power of being absolutely flexible (station nine), and therefore totally resourceful, we attain clarity (Arcanum XVII) of action.

Path Number 19

Arcanum XVIII: The Night (The Moon)
Connects stations seven and ten

Arcanum XVIII, The Night, is an essay on both the positive and negative aspects of defense. Defending oneself requires action (station seven) in the now (station ten). Negatively, when we create a shell for ourself out of a fear of growing and changing—the negative aspect of Arcanum XVIII—it's because we're unconscious (station ten) of the proper use of creative and destructive forces (station seven). This amounts to subconscious (station ten) doing (station seven).

Path Number 20

Arcanum XIX: The Dance (The Sun)
Connects stations eight and nine

Arcanum XIX, The Sun, is the interior light (Arcanum XVII, The Light) shining through the outer shell or physical matrix (Arcanum XVIII, The Night). It is the mask through which the divine actor dramatizes its cosmic role. Arcanum XIX is personality in its aspect of unity and potential perfection. Personality in this sense reveals the power (station nine) of love (station eight).

Arcanum XIX also signifies self-assurance. We cannot have true self-assurance unless we have flexibility (station nine) where values (station eight) are concerned. This does not mean adopting value systems that are formless or easily swayed. It means values that have a strong foundation in something real (station nine is also called *foundation*). Station eight represents the potential value in all things, and if we can become mentally cognizant (station nine) of this potential treasure that lies all around us, then we can effectively dramatize ourself (Arcanum XIX, The Sun) and become a mirror reflecting the divine light.

Path Number 21

Arcanum XX: The Awakening (The Sarcophagus)
Connects stations eight and ten

Arcanum XX, The Awakening, is an essay on the ideas of bondage and liberation—just as the Moon, the planetary ruler of Arcanum XX, carries out its twenty-eight-day cycle of bondage to and liberation from the shadow. Bondage is caused by the magnetic forces (station eight) of the subconscious. This means that we are subconsciously attracted or magnetized to things, and this is what creates all bondage. Liberation, on the other hand, comes through seeing the potential value (station eight) of the now (station ten). In the now we often tend to be asleep, not truly aware of what's around us or what we're really doing. When we awaken from this sleep, we may be initially horrified by the emptiness we experience. But if we can see the worth (station eight) of our immediate situation (station ten), then we are on the path to liberation (Arcanum XX, The Awakening).

Path Number 22

Arcanum XXI: The Lord of the Dance (The Adept)
Connects stations nine and ten

The Adept (Arcanum XXI) is one who makes use of the power (station nine) of the now (station ten). Such a one is capable of moment-to-moment (station ten) flexibility (station nine). This shows that adeptship is not a static state at which we finally arrive, but rather perfecting the ability to function with absolute effectiveness. The Adept is capable of making use of the power (station nine) of the subconscious (station ten). In other words, The Adept not only possesses the capacity for releasing, revealing, and realizing the power of the present moment, but draws this power from the subterranean depths of his or her own being.

PART THREE

The Minor Arcana

CHAPTER TEN

The Alchemist's Laboratory

May I rise in all forms which I desire,
without fail and forever . . .

EGYPTIAN BOOK OF THE DEAD

My system of working with the four lower elements—fire, air, water, and earth—as well as the fifth element—akasha or the quintessence—uses ancient symbols to describe their essential nature. These symbols have come down to us from Hindu philosophy and are known as the *tattwas.* Hindu philosophy defines the tattwa system broadly as the various aspects of reality and constitute human experience, expressed not only as the elements, but also as colors, chakras, and various other symbols.

THE FIVE ELEMENTS AND THEIR SYMBOLS

Earth

The earth tattwa is a yellow square, air is a blue circle, fire a red triangle, and water a silver crescent. The fifth element, which is pure energy, known as *akasha* or the *quintessence,* is depicted as an indigo egg. Sometimes the color of this fifth element is black, and sometimes the symbol used for it is a human ear.

The square of the earth tattwa reflects the number 4, which signifies creative forces working through a physical vehicle. Earth is a yellow square because yellow is the color of balance. All imbalances on other levels will ultimately find their way down to the physical realm. The number 4 is the number of awareness—we are born into the physical world to learn how to strengthen and direct our awareness as a power to be used for healing and evolution.

Yellow is found everywhere in the earthly realm. The green of plants contains it (blue plus yellow equals green), and it's found in pollen and in the brown tones of earth, rock, sand, and many other life forms. Yellow is sulphur, which is a link between the metals (the earthiest of earthy substances) and the processes of organic chemistry—life. Yellow is the most pollutable color—it shows dirt the best, which reflects the imperfections of the earthly realm.

Water

The watery realm is unique among the three other elements in terms of its form not being a simple geometric figure. Its crescent is made from two overlapping circles, a form that recalls the image of the Moon. This crescent, being made of parts of two circles, reveals a relationship to the circle of the mental realm. Thoughts grow from feelings.

Water signifies the emotions, imagination, feelings, and intuition. That most watery planet, the Moon, constantly waxes and wanes, its gravity pulling the tides, growing large then small due to illusions created by shadows. The Moon reflects the Sun, which is why the crescent's color is silvery, silver being a natural mirror.

I always thought water was blue because it seems so when looking out at the sea. But water has no color—its blue appearance comes from its mirroring the sky. The ancients gave the watery crescent tattwa the color silver, but silver is not a color—it's a reflection that changes, taking on and letting go of colors depending on what's moving around it and in what degree of light. If you meditate on that you can come to better understand the emotions.

Some imaginings are projections of our emotional body. If you hallucinate, something that seems to be external to you is actually reflecting an inner desire or fear being projected onto the screen of the outer world.

The nature of emotions is that they're always either filling up or draining away, just like the ebb and flow of tides pulled by the Moon.

Air

The air or mental realm corresponds to the color blue, because blue structures and defines, just like the mind does. It's natural for air to circulate in curves, to move in spiraling patterns as it does in hurricanes, tornadoes, trade winds (and legal documents). The thinking process also is pulled into circularity—ideas want to lead the mind to logical conclusions, tying up beginnings and endings. Blue is the sky's hue, the realm of air; and on flat land as we turn in a 360-degree arc, the sky appears all around us as a large blue circle whose periphery is the horizon. And if you wait on that flat land long enough the sky will turn black. Black is always behind blue.

Fire

The fiery or spiritual realm burns in a red triangle, because red represents growth and spiritual forces at work in all areas of life, because growth always moves toward higher consciousness. The triangle as a geometrical form based on the number 3 symbolizes activity and productivity (see Arcanum III, The Queen Mother). The triangle is the strongest shape because fire is the hardest element to contain. Fire is in a constant state of movement (Arcanum III signifies movement). The triangle has a pointed and penetrating aura because fire has the ability to pierce the physical, filling it with light.

Akasha

The egg, talisman of number 5 and the element akasha, signifies seeds and hence vibrates with the first station on the Tree of Life. Its color, black, is the same as the first and tenth stations. This reveals the ancient idea that stations one and ten are mysteriously inside each other, turning the tree into an ouroboros.

The reason the fifth element is also shown as an ear is related to the practice of silently repeating mantras, which draws the mind toward the subtlest level of the relative plane, akasha. Listening is a door to limitless power.

THE FIVE ELEMENTS AND THEIR ACTIVITIES

Each one of the elements is associated with one of the five senses. The most primitive sense, smell, is associated with the lowest element, earth. Water is associated with taste, air with touch, fire with vision (for fire is light), and akasha with hearing.

Of the four lower elements, fire and air are positively polarized, masculine, or yang, while earth and water are negatively polarized, feminine, or yin. Of the yang elements, fire is the most yang and is constantly leaping upward. Air clings to the ground unless it is made hot by being mixed with fire; then it too rises up, like a hot air balloon. Of the two yin elements, earth is the most yin, and yet is capable of being built up, as in mountains. Water always sinks and seeks a level.

The earth or physical level is the one we most obviously share with one another. Earth is the plane of appearances that scientists investigate and explore. Physical or earthly means of developing oneself are through such things as diet, exercise, physical work, or cosmetic surgery. The physical approach to things is pragmatic in that the person tuned in to the physical level is not so much interested in what they have as in what they can do with it. Of course they might investigate the nature of what they have so they can then figure out more about what they can do with it. Physical disciplines are characterized by responsibility, stability, and practicality.

The next highest level above the physical is the watery or astral plane. It's connected to the physical through the senses. Products of the imagination are born in this realm. It's not separate from the physical—the two occupy the same space. But whereas space is clearly defined in the physical realm, in the astral realm space is subjective and illusory; it all depends on feelings.

Just as humans have a physical body, they also have an astral body. This astral body (some metaphysicians call it different things) is made up of all the feelings, desires, and longings a person may have. You can feel your astral body by sitting quietly and shutting your eyes. In this state you can remember events from your past, both pleasant and unpleasant; you will note that accompanying these thoughts are actual feelings that affect your physical self. These feelings are what exists on the astral plane. This experiment shows the tie between the physical and the astral.

We have all experienced walking into a room and sensing some feeling of warmth and comfort, or tension and discomfort. Many people who have had such experiences associate the feelings they have about the room with the physical characteristics of the room, or maybe with the people in it. However, these types of experiences are actually astral in nature, meaning that the feelings that the room evokes may be due to the moods that others who have been in the room have left behind. Our astral bodies are capable of picking up on these moods that hang in the air long after the person who left them there has departed.

Water's basic nature is fluidity. We can remove a cup of water from the ocean, but once we put it back we can never take out the exact same cup of water.

Emotions are fluid—we can pick up on them from other people. If we're happy and we're around someone who's unhappy, and if there is a receptivity working both ways, our happiness will have an uplifting effect on the other person and their unhappiness will tend to dampen our mood. Fortunately, though, most people are not this sensitive. All of us tend to shut particular feelings out and tune in to others. The unfortunate thing is that often we're not consciously aware of what we're opening up to.

The astral world can have a distorting effect on identity because if we experience a bad feeling we tend to say, "I feel bad," when actually the feeling we experience may not really be ours, but something that someone else has projected onto us. The greatest danger here is one of damming up the flow—holding on to feelings rather than letting them flow as they would like to. We need to always let go of feelings so that there's room for new ones to flow in, for if we don't we can end up harboring feelings that, like stagnant water, can become dirtier and dirtier the longer they sit and collect germs.

Air, the mental level, is the seat of reason and rationality. In humans it corresponds to the mental body, which is comprised of our thoughts, concepts, and mental constructs about life and reality. This body usually becomes crystallized at a very early age and will remain this way throughout one's life unless the mind is constantly stimulated to be open, to learn more, and to grow. The mental body strives to know what and why, and to find and understand causes and relationships. We experience our mental body as the constant flow of thoughts that stream through the mind.

The mental body is rooted in the emotional body. When freed from emotions it has the power to be completely objective, though this is more of an ideal than an actual potential. Quantum physics tells us that the observer, by observing, influences the outcome of all experiments—signifying that the reflections of the astral world are not to be escaped. We feel things and then we retroactively rationalize those feelings in an attempt to make sense of them. Unless our mental body can work with feelings in at least a somewhat detached manner, our thinking tends to always be at least somewhat flawed—like looking in a mirror that's a little wavy, or with some people a lot wavy, like distortions in a funhouse mirror.

The mental body is constantly taking two ideas and putting them together—like joining the pieces of an infinitely large puzzle. The mind's genius is its ability to put diverse pieces of information together as well as its capacity for categorizing ideas and concepts on the basis of their similarities and differences.

The healthy mental body is optimally flexible and ingenious. It does not, however, create anything new. It's the etheric, or fire body, that births the new. The mental body takes what the etheric body births and puts the pieces together, organizing them.

The etheric realm is beyond reason. You have probably heard of people who can perform miraculous cures on sick and ailing people. Often these healers use very simple means. Many of them work on the etheric level. They can use simple means because the spiritual forces they're using as tools are beyond the bounds of reason. That which exists in the mental body as an extreme of complexity can be present in the etheric body in a totally simple form.

For instance, a scientist may, on the physical level, dissect a body. Then on the astral level their imagination can intuit the inner workings that their physical eye cannot see. The information is then checked out on the rational or mental level. They can then write a textbook on how the stomach digests food. The process of digestion is indeed very complicated from the mind's viewpoint, and yet through a simple but powerful affirmation of the presence of divine energy, the most complicated problems of a stomach can be cured.

Fire, too, has its limitations. To continue burning it must constantly be fed. Fire people burn out easily. Fire changes everything into itself, but if it isn't hot enough it leaves ash. This ash is the physical material that has failed fire's mutation, which can only be consumed by a hotter fire.

Everything comes from akasha, and therefore akasha kindles even fire. It's an exceedingly fine, invisible fire, filling all space. What distinguishes akasha from the four lower elements is that it has no inherently negative effects. Akasha is neither positive nor negative. It is most closely associated with the water element because it is through our emotions that we can most readily access its energy, and so akasha corresponds to the suit of Cups. But akasha's main role is harmonizer: think of akasha as a kind of invisible lubricant that is always at work bringing all the elements into greater harmony.

There are positive and negative aspects of all the four lower elements. They may operate in a manner that is harmonious and evolutionary, or discordant and entropic, depending on context. Akasha is beyond the duality of good and evil. Its presence and force descends through the four lower elements, imbuing them with energy. Its absence can weaken the four lower elements and lead to the perpetration of evil, but akasha itself remains untouched by duality.

Akasha is everywhere. It is so refined that it penetrates, creates, supports, and sustains all—just like the sea does in the physical realm. Akasha is the fecundating force of consciousness. Attention is consciousness focused in the here and now, and when it merges with akasha it becomes liberated from the here and now and merges with the everywhere and always.

Another emblem of akasha, the fifth element, is the five-pointed star. This form is a pentacle, and when it's drawn within a circle it symbolizes the suit of Coins.

Coins, as noted earlier, correspond to the air element, and the reason that air and akasha are associated with each other is because humanity's key to the use of pranic energy is found in the mind and in thinking, the mental realm that Coins signify. The word *human* comes from the ancient root *manu,* meaning "to think." Humans are thinking creatures, and it is by using thinking to focus attention that humans can attain perfect harmony on all levels. If you are accustomed to thinking of Coins, or Pentacles, as the suit of earth, then the pentacle on each coin signifies the bringing of akasha down into that densest of elements.

The main points to remember are that in the minor arcana, Wands correspond to fire, Cups correspond to water, Pentacles or Coins correspond to air, and Swords correspond to earth. Once you are familiar with these rulerships, you can delve into the associations of the four elements in order to deepen your understanding of the cards. The major arcana, meanwhile, function as a kind of fifth suit and correspond to akasha, the fifth element, since the major arcana and akasha function similarly: just as akasha harmonizes the energies of the four lower elements, the major arcana harmonize the energies of the minor arcana.

CHAPTER ELEVEN

The Numbered Cards

In chapters 1 through 7 we studied the major arcana. In chapters 8 and 9 we studied the Tree of Life. Chapter 10 was an introduction to the occult significance of the five elements, which are simultaneous planes or stages of being. You now have everything you need to read the minor arcana cards.

Each of the forty numbered cards of the minor arcana carries the vibration of a station on the Tree of Life, and also one of the four lower elements. The fifth element, akasha, occupies a special role in this scheme. Its a subtle connecting energy between the other, denser four—it works always to bring the others into harmonious and dynamic balance with each other. The number of the minor arcana card always corresponds to the same number on the Tree of Life, and the element—fire, water, air, or earth—is determined by the suit to which the card belongs.

To interpret a numbered card of the minor arcana all you have to do is first determine the meaning of the station on the Tree to which it corresponds, and then figure out the meaning of the element to which its suit corresponds. The synthesis of these two steps will determine the meaning of the card. Below is a list of the fourteen different categories you'll be working with (ten of them are the numbers on the cards, and the other four are the four lower elements).

For instance, the Five of Cups corresponds to the fifth station on the Tree and to the element of water, since Cups are ruled by that element. You'll find the meaning of the stations summarized in chapter 8, and the meaning of each of the four elements is found in chapter 10.

So for the Five of Cups you would turn to the last half of chapter 8 and see that the keyword for station five is *order.* In chapter 10 the element water relates to the emotions and feelings. Synthesizing these two we arrive at the idea of the emotions (Cups) and order (5), implying limitation and boundaries, as described in chapter 8.

So the Five of Cups can mean the overcoming of emotional confusion, since confusion is the opposite of order. It can also mean letting go of some feeling or feelings, since whenever we organize something we always tend to get rid of whatever we don't need. Each one of the stations on the Tree has many different associations, so any Minor Arcana card can have many different meanings, and they're all connected because they all resonate with the 5 vibration. Your intuition always wants to help you pick the one that will best apply to the situation your card reading is addressing and the one that will most help the person you're reading for.

THE MINOR ARCANA: THEIR SUITS AND ELEMENTS

Here's a list of keywords and phrases for each suit of the minor arcana, along with their element, followed by a list of keywords and phrases for each of the ten numbers on the cards in each suit. Following this is a list of short phrases to describe each one of the minor arcana's forty numbered cards:

Wands

Fire: creativity, transformation, putting things through a purifying fire, newness, change and regeneration, getting over things quickly, energy coming from the Higher Self, the spiritual body, things that have to do solely with you, things happening very quickly, things that could burn out quickly, joy and laughter

Coins

Air: intellectuality, mental energy, ideas, being logical, rational thinking, making connections, adjustments, relating, flexibility, communication, thinking, modifications, wavering back and forth, cleverness

Cups

Water: sensualness, emotional energy, the energy of love and feelings, universality, energy directed from the intuitive or psychic self, the emotional body, fulfillment

Swords

Earth: practicality, physical energy, the energy of manifestation and concretization, making things more definite, the physical body, repression, limitation, slowness, obstructions, sluggishness, delays, gradualness

THE MINOR ARCANA: NUMBERS, PLANETS, AND MEANINGS

Ace

Planet: Pluto

An influx of energy, transformation, obsession, one-pointedness, life force, beginning, intensification, a flowing in, the germ or seed of a new cycle

Two

Planet: Uranus

Change, creativity, independence, individuality, the unexpected, freedom, being your own person, rebellion, upsets, surprises, suddenness, unpredictability, strangeness, weirdness

Three

Planet: Neptune

Potential, receptivity, obligation, raw power, refinement, confusion, uncertainty, idealism, sacrifices made for other people, impracticality

Four

Planet: Jupiter

Growth, expansion, outreach, evolution, enthusiasm, generosity, excess, going too far, good luck, harmonization, taking on more, widening of one's horizons, overindulgence, overcompensation

Five

Planet: Saturn

Order, structure, organization, limitations, sensitiveness, confinement, seeing the spiritual aspect of something, frustration, holding back, waiting, self-questioning, crystallization, definition, blockage

Six

Planet: Sun

Balance, consciousness, awareness, will, goal, purpose, holding on to one's center, purposefulness, egotism, focusing on what's most important, self-confidence, prioritizing

Seven

Planet: Mars

Doing, persistence, initiative, building, constructive/destructive, aggression, conflict, arguments, action, assertiveness, leading

Eight

Planet: Venus

Being as opposed to doing, magnetism, attraction, enjoyment, value, aesthetics, love, beautification, sharing, temptation, satisfaction, supply, selfishness, laziness, giving in, sloppiness, appreciation

Nine

Planet: Mercury

Power, flexibility, changeability, ingenuity, cleverness, the mind, quickening, speeding up, fluidity, resourcefulness, communication, figuring out an alternative plan, getting information, problem-solving

Ten

Planet: Moon

The present moment, liberation, feelings, the subconscious or unconscious, immediate situations, changeability, the past, family, loss and redemption, end of a cycle

CHARACTERISTICS OF THE NUMBERED CARDS OF THE MINOR ARCANA

Wands

Ace of Wands

The suit of Wands blends easily with the ace, since aces naturally have a fiery feel to them. The energy of this card, though, might easily get out of control, since the burning of it has such intensity. Other aspects of this card:

A new cycle of creativity
A new lease on life
Something totally impractical
Obsessive energy that might quickly burn out
Intense creativity
Don't let petty things thwart the expression of your inspiration
A big, complete, or intense change
Obsession with being spiritual
Openness to spiritual influence
A fresh approach

Two of Wands

Both the number 2 and the suit of Wands have an unpredictable and changing quality, so this card can be highly unstable, though if you can figure out a way to make use of its bright, vivid energy, its creativity can serve you well. Other aspects of this card:

Sudden change
Sudden creative urges
New sense of freedom
Creative uniqueness
Creative experimentation
Spiritual inspiration
Flashes of insight
Being thoroughly original

Three of Wands

A highly ethereal combination that might suddenly fade away like fireworks in the sky. How mesmerizing it might be, though, while it lasts. It bears the essence of a visionary. Other aspects of this card:

Impractical ideals
Fired up by idealism
Spiritual idealism
New obligations
Renewal of one's idealism
Spiritual understanding
Things so subtle they are hard to express
Excitement over possibilities

Four of Wands

This card is about being a self-starter, generating your own motivation and having a spiritual optimism that can move you through all trials and tribulations. Other aspects of this card:

New sense of enthusiasm
New sense of harmony
Creative exuberance
Impractical knowledge
Renewal of one's zest for life
Excessive energy
Burning out of control
Expansion of creativity

Five of Wands

The number 5 and the suit of Wands don't go together so well. Fire, representing the suit of Wands, must learn to be patient, something it's definitely not into, and the number 5 indicates slowness and patience, which are qualities lacking in fire. So to make up for that you must keep the fire steady. Don't let it go out, but also don't turn it up too high. Be the patience that fire needs, and you can be like the stars, which are patient fires. Other aspects of this card:

New sense of discipline
Structuring creative energies
Focusing creative energies
Repression of creative energies
Organizing something in an impractical manner
Practical application of creative energies
Limits placed on your individuality
Creative frustration

Six of Wands

Sometimes purpose needs to be renewed again and again, which is what this card is about. It's also about self-confidence and basing that self-confidence on spiritual principles that will alleviate suffering, rather than on material things, which only lead to suffering. Always come back to what's really important, and then how could you not be happy? Other aspects of this card:

Impractical goals
Drawing together of one's energies
New sense of purpose
Renewal of vitality
Insubstantial or ungrounded goals
Feeding the fire of your self-confidence
Creative approach to goals

Seven of Wands

You do it the way *you* do it rather than trying to do it the way someone else does it. Your way will get the job done because there will be a lot of energy behind it, because it's coming from your core. Beware, though, of being too rash or hasty. Don't allow your impatience or frustrations to throw you off balance. Other aspects of this card:

Finding a new way to do something
Acting on creative impulse
Energetic constructivity
Impractical activity
Impractical way of doing things
Volatile or explosive hostility
Rash or impulsive action
Getting things done quickly

Eight of Wands

Wondrous, glowing love is here, a stimulating and warm sharing. Get into the fire of what you love and let it warm you and others. If you love yourself truly you cannot help but love other people as well, for true love is always generous. Other aspects of this card:

New sense of values
Spiritual love
Impractical love

Ease of creativity
Impractical sense of values
Renewal of love
A new love
Being satisfied with one's creativity

Nine of Wands

It is so pleasurable to get excited about ideas and to feel the fire generated by interesting communication. Say things in your own way and as you think them, for once those sparks fade away you might have difficulty recapturing them later. Think of things in new ways. Other aspects of this card:

New ideas
Creative communication
Impractical ideas
Mental energy
Insubstantial ideas
Thoughts on spiritual things
Swift thinking or communicating

Ten of Wands

Emotions need the fire of Wands, for it helps them flow. If you feel any creative stagnation you know it's time to take more risks, to try something new, to go on an adventure. Seek out whatever stimulates your feelings. Maybe this stimulation comes to you from connections with other people, or maybe your own thoughts will do it. Other aspects of this card:

Hidden creativity
Creative fulfillment
Handling the affairs of daily life in a creative manner
Emotional changes
Immediate changes
Impractical lifestyle

Emotional energy
One's subconscious is stirred up

Coins

Ace of Coins

The one thing the aces will not allow is for energy to get stuck. Sometimes the Coins like to go in circles, and if you find your mind doing this it means that your thoughts are wanting to get somewhere but on the other hand are maybe too caught in their own structures to allow this to happen. Be not afraid to say what's on your mind, even if it seems very intense—it might produce a breakthrough. Other aspects of this card:

Complete objectivity
Intensity of mind
Mental obsessiveness
Mental breakthrough
Beginning a new cycle of thinking
Intense communication
Transformation of one's thought patterns

Two of Coins

With this card you can make a connection you don't expect, which might take the form of seeing something in a new or surprising way. Hidden thoughts can come out. You may say or hear things that have a meaning that catches you off-guard. In a way this card is the exact opposite of secrets, for it tends to lay everything out on the table. Other aspects of this card:

Mental upset
Unusual or strange ideas
Sudden communication
Unique ideas
Freedom of thought
Thinking for oneself
Erratic thinking
Inspired speaking

Three of Coins

It could be easy with this energy to have what you say be misunderstood, or to misunderstand what others are saying to you. It can also mean you hear hidden messages in things, and so your psychic connections with other people might be strong and generate more intimacy. Other aspects of this card:

Mental confusion
In-depth communication
Mental idealism
Subtle adjustments
Refinement of one's ability to communicate
Adjustment of one's understanding
Psychic communication

Four of Coins

There's a wealth of ideas here and an expansion of communication. But there could also be too many ideas—they can proliferate to the point that you don't know where to focus or you can't keep them all straight. Beware of saying too much—it can cause people to miss the point. Also, timing is everything in successful communication, and when you imbue your words with enthusiasm you are more likely to get an enthusiastic response from others. Other aspects of this card:

Mental enthusiasm
Thinking too much
Mental outreach
Harmonizing ideas
Learning to be more objective
Optimistic thinking
Too many things to think about

Five of Coins

The number 5 is rather rigid and the Coins changeable, so in a way the Five of Coins keeps air in a stable pattern, but that pattern could be narrow-mindedness or an inability to take in new ideas. On the other hand the card could mean depth of thinking and the ability to be clear when communicating. Other aspects of this card:

Mental discipline
Mental depression
Organizing one's ideas
Inability to communicate
Difficulty communicating
Limited thinking
Negative thinking
Mental concentration
Stuck in the same thoughts

Six of Coins

The number 6 goes well with the suit of Coins, for it brings important ideas and an ability to prioritize thoughts according to their relative importance. Beware, though, of coming across too egotistically when you communicate. This card can help to make communication balanced and meaningful. Other aspects of this card:

Mental vitality
Objectivity where goals are concerned
Purposeful communication
Important ideas
Centering the mind
Collecting ideas together
Prioritizing one's thinking
Total synthesis of thoughts

Seven of Coins

The number 7 can whip up the Coins, causing arguments and conflict in communication. It can also make you flexible in what you're doing, which can make you more effective, but which can also destabilize your actions. It might be good to speak up, to say what's on your mind, but you need to do it in a constructive way. Other aspects of this card:

Destructive or constructive thinking
Self-motivated thinking
Thinking on one's own
Excited thinking
Building connections
Initiating ideas
Brash words or writing

Eight of Coins

Smooth and artful communication or a lazy approach to expressing ideas—this card helps you realize the value of various thoughts and maybe to use them to enhance your own prosperity. The number 8 likes giving and receiving, and certainly the Coins can stimulate and enhance this. Other aspects of this card:

Ease of communication
Putting your mind at ease
Valuable ideas
Mental rest
Lazy thinking
Communicating love
Being flexible where values are concerned

Nine of Coins

The number 9 most goes with the suit of Coins, so this card empowers thinking and communicating. It brings out cleverness and can help you get in touch with just the information you need. Beware, though, of thinking or talking too fast. Other aspects of this card:

Swift thinking
Stimulating communication
Flexible thinking
Stimulating ideas
Acumen
Synthesis of ideas
Dealing with basic ideas
Clever talk

Ten of Coins

This card can mean too many ideas, and so overthinking things. It can also mean going with the ideas that make you feel secure, which could be a good or a bad thing. Working with ideas on a more instinctive and feeling level goes with the energy of this card. Other aspects of this card:

Immediate ideas
Being in a mental rut
Emotional adjustments
Hidden beliefs
Emotional flexibility
Circular thinking
Completion of ideas
Connecting with the past

Cups

Ace of Cups

Your feelings become more intense under this influence, or maybe they change. There can be some powerful force in your subconscious that's trying to come through. If you keep everything on a love wavelength, you can't go wrong. Other aspects of this card:

Total love
Intense psychic energy
Beginning of a new emotional cycle
Psychic channeling
Emotional breakthrough
Feeling of oneness
Obsessive emotions

Two of Cups

It can be exhilarating to let your emotions out and satisfying to free yourself from their bonds. Sudden intuitions can arise, and gratification may come suddenly or in unexpected ways. If your feelings are wanting to change, let them. Other aspects of this card:

Emotional upset
Feelings of loneliness
Emotional freedom
Total freedom
Psychic inspiration
Wisdom coming through psychic channels
Sudden change of feeling

Three of Cups

The number 3 gets along really well with the suit of Cups. You may, though, be feeling so many different feelings that you aren't really sure how you feel. With this energy it helps to listen carefully to yourself, for your intuition tends to be strong. Helping other people now functions as a protective influence, bringing you much good karma. Other aspects of this card:

Emotional confusion
Receptivity to psychic impressions
Refinement of psychic energy
Total idealism
Subtle understanding
Uncertainty about how you feel
Fulfillment of an ideal

Four of Cups

Jupiter, the ruler of this number, also rules Pisces, a water sign, so this card is kind of like having Jupiter in Pisces. At its worst it can mean being overwhelmed with feelings, to the point that you do things you later regret. At best, your upbeat emotional attitude tends to win positive responses from other people, bringing you success and fulfillment. There is great fortune to be had when you enter the flow. Other aspects of this card:

Feeling enthusiastic
Emotional outreach
Feeling optimistic

Harmonious feelings
Excess of feelings
Spontaneous affection
Generous sharing of feelings

Five of Cups

This might be a card of sadness or of dark or heavy feelings. You need to look into them to understand them better. This card can also mean that you're emotionally unfulfilled and need to consider carefully what would fulfill you and how you might bring that into your life. At best it can mean sharing deep emotions with others and hence forming a profound emotional bond. This can be a card of coming into a deep understanding of how you really feel. Other aspects of this card:

Disappointment
Emotional frustration
Total concentration
Emotional caution
Repressed emotions
Sensitivity to psychic influences
Protection of one's feelings
Feelings you can't let go of
A feeling of isolation

Six of Cups

Cups like to have the sunshine of the number 6. The Sun warms the water, and you feel fulfilled by what's most important to you. And just as sunlight can purify water, this card can mean emotional cleansing—letting go of toxic feelings and gravitating toward feelings that are vibrant and life-giving. Purpose here can be fulfilled and is found through the intuition. Other aspects of this card:

Emotional energy directed purposefully
Feeling important or the need to feel important
Subjectivity where goals are concerned

Being conscious of one's feelings
Total orientation towards a goal
Emotional centering
Health coming from emotional well-being

Seven of Cups

This card is about doing things you really want to do or that your feelings compel you to do. These things may not be reasonable or practical, but they are what will bring you satisfaction. At worst it can cause spur-of-the-moment actions that you have to pay for later. Certainly it stirs up emotions and creates a desire to purge oneself of negativity. Other aspects of this card:

Dynamic self-expression
Feelings of hostility
Setting out to actively fulfill oneself
Emotional impulsiveness
Acting on feelings
Active expression of love
Rash, heat-of-the-moment actions
Emotionally riled-up
Burning passion
Actions based on intuition

Eight of Cups

The number 8 loves to be in the suit of Cups. This card can bring in deep feelings for beauty as well as emotional gratification. Negatively, it can mean emotional selfishness. Positively, it signifies sharing with others on a feeling level and all the comfort and satisfaction that beauty brings. Other aspects of this card:

Emotional relaxation
Total laziness
Selfish feelings
Intuiting the value of something
Easy flow of feelings

Total love
Psychic attraction
Fulfillment of love
Emotional satisfaction

Nine of Cups

Traditionally, this is the wish-fulfillment card of the tarot deck. It can mean communication that is gratifying or communicating feelings of love. The negative possibility of this card can be wavering feelings or ideas that are not defined enough to lead to success. The mind here is working on an instinctive and intuitive level. Other aspects of this card:

Intuitive communication
Psychic messages
Emotional flexibility
Getting to the root of one's feelings
Subjective thinking
Emotional stimulation
Communicating one's feelings

Ten of Cups

As 10 is ruled by the Moon, the most watery planet, this is a very watery card. It can mean being swamped by emotions. It can also mean feeling completely gratified or satisfied. It can signify fulfillment through dealing with everyday sorts of things and happiness at home. Other aspects of this card:

Emotional rut
Hidden feelings
Need to deal with immediate feelings at hand
Total subjectivity
Emotional stagnation
Overcome with feelings
Strong instincts
Emotional ties to family

Swords

Ace of Swords

The earth element can be very resistive, but aces can be relentless, and so combining the ace with the suit of Swords can be like liquifying rock, turning it into lava. Change might happen very slowly here and might require pressure or drastic measures. It's always asking the querent to do something definite about the situation. Other aspects of this card:

Need to be open to changes occurring on the outer level
Obsession with materialism
Intensely difficult challenge
Complete concentration on the practical
Being open to physical change
Taking a new approach to practicalities

Two of Swords

This card can signify being inspired to deal with practical and physical sorts of things in a new and creative manner. At worst it can mean the repression of one's unique gifts, which can cause inner psychic turmoil. Other aspects of this card:

Physical freedom
Inability to be uninhibited
Being free of practical considerations
Becoming unencumbered
Wisdom used practically
Gradual attainment of freedom

Three of Swords

It's difficult to bring the energy of the threes into the suit of Swords—it usually requires a lot of work. At best this card gives deep insight into the nature of problems. It can also mean doing something definite and practical to help others in need. Negatively, it can mean handling situations in a vague or chaotic manner. Other aspects of this card:

Practical idealism
Manifesting one's psychic abilities
Practical intuitions
Obligations that present a challenge
Dealing with practical affairs in a subtle manner
Inability to understand
Bringing ideals down into reality

Four of Swords

Success might come slowly or gradually with this card. It might require lots of patience, persistence and perseverance. It's a good card for saving money and accumulating resources, though negatively it can mean that any and all sorts of excesses are becoming a problem. It can help you better learn how to work with challenges and anything practical or material. Other aspects of this card:

Inability to feel enthusiastic
Trying to deal with too many challenges at once
Learning to be more practical
Learning on a practical level
Concrete expansion
Being excessively materialistic
Chronic excess
Gradual progress
Success that comes slowly

Five of Swords

This card has a feeling of stoppage or possibly a major blockage that keeps one from moving forward. To harmonize with its energy it's good to get rid of things, go on a diet, be more self-controlled, and be cautious and careful in the use of resources. It tends to bring back karma, but if you've worked hard in the past, the karma that comes back can be a reward. Other aspects of this card:

Taking practical precautions
Inability to be organized
Definite organization
Concentrating on the practical
Physical hardship
Chronic depression
A need to be careful about practicalities

Six of Swords

This card helps you to be clear about what your goals are and to find ways of being more practical where they're concerned. It can also mean the ability to cause one's goals to manifest in physical reality. Sometimes it requires a downsizing of goals. It is positive for stabilizing and improving one's self-confidence. Other aspects of this card:

Being practical where goals are concerned
Limiting one's goals
Definite goal-orientation
Defining one's purpose
Physical realization of a goal
Basing one's self-worth on material things
Obstructions where goals are concerned

Seven of Swords

This card encourages you to be careful in what you do and to not try to do too much. Accomplish what's most needed or important at the time. Patience is very necessary with this energy, and you need to keep going until you've done as much as you can, without overdoing. If you're angry it's good to be clear and as diplomatic as possible in the expression of it. Other aspects of this card:

Taking definite action
Difficulty in getting things done
Practical action
Destruction of a blockage
Inability to act

Frustrated aggression
Working slowly and carefully
Repression of anger

Eight of Swords

It's good with this card to show love in a practical way. Give your loved one something they need or something that helps them cope with the physical world. If you have warm feelings toward someone, don't hold them back, but do be somewhat cautious in how you express them. Show how much you appreciate people. Other aspects of this card:

Inability to love
A relationship of convenience
Physical satisfaction
Being practical where one's values are concerned
Defining of one's values
Materialistic values
Accumulation of money and other resources

Nine of Swords

Keep your ideas clear and well-defined, and if people aren't understanding you as well as you would like them to, try again—say it in a different way. It may be good to write your thoughts and make decisions about which ones are the most important. The number 9 represents flexibility, and earth is the least flexible of the elements. But Mercury, ruler of 9, rules the sign Virgo, which is an earth sign. So this card is like Mercury in Virgo. Beware of being too critical and stating your criticisms in a way that they won't be accepted. Other aspects of this card:

Inability to communicate
Pinning down ideas
Thinking in definite terms
Practical thinking
Communicating in a definite manner
Inability to be flexible

Ten of Swords

This card can describe being in an emotionally stuck place, and if you struggle against it you might find that you only become more frustrated. If you're emotionally stalled-out, then put more attention on your feelings, but let them be: your observation of them will have a healing effect on them. Other aspects of this card:

An emotional obstruction
Difficulties in everyday life
Practical habit patterns
Hidden obstacles or challenges
Completion of a physical cycle
Taking care of the physical aspects of home
Accepting feelings for what they are

CHAPTER TWELVE

The Court Cards

Each suit of the minor arcana has, in addition to its ten numbered cards, four court cards: 4 suits × 4 court cards = 16 court cards in all. The number 16 is significant, as are all numbers related to the tarot. We know from having studied Arcanum XVI (The Pyramid) that this number is ruled by Mars and represents action and initiative, creation as well as destruction. We can therefore deduce that the sixteen court cards symbolize an active initiatory force within humans, and that they can be both positive (creative) or negative (destructive). These are cards of personality and denote the assumption of a specific role within a situation, thus activating or initiating that situation. Anytime we assume a role, we are creating a particular relationship to the situation.

Court cards appearing in a reading show the role that has been or that should be assumed by the querent. In other words, the court cards do not necessarily refer to a person or persons within the querent's life (the proverbial tall, dark stranger), but rather they stand for the querent's need to actualize a specific relationship within the circumstances of the question. Fritz Perls, who created the psychological approach to dream analysis called Gestalt therapy, believed that all symbols within a dream are an expression of the dreamer's self-image. Likewise, within a reading, all cards directly relate to the querent's self.

The four Horsemen or Knights are the four points in time during the year that herald the changing seasons. The Horseman of Wands stands for the vernal equinox, the point when winter changes into spring. The important concept involved here is change, since each of the Horsemen symbolize the inception of a new season or cycle. As representatives of change, the Horsemen, generally speaking, are fiery in nature.

The remaining twelve court cards represent the twelve signs of the zodiac. In popular astrology people talk about their Sun signs, and by that they mean the sign of the zodiac the Sun was in when you were born. This kind of astrology is general and stereotypical because it reveals only a part of your personality. When a full horoscope is cast for someone, all twelve signs of the zodiac are present in their chart, with each sign being activated within the personality in subtly different ways.

The court cards, taking this into consideration, call for the person to accentuate a specific part of their personality within the situation. They do not call for the querent to pretend to be someone they are not, but rather, to bring forth an already-existing facet of their personality.

Just as the Horsemen are fiery in nature, the Kings vibrate with the air element—they are active and situation-oriented (involved). The Queens are representative of water, that is, passive, idealistic, and value-sustaining (nurturing). The Princesses vibrate with the earth element in that they are diversifying, practical, supportive, and helpful (synthesizing).

Role-playing is an important and essential part of expressing the self within the context of the outer world. Self-dramatization, in this manner, becomes the crucial art of effectively actualizing a part of ourself for the fulfillment of a social event. It's good when the role-player understands the power of their role and also its limitations. The following lists delineate key character traits associated with these personality cards.

The most significant idea to remember when reading the court cards is that they are telling you it doesn't matter so much what you do as how you do it. They're telling you that you can act or proceed any way you want to, but the *manner* in which you proceed and how you *think* about what you want or what you're doing is the key to benefitting from the situation.

A note about the order in which I address the court cards: Traditionally the court cards are listed Pages (which I call Princesses),

Knights (which I call Horsemen), Queens, then Kings. I order them Horsemen, Kings, Queens, then Princesses. This is because in the system I'm working with, the Horsemen correspond to fire, the Kings to air, the Queens to water, and the Princesses to earth, this order being from the rarest element to the densest element. This is the same order of elements I use in the ordering of the court cards, so that the whole thing is growing denser and denser as it goes, until we reach the Princess of Swords, which is "earth of earth."

WANDS (FIRE)

Horseman of Wands

Keyword: Spring (this card rules the vernal equinox)

Role: Forcer or Catalyst of Creative Change

Indication: The need to take charge of one's energies, to put one's energies into something new, to try something in a new way. Generally it means the need to move swiftly and creatively. Even if you don't feel creative, if you try to be creative it can prime the pump and get your juices flowing.

Negative: Inability to force a change, impracticality; rushing into things or pushing a situation too swiftly or in the wrong way; being too self-oriented and not considering the needs of the other person or people in the situation. Fate takes over and rolls over you.

King of Wands (Aries)

Keywords: I am

Role: The Pioneer

Indication: The need to aspire to something new, to start something without fear of the future, to take the initiative, to forge ahead even when you may not feel prepared to do so, to be confrontational, to explore

Negative: Acting without thinking, brashness, being headstrong, needlessly stirring up trouble, inability to keep going with things, fizzling out, ignoring or avoiding things you need to address

Queen of Wands (Leo)

Keywords: I will

Role: The Dramatizer

Indication: The need to act in a self-assured manner, to perform one's role in a dramatic way, to assert oneself, to be proud, the need to be warm and sunny and maybe to look like you know what you're doing even when you don't

Negative: Exaggerating the situation, being histrionic, egoistic, overly self-centered or self-involved, being touchy and self-concerned, upstaging other people, offending others without knowing it

Princess of Wands (Sagittarius)

Keywords: I perceive

Role: The Administrator

Indication: The need to get an overview of the situation, to take a philosophical approach, to rise above little problems, to be magnanimous, friendly, and generous; the need to not let minor or petty things stand in the way

Negative: Not dealing with the problems at hand, procrastination, wasting good luck and good chances, floating off somewhere, not getting down to business, having lots of grand ideas that aren't grounded in practical reality

COINS (AIR)

Horseman of Coins

Keyword: Autumn (this card rules the autumnal equinox)

Role: Forcer of changes, communicating or relating, taking the initiative to speak out and to make connections, pushing to make a connection, taking the chance to say something even when you aren't sure how it will be received, working to change your own thoughts

Indication: The need to change one's way of thinking, to force oneself to be more objective, to adjust in a new manner, to stop wavering and get on with it

Negative: Inability to force a change, rationalizing, wavering back and forth, diverting one's thinking into unnecessary channels, jumping from thing to thing to thing, generating lots of hot air but not getting anything significant accomplished

King of Coins (Libra)

Keywords: I balance

Role: The Producer

Indication: The need to take the initiative to relate to others, to achieve a balance within the situation, to stay active and productive; coming across smooth, poised, and diplomatic; seeking opportunities, which may mean going up and introducing yourself to people and starting a relationship

Negative: Compromising the self in order to keep the peace, being superficial, keeping the peace when peace is not what's needed, wavering in decision-making, being too focused on how they look rather than what they really are

Queen of Coins (Aquarius)

Keywords: I know

Role: The Seeker

Indication: The need to keep an open mind, to enter into experience for the wisdom you might bring to it, to work within groups when possible, to promote a sense of team spirit; making everyone feel equal, accepted, and part of the group

Negative: Being indiscriminate about where you place your energy, supporting the wrong things, going along with the group when what you really need is to think and act independently, focusing too much on the future while neglecting what's around you

Princess of Coins (Gemini)

Keywords: I think

Role: The Clarifier

Indication: The need to communicate ideas, to think things through, to be adaptable, to not be afraid to change one's mind; the need to bring one's liveliness and sparkle to activities and situations, stimulating others and getting them going on a positive track

Negative: Not giving something one's full attention, changeability, inconstancy, providing too much information that then obscures what's really important, glib and clever in a way that does not positively advance or support the situation

CUPS (WATER)

Horseman of Cups

Keyword: Summer (this card rules the summer solstice)

Role: Forcer of Emotional or Intuitive Change

Indication: The need to take charge of your emotional energy, to get hold of your feelings and direct them along positive lines, to change the way you're feeling without repressing emotions, to take the risk of acting on your intuition, letting emotions out so they can flow and be purified, going on instinct even if you can't logically justify why you're doing what you're doing

Negative: Inability to force a change, irrationality, allowing your negative feelings to run wild and carry you to places you don't want to be, feeling swamped by emotions that lead to confusion or misunderstandings, flooding people with emotions in a chaotic manner

King of Cups (Cancer)

Keywords: I feel

Role: The Protector

Indication: The need to protect or defend oneself, to be nurturing, to function from a secure base, to establish the true spiritual self within the situation, to be positively tenacious, to take care of who and what needs to be taken care of, to play the part of a teacher and help others feel more secure

Negative: Being overly defensive, hiding behind a shell, shutting yourself up at home, being unable to let go of things that give you a false security, nurturing hurts without letting others know what you're feeling

Queen of Cups (Scorpio)

Keywords: I create

Role: The Commander

Indication: The need to take command of the situation and to be on top of things, to keep silent about your feelings within the situation, to pursue your desires; the need to recreate or rework a situation so as to transform or rejuvenate it; the need to transform negativity into positivity

Negative: Manipulating a situation to one's own favor, getting hung up on resentment or revenge, anger resulting from feelings of powerlessness, getting caught up in needless power struggles, getting back at people

Princess of Cups (Pisces)

Keywords: I believe

Role: The Server

Indication: The need to commit one's energies to something beyond the self, to empathize with others, to act out of one's convictions, to just let things flow and go with the intuition; being the understanding, sympathetic person, the good listener and empathizer

Negative: Worrying and fretting, being overly concerned with or for others, feeling guilty, getting mired in confusion, coming across in a confusing manner so that no one is quite sure of what you're doing or where you're at

SWORDS (EARTH)

Horseman of Swords

Keyword: Winter (this card rules the winter solstice)

Role: Forcer of Practical or Physical Change

Indication: The need to make a definite or tangible change, to force oneself to be practical, to make something manifest, to make things happen in the physical world; the need to stop or cut off a situation; the ability to act with detachment so that you're not stressed out about what the outcome may be

Negative: Inability to force a change, lack of creative freedom, inability to overcome inertia, being too caught up in supposedly practical considerations, just letting things take their course when you could have done something positive about them

King of Swords (Capricorn)

Keywords: I use

Role: The Discriminator

Indication: The need to evaluate the situation and decide what should be done, to focus on practicalities, to be professional in one's approach; the need to focus and simplify, to come across cautiously and objectively, keeping at bay anything that does not serve practicality; coming across as the authority or the leader

Negative: Being a hard disciplinarian on the self, materialistic, overly conservative or cautious, being judgmental and too worried about many little things

Queen of Swords (Taurus)

Keywords: I have

Role: The Integrator

Indication: The need to make the most of one's resources, to pace oneself; doing things in a slow, deliberate manner in order to persevere; the need to stubbornly hold on to positive things; to come across like a rock, the pillar of stability; to be unmoving and steady in the situation; letting your own unique self come out

Negative: Inability to accept change, bullheadedness, overconcern with creature comforts, wanting to do everything by a formula, unable to try something different

Princess of Swords (Virgo)

Keywords: I analyze

Role: The Perfecter, The Servant, The Fixer

Indication: The need to analyze things in great detail, to be dutiful and responsible, to set forth standards of perfection and work toward them, finding and working with the most meaningful details

Negative: Overly critical of self and others, caught in pettiness, lacking self-confidence due to excessive self-criticism, timid, inability to act because you don't feel you're perfect enough

CHAPTER THIRTEEN

The Minor Arcana: Its Higher Numbers Revealed

What is arguably the most popular tarot deck in the world, the Rider-Waite Tarot, was created by British occultist Arthur Edward Waite and first published by the Rider Company in 1909. Each card of the minor arcana of this deck has pictorial scenes on them. What's not to like about that? People love to use this deck because the scenes speak to them. The fact is, though, that the earliest known tarot decks have minor arcana cards devoid of pictorial scenes.

The Rider-Waite deck's pictures for the minor arcana* are representations of the trials and tribulations of humankind. Here we find murder, departures by boat, riches appearing in the sky, fame, honor, troubled sleep, starvation, and lots of other dramas, all costumed in the style of the late Middle Ages and painted in the Art Noveau style popular at the time of the deck's creation. Waite never tells his readers how he arrived at these scenes. Neither Waite nor any other author I know of has ever explained any logical internal consistency to the pictures. For these reasons I decided not to use them and instead went back to a study of the older, nonpictorial minor arcana.

*The deck's illustrations were created by occultist and artist Pamela Colman Smith, Waite's colleague in the Hermetic Order of the Dawn.

In the earliest known set of tarot cards, the Tarot of Marseilles, made in France in 1390, the meaning of any particular minor arcana card is determined by two factors: the suit of the card (whether it is a Wand, a Coin, a Cup, or a Sword); and its number in the case of the numbered cards, or its "role in court" in the case of the court cards (Knight/Horseman, King, Queen, or Page/Princess). These are the criteria we'll be following in this book.

In general, many people find the nonpictorial minor arcana difficult to read because the lack of pictures on these cards other than their number, suit, and court personage gives a certain starkness to the cards. This chapter explores the implications of another factor: the specific numbers associated with each minor arcana card and their correspondences with the major arcana, the numbers of the stations of the Tree of Life, as well as the planets and the astrological signs. This system serves to bring the complete tarot together in a harmonious whole, which makes the minor arcana come alive by setting it in direct structural relationship to the major arcana.

THE NUMEROLOGY OF THE MINOR ARCANA

Much more has been written about the major arcana than the minor arcana. Though the minor arcana are an integral part of the tarot, few researchers have made extensive inquiries into its mysteries. This chapter is a study of the minor arcana based on numerology. (For a deeper dive into the subject of numerology, see chapter 15.)

The system is quite simple. Just as the cards of the major arcana are numbered from 1 through 22, the minor arcana are numbered from 23 through 78, so that one is working with the tarot based on a consistent numbering system. These numbers are the "higher numbers" of the minor arcana. The Ace of Wands is card number 23; the Two of Wands is card 24; and so on, to the Ten of Wands, which is number 32. In turn, the Horseman of Wands becomes card 33; the King of Wands card 34; the Queen of Wands card 35; and the Page or Princess of Wands card 36.

The next suit to follow is Coins, then Cups, and finally, Swords. In each suit, the cards are arranged consecutively as they are in the suit of

Wands. Here then is a complete list of number correspondences for the minor arcana according to the following system:

Ace of Wands: 23
Two of Wands: 24
Three of Wands: 25
Four of Wands: 26
Five of Wands: 27
Six of Wands: 28
Seven of Wands: 29
Eight of Wands: 30
Nine of Wands: 31
Ten of Wands: 32
Horseman of Wands: 33
King of Wands: 34
Queen of Wands: 35
Princess of Wands: 36

Ace of Cups: 51
Two of Cups: 52
Three of Cups: 53
Four of Cups: 54
Five of Cups: 55
Six of Cups: 56
Seven of Cups: 57
Eight of Cups: 58
Nine of Cups: 59
Ten of Cups: 60
Horseman of Cups: 61
King of Cups: 62
Queen of Cups: 63
Princess of Cups: 64

Ace of Coins: 37
Two of Coins: 38
Three of Coins: 39
Four of Coins: 40
Five of Coins: 41
Six of Coins: 42
Seven of Coins: 43
Eight of Coins: 44
Nine of Coins: 45
Ten of Coins: 46
Horseman of Coins: 47
King of Coins: 48
Queen of Coins: 49
Princess of Coins: 50

Ace of Swords: 65
Two of Swords: 66
Three of Swords: 67
Four of Swords: 68
Five of Swords: 69
Six of Swords: 70
Seven of Swords: 71
Eight of Swords: 72
Nine of Swords: 73
Ten of Swords: 74
Horseman of Swords: 75
King of Swords: 76
Queen of Swords: 77
Princess of Swords: 78

When I first looked at this system I was skeptical, for it seemed maybe too obvious, arbitrary, and artificial. Still, I sensed a certain astral light in it and decided to test the system so that I could decide on its validity myself.

Then one night just after going to bed, I heard a voice in my ear whispering, *Get up and add together the numbers for all the court cards of the minor arcana.*

You can add them up yourself using the numbering system above, and if you do you'll find what I found: they add up to 888. This number signifies Christ, who represents a synthesis of all humans, with humanity represented by the sixteen minor arcana court cards.

Another thing that occurred to me is that the Tree of Life has traditionally been given the symbolic number 32 because it consists of ten stations connected by twenty-two pathways: 10 + 22 = 32. You will see on the list that 32 corresponds to the Ten of Wands, the Ten Wands being the "branches" of the Tree itself.

I want to remind you that in my system, **Wands go with fire, Coins with air, Cups with water, and Swords with earth.** Some people change the elemental rulerships for Coins and Swords. If you do this, then you should also switch the numbers in my list, so that the Ace of Coins will correspond to the number 65 and the Ace of Swords with 37.

The more I've contemplated this system of numerological correspondences for the whole deck, the more I've come to realize that it provides indispensable insight into some of the deeper meanings of the minor arcana.

Now let's go over the minor arcana card by card and discuss the relationship between the number ascribed to that card and the card itself. If there are concepts and terms in this section you don't understand or that you want to know more about, it will be helpful to review chapter 15, which is devoted to the subject of numerology.

WANDS

Ace of Wands: 23

Wands are the suit of fire, the element of creativity and change. Pluto, which rules the aces, is the planet of intensity and transformation. Hence, the Ace of Wands symbolizes **creative transformation.**

Aleister Crowley, in his collection titled *777 and Other Qabalistic Writings,* says that the number 23 symbolizes "nascent life," nascent meaning "beginning to form, grow, start, or develop." The beginning of life, then, represented by the number 23, is a creative (fire) transformation (Pluto). The Ace of Wands is a card of intense changes, the changes that occur when a seed or germ starts to grow or sprout.

It's beautiful that the minor arcana begins with the number 23, the digits of which add up to 5, which is Jupiter, meaning that the whole suit of Wands is about growing and learning.

Two of Wands: 24

The wands are spiritual in nature, and since Uranus, the planet of freedom, rules the twos, the Two of Wands is a card of **spiritual freedom.** The twenty-four books of both *The Iliad* and *The Odyssey* are symbolic of Odysseus gaining this spiritual freedom by being tested by the gods.

As both number 2 and the suit of Wands signify creativity, this is one of the most creative cards in the deck. It means much to me that 2 + 4 = 6, meaning that the pure creativity of this card comes from Venus (Arcanum VI, The Crossroads), or love. This theme is stated in another way, since 3 × 8 = 24, meaning that the number 24 is love (Venus is station eight on the Tree) activated (Arcanum III, The Queen Mother).

As 24 is the fourth abundant number, an abundant number being a number where the sum of all its proper factors is larger than the original number. It signifies any and all sorts of transformations and a fullness or abundance of creative energy. I have often thought of the number 24 as a labyrinth, for it is only when we've walked every path of our own inner labyrinth that we come to our center and hence attain spiritual (fire = Wands) freedom (2).

Three of Wands: 25

Here we combine Neptune (station three) with fire (Wands). The number 25 is the square of the number 5. Whenever a number is squared, the resulting number symbolizes the original number becoming manifest in physical form. The Three of Wands is then the number 5 manifesting in physicality, while 5 is the number of life, learning, and teaching. Neptune is the planet of idealism, so the Three of Wands, a fire card, is

spiritual idealism manifesting in form, or living, learning, and teaching becoming a physical reality.

Astrologer and visionary Ellias Lonsdale says that the challenge of the number 25 is to bring spiritual energy down into the physical world. Because this energy is so ethereal, when we try to capture it in a form that can be communicated, we can be in for a difficult task, hence the rarified and elusive nature of this card.

Four of Wands: 26

Whenever a number is multiplied by 2, the resultant number represents the sustainment of the first number, that is, the reinforcement of a number by multiplying it. Hence 26 is the sustainment of 13 (2 × 13 = 26). The number 13 in the major arcana is the number of death and rebirth, so 26, the number of the Four of Wands, is the "sustainment of death and rebirth," meaning **spiritual growth through the cycles of incarnation.**

The number 4 is ruled on the Tree of Life by Jupiter, the planet of growth. So we have the equation "creative (fire) growth (Jupiter) is the sustainment of the process of dying and being reborn." The number 26 is also 8 on the level of 3 (the sequence of unfoldment for the 8, that is, its successive appearances in the natural order of numbers being 8-17-26). By "on the level of 3," I mean that as you count onward from 8, the next time you'll meet 8 when you add the digits of a number together is at 17 (7 + 1 = 8), so 17 is 8 on the level of 2, and then the next time you'll meet 8 will be at 26 (2 + 6 = 8), so 26 is 8 on the level of 3. The number 26, then, can signify karmic (8) relationships (3), or, at its highest, creating of good karma (8) through relating (3).

The ancient Hebrew name YHVH, a name that isn't spoken and which nobody knows how to correctly pronounce anyway, has been translated in the Christian Bible as Jehovah. The letters of this word add up to 26.

Five of Wands: 27

Here we have the card of change (fire) and order (Saturn = 5); 3 × 9 = 27. Whenever a number is multiplied by 3, the original number becomes activated, 3 being the number of activity. Hence 27 is active wisdom (9 in the major arcana being The Sage). So **active wisdom through order** (3 × 9 = 27) is a matter of seeing the ever-changing (fire) order (5) of things.

This card requires working at balance, because here Saturn wants to put out the fire, and the fire would like to escape the confinement of Saturn. I think of this as the alchemical furnace in which creativity (fire) is used in a highly focused and concentrated way. Confining fire intensifies it, raising its temperature.

Six of Wands: 28

Crowley says that the number 28 is the mystic number of Netzach, the seventh station of the Tree of Life, called Victory. The number 6 in the minor arcana is ruled by the Sun, the planet of purpose. So **attaining mystical victory** (Netzach) is one's spiritual (fire) purpose (6).

The number 28 is the second perfect number. Perfect numbers are those that have all the numbers that will evenly divide into them add up to the numbers themselves. The first perfect number is 6, because the numbers that divide evenly into it are 1, 2, and 3, which add up to 6. There are no other numbers in the rest of the tarot deck that are perfect after 28, because the next after 6 is 496, which is followed by 8,128. So the number 28 is all about perfection achieved on the level of Virgo (Arcanum II), a sign that is already about perfection, but which is also about work. So we could say that this card is about **perfecting our work,** which is the highest spiritual (Wands) purpose (6).

As Ellias Lonsdale once reminded me, "We must start from the assumption that everything is already perfect exactly as it is." This is one of the most profound mysteries.

Seven of Wands: 29

Crowley says that 29 is the number of "the Magick force itself." The number 7 is ruled by Mars, the planet of action. So we see here that "the Magick force itself" equates with creative (fire) action (Mars), or we might also say that high magick is spiritual (fire) striving (Mars). This is very much a card about **taking creative risks,** which is the only way to produce true art.

Eight of Wands: 30

The number 8 is ruled by Venus, the planet of love, so the Eight (love) of Wands (fire) symbolizes **spiritual love.** Crowley, in his book *Gematria,* says that 30 is the number of truth, so we have the equation that spiritual love equals truth.

The number 30 is also the number of Pisces on the cosmic scale, which is a system of numbers used by the Egyptians, and which will be more fully explained a little later. The cosmic scale shows the most spiritual manifestation of the number it refers to, so 30 is a high spiritual manifestation of Pisces. As every sign of the zodiac has 30 degrees, this shows how the Pisces energy permeates all the signs. The number 30 is Pisces in its most light-filled, exalted form.

The number 30 is also the fifth abundant number, so it signifies the richness (abundance) of generosity (Jupiter = Arcanum V, The Pentagram), which is the finest way to express love.

Nine of Wands: 31

The number 9 corresponds to Mercury, the planet of mind and communication. So the Nine (communication) of Wands (fire) symbolizes **creative communication** or mental (Mercury) changes (fire). The number 31 represents the 3 moving toward 1 (3-1 or 31). The number 3 is the number of relationship and activity, and 1 is the number of synthesis, so creative communication (Nine of Wands) equates with the idea of relationships attaining synthesis or oneness. Note that the digits of the number add up to 4, showing the Scorpionic aura of the burning Mercury, for Arcanum IV is ruled by Scorpio. Also, as fire is the most irrational of the elements, this card can mean irrational thinking and communicating, which at its highest can deliver the unbridled truth in startling new forms.

Ten of Wands: 32

The Hebrew word for "forked lightning" is transliterated as HZYZ; this adds up to 32, and 32 is 2 × 16, the number 16 being the arcanum of the lightning-struck Tower (or in our Egyptian deck, The Pyramid). The number 32 is the sustainment or reinforcement of the number 16

(2 × 16). The tenth station on the Tree is called Kingdom and signifies fulfillment, so the Ten (fulfillment) of Wands (fire) signifies **spiritual or creative fulfillment.** Therefore, the sustainment, or reinforcement, of the process of construction/destruction (Arcanum XVI) is the key to creative fulfillment. Failures feed the work with whatever we've learned from them.

Horseman of Wands: 33

The number 33 is 3 × 11, or idealism (Arcanum XI, The Maiden) in action (× 3). The Horsemen are the forcers of change, and here the Horseman of Wands is doing this on a spiritual or creative level. His role is therefore one of **active idealism** (3 × 11).

Negatively the card could be chaos (11) in action (3).

King of Wands: 34

The number 34 is 2 × 17, or the sustainment of 17, or Arcanum XVII, The Star, which symbolizes, as C. C. Zain puts it, "the interior light which illuminates the Spirit." So the role of Aries (ruler of the King of Wands) involves **aspiration, pioneering, and renewal.** This is the action that sustains the interior spiritual light.

It can also be seen as triumph (3 + 4 = 7) on the level of transformation. As we count through the numbers that are 7 on the level of 1, 2, 3, and 4—7, 16, 25, 34—the fourth time 7 appears is as 34.

Queen of Wands: 35

Crowley tells us that 7 × 5 = 35, which is a blending of high-mindedness or transcendence (7) and enthusiasm or generosity (5). The Queen of Wands is ruled by Leo, the powerful monarch of the animal kingdom. She manifests as **transcendent generosity.**

All the court cards have to do with role-playing, and no sign likes to role-play more than Leo, the ruler of this card. Numerologically, 35 reduces to an 8, signifying that Leo's role-playing always creates karma, and so it's important for it to attempt to create good karma by playing roles that uplift and spiritually support others.

Princess of Wands: 36

The number 36 is obtained by adding all the numbers from 1 to 8. The number 8 on the Tree of Life is ruled by Venus, the planet governing love, values, and appreciation. The Princess of Wands is ruled by Sagittarius, the sign of philosophy, so true philosophy is a summation of values.

It can also be seen as a summation of love, meaning complete love. And since 36 is also the sixth abundant number, it reinforces what was just said, for it shows the **abundance of love** that this number expresses.

If we think of Venus in a negative sense, the card can mean someone who, for selfish reasons or motives of laziness, completely and abundantly avoids whatever they do not wish to deal with.

COINS

Ace of Coins: 37

Crowley calls the number 37 "Man's Crown of Power." Since the Coins govern air, the element of thinking and communicating, and since the aces are governed by Pluto, the planet of transformation, then a person's crown of power is their ability to cause **transformation through mental power** (mind and ideas).

Note how the tattwa for air is a blue circle, and 3 + 7 = 10, Arcanum X being The Wheel.

Two of Coins: 38

This is the Uranus (which rules the number 2) of air (the element governed by the suit of Coins), or freedom and inspiration (Uranus) in thinking and communicating (Coins). The number 38 is the sustainment of 19 (2 × 19 = 38)—in other words, it reinforces the number 19. The number 19 in the major arcana is the Dance/Sun, which is ruled by Leo, the sign of self-expression. Therefore, self-expression (19) is sustained (× 2) by **inspired thinking and free communicating.**

Also, 3 + 8 = 11, so creative (2) thinking (Coins) involves intuition and subtlety (11).

Three of Coins: 39

This card symbolizes the refinement (station three, Neptune) of thought processes (Coins). Occultist and astrologer Marc Jones defined alchemy as "the refinement of thinking for the sake of the thinker." The number 39 is 3 × 13, or active (3) renewal (13); so alchemy, or the **refinement of thinking,** is practiced by constantly and actively renewing or reviewing one's mental patterns. The number 39 as 3 × 13 can also mean renewal (13) of connections (3).

Negatively, this card can signify mental (Coins) confusion (Neptune), which is what alchemy as defined by Jones clears up.

Four of Coins: 40

Here we have mental (Coins) growth and expansion (Jupiter, ruler of station four). The number 40 is a famous one—the number of days and nights that Jesus spent in the wilderness and the number of days and nights that Noah was in the Ark; it is the number of cosmic crisis, in which the spiritual self's power of thought and communication (with Creative Intelligence) is expanding. As well, the numbers you can multiply together to make 40 are 2 × 2 × 2 × 5, which add up to 11, meaning that **cosmic crisis leads to refinement and potentiation** (Arcanum XI, the Maiden, and station three on the Tree of Life—which corresponds to Neptune—signify refinement and potential) of the soul.

Five of Coins: 41

Crowley refers to the number 41 as "The Mother, unfertilized and unenlightened." The Five of Coins is the number of mental (Coins) limitation (5 = Saturn). The number 41 is the fourteenth prime number and therefore is the evolution of 14.

Prime numbers represent the evolution of a number that is determined by writing the prime numbers starting with 1 in sequence and then counting them consecutively. The mathematical definition of a prime number is a number greater than 1 that only has two factors, 1 and the number itself. This means that a prime number cannot be divided by any number other than 1 and the number itself without leaving a remainder. For example, 7 is a prime number in that it only has two factors, 1 and 7 (itself). I use another definition of a prime number, which *includes* the number 1. I feel this moves the definition away from duality and generates a series of prime numbers that is more spiritual, whole, and complete in nature. Both definitions are valid. The difference between the mathematical definition of a prime number and my definition is that the sequences they generate are one off from each other. For example, according to the mathematical definition, 7 is the fourth prime number; according to my definition, 7 is the fifth prime number. See chapter 15, "Numerology," for more on prime numbers.

The number 14 in the major arcana is The Alchemist, which is ruled by Taurus, the sign of integration. Therefore mental (Coins) ordering (Saturn) is **the evolution of integration** (14). This card can also mean transformation (Arcanum IV, The Commander) leading to unification (Arcanum I, The Messenger). I derived this by reading 41 as 4 progressing to 1. You can do that kind of progressive reading of the digits for any number, and it gives you more information about it.

Six of Coins: 42

This is the card of mental (Coins) centering (station six, the Sun). It's also the sustainment of 21, since 2 × 21 = 42. Major Arcanum XXI is The Adept, which is ruled by the Sun. The Sun signifies will and purpose, so the sustainment of will and purpose depends on one's ability to achieve mental centering or conscious (Sun) communication (Coins)—in other words, **conscious communication with oneself.**

Seven of Coins: 43

This is the card of **constructive communication** (7 = Mars, Coins = communication). The number 43 is the fifteenth prime number (see as well chapter 15, "Numerology") and hence signifies the evolution of forms and definitions (Saturn rules both concepts as well as Arcanum XV, The Musician) so the Seven of Coins depends on one's ability to evolve effective forms of communicating as well as adequate and clear definitions for the symbols used.

Eight of Coins: 44

This card symbolizes valuable or beautiful (Venus = 8) ideas (Coins). Venus rules easiness, so we might call this card **ease of**

communication. The number 44 is 4 × 11. In the major arcana, Arcanum IV, The Commander, is ruled by Scorpio and signifies awareness, while Arcanum XI, The Maiden, is ruled by Neptune and signifies refinement. Therefore beautiful and valuable ideas and the ability to communicate artfully and easily (Venus rules art) depends on how refined one's awareness is.

Nine of Coins: 45

The number 45 is 1 through 9 added together and so represents a summation of the number 9, which is the number of Yesod (station nine) on the Tree of Life. Yesod is ruled by Mercury, the planet of communication and mind. We can read Yesod as "flexibility." Hence complete flexibility (45 as the summation of 9) equates with **mental power** (Coins = mind, power of knowing = station nine, Yesod).

Also, 45 is the sum of 3 × 3 × 5, three numbers that add up to 11, meaning that mental power is always psychic (Arcanum XI, The Maiden) in nature.

Ten of Coins: 46

Station ten, called Kingdom on the Tree, symbolizes totality, so the Ten of Coins symbolizes total (10) communication (Coins). The number 46 is the sum of 2 × 23, and 23 is the number of the Ace of Wands, the card of creative intensity. Therefore **total communication** is the sustainment of creative intensity. Total communication means communication with the cosmos, both the inner and the outer cosmos, which are the same.

Horseman of Coins: 47

This card symbolizes the forcing (Horseman) of communication (Coins). The number 47 is the sixteenth prime number, which is the evolution of Arcanum XVI, The Pyramid, which is ruled by Mars. So the evolution of constructive action (Mars) depends on one's ability to **force communication with the self**—meaning that one becomes aware of any tendency to be in denial about one's real and imagined identities and consciously works to build lines of communication to connect with those energies that one has ignored or repressed.

King of Coins: 48

This is the Libran court card that symbolizes humanity's ability to achieve dynamic balance between all aspects of life. The number 48 is 2 × 24, and 24 is the number of the Two of Wands, which symbolizes spiritual freedom. The equation is simple: **spiritual freedom attained through dynamic balance** between all aspects of life .

Queen of Coins: 49

This is the Aquarian role model card that symbolizes humanity's ability to gain wisdom from openly and freely experimenting and experiencing. The number 49 is 7 × 7, or the realization in form (square) of evolution (Arcanum VII, The Victory). Evolution manifests as a **wisdom gained.** Here we must not limit wisdom to mental activity and intellectual logic. Wisdom as here used is the wisdom that a bird uses to evolve feathers and wings if it wants to fly.

Princess of Coins: 50

This is the Gemini role model card symbolizing humanity's ability to be ingenious and to adjust to anything and everything. The number 50 is 2 × 25, or the sustainment (× 2) of the Three of Wands, whose number is 25, where the Three of Wands expresses the idea of learning and teaching becoming a reality. **Ingenuity through learning and teaching** is the result of the ability to make adjustments.

CUPS

Ace of Cups: 51

The Cups, which rule water, govern the psychic and astral realms. The Ace of Cups is the card of psychic (water) intensity (aces = Pluto). The number 51 is 3 × 17, or the activation (× 3) of the interior light that illuminates the Spirit. When the light of Creative Intelligence is activated, **psychic intensity** is the result.

Two of Cups: 52

This is the card of psychic (Cups) inspiration (2). The number 52 is the sustainment of 26 because 52 = 2 × 26. As well, the number 26 is the

Four of Wands, or spiritual (Wands) growth (4). Spiritual growth is sustained by **psychic inspiration** via connection with our spirit guides.

Three of Cups: 53

This card symbolizes the fulfillment (Cups) of an ideal (3 = Neptune) The number 53 is the seventeenth prime number, symbolizing the evolution of Arcanum XVII, The Star, and symbolizing the inner light. As both the planetary ruler of this card and its suit are highly intuitive, this card signifies **deep communion with one's inner light.** Of course its negative possibility—emotional confusion—can come from the proliferation of Gemini's (Arcanum XVII) tendency to scatter energy and thereby diffuse focus.

If we want to look at prime numbers in a negative way we can see them as signifying devolution rather than evolution—a breaking down rather than a developing.

Four of Cups: 54

This is the card of psychic (Cups) expansion (4 = Jupiter). The number 54 is the sustainment (× 2) of 27, the Five of Wands, which is the card of active wisdom. A beautiful meaning here is generosity (Jupiter) of love (Cups), which equates with the element of akasha (5), which suffuses the four traditional elements (5 to 4 is 54). I have always associated this number with quartz, a mineral highly supportive of this card's meaning—**psychic expansion.**

Five of Cups: 55

The number 55 is the addition of all the numbers from 1 through 10, and so it is the mystical number of Malkuth, the tenth station on the Tree of Life. Malkuth is either the realm of stagnation or fulfillment, so 55 symbolizes either complete stagnation or complete fulfillment. The Five of Cups can be read as psychic (Cups) limitation (5 = Saturn). Psychic limitation spells eventual and complete stagnation. Saturn, though, is also the planet of focus, and so we might say that this card signifies **complete fulfillment through psychic focus** (Cups = psychic, 5 = Saturn). The number 55 is a very beautiful number, as 5 likes to proliferate, as it does here.

Six of Cups: 56

There are fifty-six cards in the minor arcana, so the Six of Cups tells us that the minor arcana has to do with the fulfillment (Cups) of purpose (sixes = Sun) as outlined in the major arcana.

The number 56 is 2 × 28, the sustainment of the Six of Wands, the card of spiritual purpose. Here we have the simple equation that the **fulfillment of purpose** (Six of Cups) is equivalent to spiritual purpose (Six of Wands). We can clarify this by saying that the fulfillment of any purpose—that is, simply being purposeful—ultimately contributes to an overall spiritual purpose. That is why Crowley always said that the first thing a magician must always do is what they say they are going to do. Anything else represents nonpurposefulness. Therefore, the evolution of the inner light is the fulfillment of the ideal.

Seven of Cups: 57

The number 57 is 3 × 19, or active (× 3) self-expression (Arcanum XIX, The Dance). The seventh station on the Tree of Life is often referred to as Victory, so we might read the Seven of Cups as the fulfillment (Cups) of victory (station seven). The **fulfillment of victory** is attained through active self-expression, the expression of the true and real Higher Self.

Eight of Cups: 58

Venus, which rules station eight on the Tree of Life, is the planet of attraction and magnetism, so we might read the Eight of Cups as **psychic attraction and magnetism.** The number 58 is the sustainment (× 2) of 29, the number that Crowley refers to as "the Magick force in action." So psychic attraction sustains the activity of the magick force in action. Need we say more?

Nine of Cups: 59

The number 59 is the eighteenth prime number and so symbolizes the evolution of Arcanum XVIII, The Moon, which is ruled by Cancer. Cancer is the sign of security and protection. We can read the Nine of Cups as psychic (Cups) communication (9 = Mercury). Therefore, the ability to be in **psychic communication with oneself and the**

surrounding reality is a way of attaining greater and more effective security and self-protection.

Ten of Cups: 60

Crowley refers to the number 60 as restriction, and we could call the Ten of Cups psychic (Cups) stagnation (10 = the Moon, stagnation being a negative keyword for the Moon). So we have the equation that restriction is psychic stagnation. The number 60 is twice 30, and 30 corresponds to the Eight of Wands (see Eight of Wands above). So we could call the Ten of Cups the complete (10) **psychic attunement** (Cups) that sustains spiritual love (a meaning for the Eight of Wands).

Horseman of Cups: 61

The number 61 is the nineteenth prime number, hence the evolution of Arcanum XIX, The Sun, which corresponds to Leo. Leo is self-expression and self-assurance, hence 61 is the **evolution of self-expression and self-assurance.** This comes through the Horseman of Cups, which symbolizes the forcing (Horseman) of emotional (Cups) changes. Doing this evolves the ability for self-expression and self-assurance.

I love the way 61 is 19 upside-down, and also the fact that 41 is the fourteenth prime number, and the two numbers are each other reversed.

King of Cups: 62

The King of Cups is the Cancer court card, the nurturer and protector. The number 62 is the sustainment of 31 (2 × 31 = 62). The number 31 is the Nine of Wands, meaning creative communication (9 = Mercury, ideas; Wands = creativity). **Creative ideas sustained through nurturing, feeding, and protecting them** is the significance of this card. Note that Cancer rules the mammary glands, and even though Cancer is the most feminine of the signs, its cardinality gives it a strong masculine tone.

Queen of Cups: 63

This is the Scorpio court card (63 = 3 × 21) or the activated (× 3) will (Arcanum XXI, The Lord of the Dance). Scorpio is the commander and ruler whose will is in active operation. This queen, similarly, is on top of things, has penetrating insight into hidden truth, and is willing to lead her subjects through any changes that will result in a fuller and more spiritual life. If she manifests negatively, she might be jealous, vindictive, and secretive about selfish motives. We could call this card **active willing.** As Marc Jones gives *creativity* as the primary word to describe Scorpio, the Queen of Cups can be thought of as the role of the artist.

Princess of Cups: 64

This is the Pisces court card. The number 64 = 8 × 8, or the physical manifestation (square) of karma (Arcanum VIII, The Balance/Justice = karma). The Hebrew word for *justice* adds up to 64. Pisces is the sign of commitment, the idea here being that personal commitment manifests **divine or cosmic justice.**

SWORDS

Ace of Swords: 65

The Swords are the suit of physicality and manifestation, and aces are transformative. Hence, the Ace of Swords means physical (Swords) transformation (ace) or a new cycle (ace) of manifestation (Swords). The number 65 is 13 × 5, a blending of renewal (Arcanum XIII, The Rainbow) and learning (Arcanum V, The Pentagram). This card expresses the idea of **new cycles of manifestation renewing the learning process.**

Two of Swords: 66

The Two of Swords is freedom (2 = Uranus) made reality (Swords). The number 66 is the sum of all the numbers from 1 to 11, hence the completion of Arcanum XI (The Maiden) is refinement. Freedom is made a reality through **complete refinement of the self.** This means that when the self is unclouded and clear in its selfhood, it becomes completely free.

Three of Swords: 67

The Hebrew word for the third station on the Tree of Life, BINH, adds up to 67, and 67 is the twentieth prime number. Arcanum XX,

The Awakening, is ruled by the Moon, the planet of emotions and feelings. Hence 67 signifies the **evolution of the feeling nature** in terms of complexity and subtlety. This substantiates or makes manifest (Swords) psychic awareness (station three = Neptune = psychic awareness).

Four of Swords: 68

The number 68 is the sustainment of 34 (2 × 34 = 68), and 34 corresponds to the King of Wands. The Four of Swords can thus be read as the physical manifestation (Swords) of enthusiasm (4 = Jupiter). The King of Wands is Aries, the pioneer, he who forges on into unknown territory. This activity of the King of Wands is sustained (× 2) by his manifesting in concrete form his enthusiasm and exuberance, hence the meaning: **enthusiasm made manifest.**

Five of Swords: 69

The Five of Swords is the card of physical (Swords) limitations (5 = Saturn). The Hebrew word ABVM, meaning "enclosure," adds up to 69. The number 69 = 3 × 23, and 23 is the Ace of Wands, or creative (Wands) transformation (aces). Active creative transformation (3 × 23) is accomplished by physically (Swords) focusing and defining (both keywords of Saturn) one's creative energy. Thus **physical limitations bring about creative transformation.** If the energy is left unformed and unenclosed, it will not have a direct effect in the physical realm. The directing of creative energy into physical form is the goal of alchemy.

Six of Swords: 70

This card symbolizes the manifestation or concretizing (Swords) of will (6 = Sun). The number 70 is the sustainment of 35 (2 × 35 = 70), and 35 is the number of the Queen of Wands, the Leo court card, Leo being ruled by the Sun. The **manifestation of willpower** sustains one's self-assurance and the ability for self-expression (Queen of Wands).

It's interesting to note that in the cosmic scale of numbering described in chapter 15, 70 corresponds to 16, which is Mars (Arcanum XVI, The Pyramid). This means that achieving balance (6) in the physical realm (Swords) requires action, initiative, and effort—activities ruled by Mars.

The number 70 is 10 × 7, blending Uranus with Sagittarius, meaning that our own unique (Arcanum X, The Cycle) overview of life (Arcanum VII, The Victory) is what helps us perceive meanings (station six = meaning) in the physical world (Swords).

Seven of Swords: 71

The number 71 is the twenty-first prime number and hence the evolution of willpower (Arcanum XXI, The Lord of the Dance = willpower), or we might say the enlivening and harmonizing (keywords for prime numbers) of meaning (Arcanum XXI).

The Seven of Swords is action (7 = Mars) manifesting in the physical realm (Swords). Taking **direct, constructive action** in physical reality advances the growth and development of willpower. This is a traditional concept found in almost all mystery schools.

Eight of Swords: 72

The number 72 is 6 × 12, or a blending of love (Arcanum VI, The Crossroads = Venus) with commitment (Arcanum XII, The Devotee = Pisces). The Eight of Swords is the concrete manifestation (Swords) of love (8 = Venus). When love is imbued with dedication and commitment, it becomes a manifest reality, hence the meaning: **love manifesting through commitment.**

Kabbalists say that God has seventy-two names, which makes sense, as God is love (6) of the totality of creation (Arcanum XII is ruled by Pisces and contains within it the totality of all the signs that came before it).

Nine of Swords: 73

The Hebrew word for the second station on the Tree of Life is ChKMH (Chokmah); this word adds up to 73 (8 +20 + 40 + 5, using the cosmic scale of numbering, described in chapter 15). ChKMH means "wisdom." **Wisdom is mind made manifest** (station nine = Mercury = mind; Swords = forcer of change). It is mind acting through physical reality. The number 73 is the twenty-second prime number, that is, the evolution of Arcanum XXII, The Fool, which is ruled by Pluto, the planet of relentless obsession. As this obsession evolves, the person thirsts for union with all space and time, and through this eventually attains wisdom.

Ten of Swords: 74

The Ten of Swords is the card of complete (10 = Moon) manifestation (Swords). The number 74 is the sustainment of 37 (2 × 37), which is the Ace of Coins, "Man's Crown of Power," as Crowley calls it. The Ace of Coins is the highest level (ace) of mind energy (Coins). Complete manifestation of the life force energy sustains this **ultimate mind power.** Until the revealing or unveiling (manifestation = Swords) of truth is complete (tens) within the Self, the mind does not possess full force.

Horseman of Swords: 75

The Horseman of Swords is the forcer (Horseman) of physical change (Swords). The number 75 = 3 × 25, or the sustainment (× 3) of 25, which is the number of the Three of Wands. We might call the Three of Wands the card of new (Wands) potentials (station three = Neptune, the planet of potentiality). So we have the equation that **forcing physical change activates new potentials.**

You may wonder why the number of this card, 75, adds up to 12. First of all, 75 is the sixth time 12 appears when we begin counting levels of 12 upward from 1: 12, 39, 48, 57, 66, 75 are the numbers in order with digits that add up to 12. So it's about acceptance (12) on the level of values (6), meaning accepting whatever of value comes forth from our actions.

King of Swords: 76

This is the Capricorn court card representing **taking command.** Capricorn represents one's ability to decide, judge, and use. The number 76 is 4 × 19, or a blending of Scorpio (Arcanum IV, The Commander) and Leo (Arcanum XIX, The Sun). To develop the ability to make decisions and judgments as well as making effective use of anything requires a blend of taking command of situations (Scorpio) and being self-assured (Leo).

Queen of Swords: 77

Crowley says that the number 77 means "magickal power in perfection." The Queen of Swords is the Taurus court card. Taurus symbolizes a human's ability for stamina—a slow, patient, and steady pacing of the self. It is through developing this ability that magickal power attains perfection. Magick, according to Crowley, is the art of producing changes through **conscious direction of the will,** and this is best done slowly, evenly, and patiently.

It's interesting how this number adds up to 14, the Arcana XIV (The Alchemist), which is ruled by Taurus. Here it is divided into two 7s, signifying the yin and yang of each of the seven planets, 14 being the number of alchemy. The number 77 is also 7 times 11, or the refining and potentiation (11) of one's understanding (7).

Princess of Swords: 78

This is the Virgo court card. The number 78 is obtained by adding together all the numbers from 1 through 12, hence it is the completion of 12, which is the major arcanum ruled by Pisces (Arcanum XIV, The Devotee). Virgo is a human being's ability to effectively work, solve problems, and perfect things. Hence this card's meaning: **accomplishment through commitment to the work.**

Note that 7 + 8 = 15, the number of Saturn. Also, this is the third time we find 15 as we count forward. The first time is 15, the next is 69, and the third is 78. (There is no number below 69 whose digits will add up to 15, and then after 69 there is not another number whose digits add up to 15 until we arrive at 78.) And so 78 is Saturn (Arcanum XV, The Musician) manifesting on the level of Libra (Arcanum III, The Queen Mother). This means that the role of Virgo is to work with structure and limitation (15) in a balanced and harmonious way (3).

This system of numbering the minor arcana opens up whole new vistas of correspondences and meaning for the cards. I have not even begun to cover it fully in the above analysis, but I hope that I have pointed out enough so that any reader with an inquiring mind can pursue it further on their own.

It is noteworthy that the atomic number for the element gold is 79. It is a basic principle of numerology that any number is the basis or groundwork for the number that immediately follows it. The tarot as a whole has 78 cards and so is associated with the number 78; the number 78 is the foundation or basis for 79, which is the number of gold. This to me represents another link between the tarot and alchemy. It could be argued that the creators of the tarot did not know about the periodic table of the elements. My answer to that objection is that it cannot be proven. Also, is it not possible that a sensitive person could feel the 79 vibration coming from gold?

Another beautiful facet of this system is that it can be used by the student as a basis for deeper understanding of the numbers 23 through 78. If one encounters these numbers in divination, daily life, and so forth, they can be directly referred back to the specific cards they rule.

Numbers are vehicles for contemplation and meditation, as well as an important aspect of magick work, and this particular system of numbering the minor arcana supports the contemplative approach by enriching our understanding of numbers via the cards.

PART FOUR

Advanced Practices

CHAPTER FOURTEEN

The Metaphysics of the Question

> *The life-voyager wishing to be taught by Proteus (a mythological god) must grasp him steadfastly and press him yet the more, and at length he will appear in his proper shape. But this wily God never discloses even to the skillful questioner the whole content of his wisdom. He will reply only to the question put to him, and what he discloses will be great or trivial, according to the question asked.*
>
> Joseph Campbell, *Hero with a Thousand Faces*

Many of the difficulties of reading the tarot stem from improperly phrased questions. Questions are associated with Arcanum VIII, The Rainbow. This arcanum is also associated with karma, which is the truth that whatever you put out, you get back. It's a law of the universe that's at work at all times and in all situations. Everything we do is answered by an echo—one that we might hear soon, or maybe in one or more lifetimes from now.

The law of karma is closely associated with the idea of asking questions. If the questions we ask are valid, that is, if we really want to know the answer and are open to understanding it, then the answer will always be forthcoming. Many times, though, people ask questions that aren't valid. Many questions are just self-indulgent, that is, we already know the answer but are looking for confirmation, or we're vainly hoping that the answer we know to be true could be answered in some other way that would make it easier for us.

Other questions are anxiety-driven, coming from a place in us that fears or expects the worst.

At other times we may ask questions when we're not ready to hear the answer because our mind isn't in tune with what's being told to us. The basic assumptions hidden in our psyches can make answers invisible.

In Workshop Two we discussed the importance of not asking yes or no questions. The main reason for this is that it's metaphysically invalid to do so. The laws of metaphysics show that since free will is a reality, there are no situations in life that are so cut-and-dry that they are solely one way or another. The tarot is meant to give advice and to point the way to expanded consciousness and awareness, rather than to give pat answers.

As a metaphysical tool, the tarot is a passive instrument, meaning that it's only as effective as the person using it. In this sense it's very much like playing the piano: reading the tarot is an art rather than a mechanical process, and as an art there are no limits to how well it can be done or on how much insight can be gained from it.

We have had students ask, "Just how long does it take to learn the tarot, to really get into it?" I usually tell them that it takes just as long and there is as much involved as there is in mastering any other subject such as physics, chemistry, or psychology. We need to have respect for the complexities involved in our study, but we also need to cast aside any fears that center on those complexities. Many students say, "I didn't realize there was so much to it. I wonder if I'll be able to ever really understand it." This sort of student is reacting negatively to the complexities.

Actually, you can begin to read all the cards right now by studying the following:

- The summary of the major arcana cards found in chapter 7
- The summary of the minor arcana cards found in chapter 11
- The summary of the court cards found in chapter 12

If you only use these keywords and phrases for the cards found in these chapters, you should be able to do a clear and helpful basic reading for both yourself and for others, even without reading the rest of this book.

You may well ask, "Well, if all I need to read the tarot are these keywords, then why pore over all the other chapters?" The answer is that deepening your knowledge of the cards and their relationships gives you a more profound understanding of the nature of reality and life itself. So when you're ready to take in the other chapters, do so, for it's a way of manuring your tarot garden.

As your understanding becomes more and more refined and fertilized, you will be better able to perceive more about the various levels of meaning and subtleties of the cards and how they relate to everything in the world around you. Since we only get out of the tarot what we bring to it, it's good to constantly be deepening our knowledge of it if we expect to receive something of high value in return.

The tarot can be used to solve practical issues, but a primary mistake that's often made is that petty or trifling issues are brought to it. If this is done, we can only expect to receive petty and trifling answers in return.

For instance, a woman comes to me with the question, "What are the vibrations surrounding my buying a new dress?" On the surface, this question is quite mundane. The first thing I would do in this instance is ask her, "Why are you concerned about a new piece of clothing?" Then let us imagine that she says to me that the dress in question costs $1,200 and is a designer original, and that if she buys the dress she'll have to do so with her husband's money, and without his knowledge. Furthermore, she is sure that he would disapprove.

By my asking her the simple question "Why?" I have uncovered a whole set of attitudes and relationships that are far more important than purchasing a piece of clothing. The average person would feel that by having this added information about the question, the focus of interest has been shifted from just an article of clothing to a large sum of money and a potential deceitful act. This question could be answered by phrasing it in this manner: "What part does the choice involved in this possibility play in the development and evolution of this person?"

We have then taken a materialistic, mundane question and elevated it to a spiritual level. I have phrased this question to correspond to a metaphysical law that states, "Living is learning." The person in question has something to learn from the situation, and the tarot reader has the potential to help her learn it.

It's much easier to state several positive and foolproof ways of asking questions than it is to catalog all the wrong ways questions can be asked. Because of this, we'll only point out the major pitfalls that most people encounter when asking questions, and then go on to describe tried-and-true question formulas.

HOW TO EFFECTIVELY FORMULATE A QUESTION

A major pitfall arises when questions are phrased in a quantitative manner, such as "How much will I gain from going to school next semester?" *Gain* in this instance cannot be measured in specific units, such as miles or pounds. We can't just lay out three cards, look at them, and then tell the person, "Oh, you'll gain bunches and bunches!"

Another example of this kind of question is, "How much does so-and-so love me?" It is only in popular songs that love is measured in bushels and pecks.

Multiple option questions, although they may not go against metaphysical laws, are also difficult because the reader has to try to deal with two or more opportunities or possibilities simultaneously within the reading. An example of a multiple-option question is "Should I go to Wyoming, Colorado, or Nevada on my camping trip?" If an inexperienced reader were to lay out three cards on this question without modifying it, they might feel as if they had nothing to say, or had no information to give that could be derived from the cards.

This question is actually three questions that could be stated: "What may I positively gain from going on a camping trip to Wyoming?" Then state the same question using the other two locations. The cards will not tell the querent that any one of the alternatives is better than the others, but they will indicate that there are different things to be gained from each of the three different places.

It's then up to the querent to decide where to go on the basis of what the cards have told them and comparing that to what they would most like to gain from the trip.

Another big pitfall is a reading that is based on faulty information from the beginning. For instance, let's take a person who has previously been to a psychic and then goes to a tarot reader. The psychic has told her that the woman's child has an illness, and the woman asks the tarot reader, "Should I take my child to a specialist or to a regular doctor?" Again, we have a multiple option question, but the real crux of the matter here is that we cannot be sure that the impressions picked up by the psychic are even valid to begin with. If the psychic impressions were not valid, then any tarot reading on the question cannot be valid either.

It's important for the reader to get as much information from the querent as possible. Often if you as a reader try to do this, the person may say, "But I thought you were psychic—why do I need to tell you so much?" The answer to this is that things are often not what they seem, and therefore the question that the querent has as it is first stated to you may be hiding a deeper and more pressing question. As a reader we need to state firm, positive, metaphysically valid questions, but we cannot expect those we are reading for to have mastered this art.

The simplest sort of foolproof question that we can ask is, "What is the major vibration surrounding this situation?" Or another way of stating this is, "What is the nature of the inner core of this matter?" Or you could say something like, "What is this situation really about?"

For instance, let's say a person asks, "Will I be happy at my new job?" We can rephrase this question by saying, "What does this new job represent to this person—what is the inner core of this matter?" If I pull a single card on this and come up with Arcanum XIII, The Rainbow, we can then interpret the card by saying that the vibrations surrounding the situation are ones of change—change that begins a new cycle, one that could be refreshing or renewing, and although it may be jarring, is quite promising provided the person can meet the change openly and head-on.

All difficult questions can be changed to, "What is the person learning from this?" This manner of phrasing the question will nearly always ensure a positive and effective start to a reading.

I think it is good to beware of all questions in which the querent is not present, meaning questions a person might pose about other people or about situations in which they are not directly involved. It is not that you can't ask these questions and get valid answers. I have had many people come to me and ask about their children and friends, for instance, and sometimes I will go ahead and answer these questions with the tarot. But I always try to guide the person back toward posing questions that will enrich and support their own inner being. A primary metaphysical law is that we are here to be active, to work. Therefore, another good way to begin a question is: "What can I do . . ." Since all doing is based on attitude and outlook, and depends strongly on approach, an even better way to ask such a question is: "What approach would be most effective in this situation," or "What is the best attitude for me to take in this situation?"

PAST, PRESENT, AND FUTURE CARDS

Most people who come for a tarot reading want to know things about their future, but on the whole most of us concentrate far too much of our energies on the future rather than thinking about the past in such a way that we can gain expanded insight from it; even more importantly, we tend to not pay attention to what we're doing right now. It seems to be easier for people to dwell on the future because it does not yet exist and thus is a nice, blank page on which to paint our hopes, wishes, and fantasies.

The reason that we as readers usually lay out the cards that correspond to the past as well as the present and the future is because all present involvement is built on what has already happened. In a three-card reading, the present and future cards always have to be interpreted in the light of the past card. That past card is not there just to show the querent that we can intuit or psychically pick up on past events in their life; it's there to show us the matrix of the whole situation. It provides us with a vision of the groundwork that's the basis of all subsequent involvement. If the present card is the Five of Coins, for example, which in chapter 11 is given the meaning of the structuring of ideas; and the past card is the Two of Cups, which is an emotional change or even upset; then we know that this structuring of ideas, which is necessary now, is needed because the person has been through emotional changes.

When laying out the cards in a sequence, always think of the energy vibration of each card growing out of the one before it, and then leading on to the one that follows it.

Most new students have a tendency to try to explain all these ideas to the person for whom they are reading. Often this is not necessary, and in fact sometimes it can be confusing to the querent. The querent is usually not so much interested in how the reading is being done as they are in the answer to their question. Because of this it's sometimes easier for the reader to phrase the question to herself silently, and then give the answer to the querent.

A good example of this is the person who comes to the reader and says, "I'm not sure of the question I want to ask, I just want a general idea of what's going on in my life." If this is the basic attitude of the person, it's good for the reader to ask what this person is having difficulty handling in their life, or what they feel their major challenges are in life. If the person then mentions their marriage as being a major area of concern, the reader can silently ask the question, *What does this person need to learn from this challenge in their marriage?*

HOW TO HANDLE A GENERAL READING

Most people who come to a tarot card reader have problems or they wouldn't be there in the first place. It's the reader's job to figure out what the crux of the problem is, and to do this it's usually necessary to pose some questions to the querent. A good rule of thumb is that it's better to have more than enough information about the situation from the querent than too little.

On the other hand, as a reader you might run into people who tend to go on and on, giving you many insignificant details about a situation. Sometimes it's good to let the querent talk in this manner—they must be receiving some satisfaction or sense of release talking about their situation. But it's also important to keep the reading smooth so that we don't get bogged down in a lot of inconsequentials. Most people who come to a card reader are suffering in one way or another, and metaphysically speaking, all suffering aims at trying to get us to see something that we've overlooked or that we're avoiding. For this reason it's sometimes good to silently ask the question, *What is this person's blind spot—what is it they are missing?*

UNSOLICITED READINGS

In the spirit of helpfulness we might feel compelled to do readings for friends, but one should be very careful about doing readings that are not solicited—which the person did not ask for. This is because all readings are a form of healing, or should be, and according to the laws of metaphysics, no healing is valid until the person receiving the healing realizes that there is something wrong and then asks for healing.

Say we see that a friend is having a problem relating to a family member. We might be talking to this friend on the phone and say, "I did a reading on this situation for you and this is what I came up with . . . " Often when we tell the person what we gleaned from the cards, the person will be curiously unreceptive to our insights and advice. This may be because we gave it at the wrong time, and without their showing any desire for a tarot card reading.

This sort of thing can also happen with people who request a reading. In talking to them, we may feel that they need to know about something that they seem disinclined to talk about. It's better to leave subjects of this nature alone, because whatever the person wants to know about at the time is exactly what they should know about. Healing is not something that can be forced. As a famous Sufi holy man once said, "Think twice before trying to wake someone up—they may need their sleep."

FUTURE-ORIENTED QUESTIONS

A special word of caution should be said concerning the cards in a reading that deal with the future. These cards show what the person needs to orient toward. In effect, they indicate a beneficial direction to take. In the time-space environment in which we live, the future does not exist. If we are going to Los Angeles by car, we are either there or we're not. If we're not there, then Los Angeles is something that we're looking forward to, and to get there we have to take the proper route. The future card alludes to this idea of the proper route—the direction in which the person is heading. It does *not* predict what is going to happen in any kind of concrete or definite manner. All the cards in a reading describe the *qualities* of events and situations and not the events and situations themselves. This is based on the idea that the cards are archetypal forces, and as such they are neither positive nor negative, but can be used positively or negatively.

A better way to state this is to say that the forces can be used effectively or ineffectively. We as readers should be attempting to help others use the forces at hand more effectively. The positive use of the cards involve advising the querent, whereas the potentially negative use of the cards would be to caution the querent about what *not* to do or how *not* to be. The negative force of a card can be canceled through the positive use of its force. This is based on the metaphysical principle that all problems contain their solutions.

HANDLING THE CARDS

Finally, there is the whole matter of how to handle the cards, that is, how to shuffle them, cut them, and lay out the reading. All this is a matter of ritual, and ritual is simply a tool to bring the proper atmosphere to a reading, as well as an important means of focusing one's intent. The power in rituals lies in the consistency of your ritual process, which will develop as your ritual becomes a habit. Furthermore, rituals are a rehearsal of the attitude or relationship that is being assumed by the reader toward the reading and even toward the tarot itself. As the reader begins a reading, much depends on their mental attitude: if their mind is scattered, with part of it left behind, still pondering the newspaper or their lunch, the reading will suffer. So ritual is a way of focusing on the purpose for casting the reading.

It's really best for us and everyone involved if we can accept the metaphysical truth that we cannot lay out the wrong cards. There is no such thing as shuffling too much or not enough, and thereby getting the cards in the wrong order. The cards are always in the right order. If we have difficulty interpreting the cards, the difficulty is to be solved within ourself, and not in declaring a misdeal and starting over.

This is in line with the metaphysical law of divine order, which alludes to the idea that all is as it should be, that everything is perfect right now, just as it is. This law is not to be used as an excuse for being passive or lazy. It means that up until now we have been doing as well as we can, and the present is the point always at which it is time to be more effective, which sometimes and often means letting go, relaxing, and allowing an influx of Creative Intelligence.

FOLLOW YOUR INTUITION

There's one last and most important thought I have to deliver to you: even though this book is a storehouse of intellectual constructs, what matters most is your own intuition. The more you use the cards, the less factual information you'll need to have to read them. And if ever there is a conflict between the meaning of the cards given in this or any other book and what your intuition is telling you, *always* go with your intuition.

The cards have countless hidden meanings we often do not yet know, but the spirits who inhabit them are always in clear communication with your inner knowing. Set the intention that you're allowing that inner knowing to flow forth from you, then let yourself speak it spontaneously.

CHAPTER FIFTEEN

Numerology

The purpose of studying the cards through numerology is that it serves to enrich our understanding of them so that their meanings will become clearer and clearer.

In one way of working with the tarot, every card *except* for the court cards has a number—each major arcana card has a number (1 through 22 traditionally, or 0 through 21 alternatively) and each numbered minor arcana card has a number (1 through 10). In another way of working with the tarot, the minor arcana *including* the court cards are assigned numbers higher than 22—these are the "higher numbers" of the minor arcana (see chapter 13 for more on this). These numbers associated with each tarot card are not arbitrary—their vibration is exactly the same as the card to which they belong.

Every number has its own specific properties and meanings, and since numbers are found everywhere in reality, the study of numerology is significant to all branches of knowledge. In one respect the tarot is a textbook on numerology, because if we understand the cards we automatically understand the meaning of numbers. For instance, if we repeatedly come across the number 17, we know immediately that this corresponds to Arcanum XVII, The Light/The Star.

There's an infinite quantity of numbers, so to make our study of numerology more simple and convenient we use an easy method to reduce numbers so that we can more readily work with them. This method is called **casting out 9s**, and here's how you do it: To cast out the 9s from any number, all you have to do is add the digits in that number together. For instance, the number 1492 becomes 16, because 1 + 4 + 9 + 2 = 16. This shows that the number 1492 is on the 16 vibration, and therefore corresponds to Arcanum XVI, The Pyramid. I could have continued the process of casting out the 9s from 1492 by casting out the last 9 by adding the digits of 16 together: 1 + 6 = 7. I did not do this because there is a card numbered 16 in the major arcana and it's better to use the meaning of that card rather than reduce the number even more; if you did that and interpreted the further reduced number (7) to understand the vibration of 1492, it would make your understanding less specific and more general. In other words, the number 16 is "readable" because there is a major arcanum with that number. The 9s are not completely cast out of a number until our answer contains only one digit, but since there are twenty-two cards in the major arcana, for tarot interpretations we only cast out the 9s until we arrive at an answer which is 22 or less. Of course, if you use the higher numbers for the minor arcana, which we discussed in chapter 13, you can then reduce any number by casting out 9s until it falls below 78.

If you wonder why this technique is called casting out 9s, note that 16 – 9 = 7, so casting out 9s also means subtracting 9 as many times as we can until we arrive at a number below 22—the number of the last card of the major arcana. If you want reassurance that I'm right, you might try subtracting 9 over and over from 1492. It would be rather boring and tedious, but I promise you that you will eventually end up with the number 16. An easier and faster way to get there is, as I said before, to simply add up the digits of 1492, which causes the 16 to appear very swiftly. In other words, casting out 9s is the same thing as finding a number's digit sum, or adding the number's digits together.

Also, each number is the product or "child" of the number that comes before it, and the "father/mother" or progenitor of the number that follows it. For instance, Arcanum XVI, The Pyramid, which signifies destruction/construction, is born out of Arcanum XV, The Musician, which signifies structure. This means that if the structure of something is right, then we can build on it. If the structure is weak, destruction might eventually be the result. Arcanum XVI then leads on to or gives birth to Arcanum XVII, The Light. This means that construction or destruction tends to vivify and clarify (keywords for Arcanum XVII) our true sense of being. All the cards of the major arcana can be studied in this manner.

Whether you are using the higher numbers of the minor arcana or not, you will always be able to consider the numbers associated with the major arcana—either 1 through 22 (traditionally), or 0 through 21 (alternatively). There are two different ways we can read the numbers on the minor arcana cards. The simpler way is to use the numbers from 1 through 10 that are assigned to the numbered cards of the minor arcana in the deck (Ace of Cups = 1, Two of Cups = 2, and so on). If we associate the numbers this way, we don't assign any numbers to the court cards, since traditionally they have never been assigned any. When the court cards aren't numbered we can ignore them, numerologically speaking, or consider their numerical value as 0, when we are adding the numbers together in a reading.

The other way of reading the numbers on the minor arcana cards is to use the higher numbers, from 23 to 78, for the minor arcana that we explored in chapter 13. This way of reading the numbers will always yield a higher number and a more specific and detailed analysis, since the higher we go in the numbering system the greater complexity and mixing of energies we find.

Of these two ways of reading the numbers on the minor arcana cards, one is not necessarily better than the other. The first, simpler method yields more of a summary. The second method, using the higher numbers of the minor arcana, yields more specificity. I always do both and then take both results into consideration.

There are many ways to bring numerology into your understanding of the tarot. You can interpret the meanings of numbers associated with individual cards during readings or as you familiarize yourself with the cards. You can also reduce larger numbers, like years, such as 1492, or the sum of the numbers of all the tarot cards in a reading and then relate the reduced numbers back to individual arcana based on their numbers. When we get to gematria (see chapter 16), we'll learn how to interpret a person's name numerologically, resulting in numbers that can also be related back to individual arcana. By learning how different numbers relate to each other, you can explore the ways *any and all* numbers relate to the tarot.

PRIME NUMBERS

Prime numbers are those that can only be divided evenly by themselves and 1. For instance, 17 is a prime number because no other number (besides itself and 1) will divide into it evenly. Prime numbers are new, unique, and original manifestations of the number they correspond to in the list of primes, and as such tend to be more unique and original than other numbers.

The major arcana cards that are ruled by prime numbers are numbered 1, 2, 3, 5, 7, 11, 13, 17, and 19. Oddly enough, they all add up to 78—the number of cards in a tarot deck! In this list of major arcana that are prime numbers I have included the number 1, which modern mathematicians tell us is not a prime. There are disputes about this that I won't go into at this point since it wouldn't help you understand what I'm saying. Suffice it to say there are two ways to list prime numbers: one way that lists 1 as the first one (which I use to interpret the tarot), and the other way that starts the list with 2. I call the list starting with 1 the "fiery" or "spiritual" list, whereas the list starting with 2 is the "earthy" or "physical" list. This is in line with a major concept from Kabbalah: there are no wrong ways to do things, or wrong systems, because every system carries meaning.

The prime numbers I gave you above starts with 1, so it is part of the spiritual list. In this list, 17 is the eighth prime, meaning that 17 is a unique and original manifestation of 8.

What does this really mean? It's saying that Gemini, the astrological ruler of Arcanum XVII, The Light, is about being original when it comes to using things, while Capricorn, ruler of Arcanum VIII, The Balance, signifies using in general. It can also mean that our relationship to our interior light (Arcanum XVII) is our own unique relationship to karma (Arcanum VIII).

The earthy or physical list of primes starts out like this: 2, 3, 5, 7, 11, 13, 17, 19, and so forth. In this list, 17 is the seventh prime, meaning that in the physical realm 17 is a unique manifestation of 7, or we could say that communicating and information-gathering (Arcanum XVII) can be a unique or original way of gaining an overview (Sagittarius rules Arcanum VII) of the world.

If you love math you can explore all the cards in this manner, and if you don't love math it can certainly be a lot easier to *feel* your way into the network of all these meanings rather than trying to figure them out on paper and then trying to logically and rationally explain them.

NUMBER MIXOLOGY

All the other cards of the major arcana are nonprime numbers or composites or mixtures of other numbers. For instance, Arcanum XV, The Musician, is numbered 15, which is a mixture of 3 and 5, because 3 × 5 = 15. The number 3 signifies activity, and 5 signifies harmony, so 15 signifies acting in harmony, which is the idea of perfect structure (15 = structure). If you think of 15 as self-questioning (a keyword you'll find under Arcanum XV in chapter 7), you'll see that self-questioning (Arcanum XV) equals productive (3) growth (5). All the other cards of the major arcana can be studied in this same manner.

Numbers can also be added to one another as a means of further understanding their significance. For instance, we can say that Arcanum VII (The Victory) plus Arcanum VI (The Crossroads) equals Arcanum XIII (The Rainbow). This means that love (Arcanum VI), which rises above the material plane (Arcanum VII), is transformative (Arcanum XIII) in nature. Or we might also say that aspiration (Arcanum XIII) is actually transcending (Arcanum VII) the path of least resistance (Arcanum VI). There are, of course, many other ways to rephrase this equation.

The difference between adding and multiplying two numbers is that when you add them up you're only combining the two forces in question, whereas when you multiply two numbers together, you're completely *blending* them. For instance, 2 + 3 = 5 means that harmony (5) is the combination of perfection (2) and equilibrium (3); whereas, 2 × 3 = 6 means that love (6) is the complete mixture of purity (2) and activity (3).

NUMBER LEVELS IN NUMEROLOGY

Another means of analyzing any number is to figure out its **level.** Let's say you add up the numbers of all the cards in a tarot reading and the resulting number is 89. To determine the potential significance of this number, first cast out its 9s by adding the number's digits together. Casting out the 9s from 89 gives you 17 (8 + 9 = 17), so you can immediately connect the number 89 to Arcanum XVII, The Star. The next step in determining the level of a number is to take your answer after you've cast out the 9s and subtract it from the original number. Continuing with the number 89 as an example, we would subtract 17 from 89, which leaves 72. The next step in figuring out the level of a number is to take the last answer and divide it by 9. The reason we divide by 9 is because each cycle of 9 represents a cycle of completion. We find out how many of cycles of completion there are in a number by dividing it by 9. If you find when you divide this answer by 9 that you have a remainder, you can be sure of one thing: you divided wrong, so go back and check your work. You will always find that this number is evenly divisible by 9. The last step in determining the level of a number is to add 1 to the previous answer. Once we know how many cycles of completion there are in a number, we can determine the number's level by adding 1, since the number's level will be *one more* than the number of cycles of completion it contains. In our example, we divide 72 by 9, and get an answer of 8. The last step is to add 1 to the last answer, which results in 9 (8 + 1 = 9). The final answer, then, is 9, so we may say that 89 (our original number) reduces to 17 (its basic vibration) on the level of 9 (its secondary vibration).

To summarize, there are four steps to determining the level of a number:

1. Cast out the nines by adding together all the digits of the number until you arrive at a number less than 22. (Review the process for casting out 9s laid out earlier in this chapter if you are unclear on how to do this.)
2. Subtract this answer from the original number.

3. Divide the answer you obtained in step 2 by 9.
4. Finally, add 1 to the answer you obtained in step 3, and that will show you the level.

The level of a number tells us in what realm it is operating. So the number 89 is 17 on the level of or in the realm of 9, which means that it is clarity (17) in the realm of wisdom gained through experience (9).

THE COSMIC SCALE IN NUMEROLOGY

The ancients used a special number system known as the cosmic scale. In tarot, the cosmic scale can be used in a numerological analysis of a purely spiritual and occult nature, whereas the regular scale deals more with tangibles.

The first ten numbers of the cosmic scale are just like the regular system of counting: 1, 2, 3, 4, 5, 6, 7, 8, 9, 10. After 10, though, comes 20, rather than 11, and we then proceed, counting by 10s until we reach 100. From here on, we count by hundreds to 1,000. The number 1,000 is the last number in the cosmic scale because it is thought of as the number of completion.

The major arcana can also be numbered by the cosmic scale, so that Arcanum XI (11) then becomes Arcanum XX (20).

The following list shows the correlation between the regular number system and the cosmic scale:

1 regular = 1 cosmic	11 regular = 20 cosmic	21 regular = 300 cosmic
2 regular = 2 cosmic	12 regular = 30 cosmic	22 regular = 400 cosmic
3 regular = 3 cosmic	13 regular = 40 cosmic	23 regular = 500 cosmic
4 regular = 4 cosmic	14 regular = 50 cosmic	24 regular = 600 cosmic
5 regular = 5 cosmic	15 regular = 60 cosmic	25 regular = 700 cosmic
6 regular = 6 cosmic	16 regular = 70 cosmic	26 regular = 800 cosmic
7 regular = 7 cosmic	17 regular = 80 cosmic	27 regular = 900 cosmic
8 regular = 8 cosmic	18 regular = 90 cosmic	28 regular = 1,000 cosmic
9 regular = 9 cosmic	19 regular = 100 cosmic	
10 regular =10 cosmic	20 regular = 200 cosmic	

And so on, so that 29 regular would = 2,000 cosmic and 30 regular would = 3,000 cosmic.

As you can see from this list, the number 1,000 in the cosmic scale corresponds to 28 in the regular scale. The number 28 has special significance in that there are twenty-eight lunar mansions in Vedic astrology. The lunar mansion is a very old type of astrology used in Vedic astrology. Let's take a quick look at how this system works in the following example, using the number 28:

- The number 28 reduces to 10 (2 + 8 = 10; also known as casting out 9s)
- The level of 28 is 3 (28 − 10 = 18, 18 ÷ 9 = 2, 2 + 1 = 3); for a review of these calculations, see steps 2 through 4 above under "Number Levels in Numerology."

Therefore, 28 is pure creativity (10) in the realm of activity (3). We can also say that 28 is 4 × 7, meaning that it is a blend of creativity (4) and transcendence (7). We refer to 10 as pure creativity, and to 4 as just creativity. This is because 4 always implies creativity within a material or tangible form, and therefore it's related to the basic animal drive to procreate, whereas the creativity of 10 is unbounded—beyond physical laws, original, and therefore inspired. The number 28 can also be seen as 2 × 14, or perfection (2) blended with integration (14).

It is not necessary to use both scales in all your tarot work, although you can do this if a deeper analysis is desired. The cosmic scale helps to explain why certain numbers are used in sacred writings, such as the forty days and nights that Noah spent in the Ark. As you can see, the number 40 in the cosmic scale corresponds to 13 in the regular scale, and 13 corresponds to Arcanum XIII, The Reaper, a symbol of transformation, the crisis of new beginnings, and dying to the old.

Another example from the Bible refers to the time allotted to a human being as "threescore years and ten" (Psalm 90:10), where a score is twenty years, making a total of seventy years. The number 70 in the cosmic scale corresponds to 16 in the regular scale. The number 16 corresponds to Arcanum XVI, The Pyramid, which in some decks is called The House of God, meaning the physical body. This card can thus signify the destruction of the physical body.

The two different scales of numbers, the regular and the cosmic, should never be mixed and should always be kept separate from each other. They represent alternate methods of numerological analysis.

SQUARES IN NUMEROLOGY

Another important branch of numerology is the study of squares. A square number is one that is multiplied by itself, such as 4, which is the sum of 2 × 2; or 9, which is the sum of 3 × 3. We always refer to the larger number as a perfect square, and the smaller number that yields the larger number its square root. The perfect square always shows how its square root operates creatively in the realm of physical reality. For instance, activity (the number 3), operates creatively in the realm of physical reality to yield wisdom through experience (9, or 3 × 3). This signifies that wisdom through experience comes, in one sense, from activity and productivity (3) on the material plane. If we were not active in the material realm, how can we have experiences through which wisdom can be gained?

APPLYING THE TEACHINGS OF NUMEROLOGY

Of all the possible means you have at your disposal to study the cards, I personally have found numerology to be the most effective. To study a card from a numerological standpoint, pick one—for instance, Arcanum XVIII, The Night—and begin to work with it. In this example, the number in question is 18, and 18 is 9 × 2 and 3 × 6, as well as 1 + 17, 2 + 16, 3 + 15, 4 + 14, 5 + 13, 6 + 12, 7 + 11, 8 + 10, and 9 + 9. Some of these combinations will be easily understood as you attempt to fit the proper keywords together. Others will stump you, and when this happens, you can rest assured that you're working with an aspect of number 18 that you do not understand, and which you therefore need to think through carefully, for when something stumps you, you know you've stumbled onto a treasure that can teach you much.

Numerology can be used within an actual reading, and this is quite powerful—something I do all the time. For instance, if you are doing a three-card reading, you can add the numbers of the reading as a whole. As an example, say that you lay out the cards for a three-card spread and get Arcanum XXI, The Lord of the Dance, as the first card; the Nine of Wands as the second card; and the Three of Coins as the third card. You would simply add 21 (for Arcanum XXI) plus 9, plus 3, which equals 33. You would then reduce the 33 to 6 (3 + 3 = 6). This tells you that the reading as a whole is concerned with the idea of 6, and of course you would use Arcanum VI (The Crossroads) as the basis for understanding the number 6. Because the study of numerology is endless and can be as complex as you want it to be, you should be careful to not get carried away by bringing too many factors into a numerological analysis, to the extent that your mind becomes overwhelmed and the whole thing becomes confusing.

The most important factor in analyzing a number will always be the reduction of the number in question by adding up its digits. This is the main way of identifying the number. All the other techniques and ideas in this lesson can be applied to numerological analysis, but it must be remembered that they are basically giving you an idea of the subtler overtones and colorations inherent in numbers. Numerology is a fine study for students of both the tarot and metaphysics in general, because it trains the mind to think clearly in abstractions.

The concept of numbers is unique because it stands halfway between the seen and the unseen. Numbers are at the midpoint between the intangible and the tangible. We can compare number concepts with other abstract concepts and see that numbers are much more definite. For instance, the idea of 17 is much more definite than the idea of clarity, because clarity is relative, whereas 17 is quite specific. Because numbers bridge the gap between the real and the ideal, they are associated with magic. They are humanity's link with the unmanifest, yet ever-present forces of the universe. Each number is a being in and of itself, with a whole set of traits and properties and energies that mirror its living uniqueness; and yet each number is not separate from the rest of reality—it is intimately linked with all else, through the mystery of the One.

Often in books on numerology there are long lists of numbers, some even going up into the hundreds, with meanings given for each one of them. This is far too much material for most people to memorize, which is why we should concern ourselves more with techniques of working with numbers rather than just a catalog of the significance of all the many different numbers.

If you have a good grasp of some basic number theories—for instance how to reduce the bigger ones—then find their level, as well as the concept of blending them by multiplying them, then you can figure out the meaning of any number.

Another problem with long lists of short analyses of numbers is that a single number can mean a wide variety of things depending on the context in which it's found. Numbers speak their own language, and we can't help but lose some of what they're saying when we try to translate their vibrations into everyday words. The way to meet this challenge of translation is through constantly rethinking and retranslating, so that our analysis is in harmony with the specific situation we're dealing with.

Now that you've been introduced to the basic ideas involved in numerology, it would be good for you to go back to the major arcana and look closely at all the cards higher than Arcanum IX. The first nine major arcana cards could be called the "root arcana" because the major arcana above Arcanum IX (9) can all be reduced to the number 9 or smaller. For instance, 13 can be reduced to 4. This means that 13 is actually a manifestation of 4, but on a different level—in this case, the level of 2. I found this out by adding the 1 and 3 of 13 to get 4, then subtracting 4 from 13 to get 9, then dividing this answer by 9 to get 1, and then adding 1 to that to get 2. You can readily see here that if you start counting from 4 onward, the next time you will come to a number whose digits add up to 4 is when you come to 13, so 13 is the second time in counting that you encounter a 4—which is another way of seeing that 13 is on the level of 2. Arcanum XXII (22) becomes still another manifestation of 4, this time on the level of 3. I derived this by adding the digits of 22 together to get 4, then subtracting 4 from 22 to get 18, then dividing 18 by 9 to get 2, and then adding 1 to 2 to get 3. You can think of all the cards from Arcanum X to XXII in this manner. This kind of study can yield wonderfully fruitful results in terms of uncovering deeper understandings.

☽ *Workshop Three: Using the Higher-Numbered Cards of the Minor Arcana*

If you wish to get into a more detailed reading of the cards you can use the higher numbers given for the minor arcana in chapter 13. Here's how this works:

Let's take as an example a three-card reading in which we've turned over the following cards.

Arcanum VIII (The Balance/Justice), Three of Coins, and Princess of Swords

The question the querent asked is: "What is the best way to approach the writing I'm currently working on?"

In our usual way of working we would add these three cards up in this way: 8 (for Arcanum VIII), plus 3 (for the Three of Coins), plus 0 (for the Princess of Swords, since in our usual way of adding the court cards have no numbers). This yields the sum of 11, which signifies that the person's best approach to their writing is to use their imagination and follow the direction to which their intuition is guiding them.

Here we've only interpreted the addition of three cards to get the overview for the whole reading. Of course, we could also look at each of the three cards individually, but for right now, instead of doing this I want to show you how to work with the higher numbers of the cards.

If we decide to amplify this reading by using the higher numbers for the minor arcana given in chapter 13, we have the following: 8 (for Arcanum VIII), plus 39 (the number of the Three of Coins), plus 78 (the number of the Princess of Swords). This yields the sum of 125, which is 8 on the level of 14 ($1 + 2 + 5 = 8$, $125 - 8 = 117$, $117 \div 9 = 13$, and $13 + 1 = 14$).

The number 8 on the level of 14 means Capricorn energy (Arcanum VIII, The Balance) working in the realm of Taurus (Arcanum XIV, The Alchemist). Capricorn always focuses on the essentials of anything—it gets down to the bones of an issue, and this manifests in the realm of values (ruled by Taurus).

You don't have to use these higher numbers in every reading; in fact, if you don't wish to you don't need to use them at all. What you want to keep in mind is that the higher numbers show more of the complexities going on, though these can also be accessed through your own intuition. Always go with what you're most comfortable with.

☽ *Workshop Four: Numerological Synthesis in the Three-Card Reading*

In working with the three-card spread (see Workshop Two: The Three-Card Spread), remember that each card springs from the one preceding it—the present card comes out of the past card, and the future card grows out of the present card. This is a good way for you to intuitively feel the connections between the cards.

Each phase of a cycle evolves into the next phase. By adding the numbers of the cards in a reading you can perceive the transitions between the phases. It's a way of reading between the lines to gain more information. Given the past and the present, you can gain insight into the process through which the energy of each card is evolving from one into the other.

The way you gain this insight is by adding the numbers of the cards and then looking up the meaning of the sums you obtain. After a while, you'll know the cards so well you won't have to look any of them up.

There are four possible ways of adding up the three cards:

1. Add the past and present cards.
2. Add the present and future cards.
3. Add the past and future cards.
4. Add all three cards together.

It's good to add the cards in the order presented here, because that way you'll be reading the transitional processes (that is, the numerical sums) naturally as they come up in the reading.

After you've interpreted the past and present cards, you can add their numbers together to get insight into the process at work between the past and the present.

Then you can move on to examine the future card. Once the future card has been fully explained, you can read the meaning of the sum of the present and future cards, and then follow this by examining the process going on between the past and future cards.

Finally, by adding the numbers of all three cards, you can see the overall process going on in the entire reading.

✦ Summary of the Positions of the Cards in a Three-Card Reading

Past card: This describes the quality of the past, which provides the foundation for the present situation. You can think of this card as the root or basis of the question. It's the seed where it all got started.

Present card: This describes the feeling around the situation as it now stands. It reveals the sort of positive energy needed in the now—in other words, it shows the kind of action to take to help the situation positively unfold.

Future card: This describes the potential evolution of the situation. It points out how any conflict in the situation might get solved. It also shows what can be positively sought for in the situation.

✦ Summary of the Numerological Steps of Synthesis in the Three-Card Reading

Step one: Past card + present card = the evolution of the present situation or how it came to be what it is. The sum of the numbers of both cards shows the pattern of growth from the past to the present, so you can think of this addition as revealing an underlying tone that's affecting the current situation.

Step two: Present card + future card = the possible evolution of the situation in the future. The sum of each of these cards shows the pattern of growth from the present into the future, as well as how to proceed toward the best possible outcome for the future.

Step three: Past card + future card = the dynamic balance between the circumstances of the past and the possibilities of the future. This sum shows the process of growth between the foundation (past) and the final outcome (future). It shows what the past is trying to become.

Step four: Past card + present card + future card = an overview of the dynamic inherent within the entire situation. This sum shows what's to be gained or learned from the situation.

✦ Summary of Rules for a Numerological Synthesis of the Three-Card Reading

Rule 1: Since court cards don't typically have a numerical value (see chapter 15, "Numerology"), when they appear in a reading, they are given the value of 0. For example: King of Wands + Two of Cups + Arcanum XII = 0 + 2 + 12 = 14. (Unless, of course, you're using those higher numbers for the minor arcana as discussed in chapter 13, which I suggest you do if you want more in-depth information about the situation.)

Rule 2: Add the numerical values of the major arcana cards to those of the numbered cards of the minor arcana without differentiating between the arcana. As in the example described in rule 1, the minor arcana card, the Two of Cups, can be added to Arcanum XII (12), which yields the sum of 14. (Or, by the number given in chapter 13, 52 is the number of the Two of Cups, so the sum is 64, because 52 + 12 = 64).

Rule 3: If the sum of the cards is greater than 22, the number should be reduced by adding its digits. For example: Nine of Cups + Arcanum XVI = 9 + 16 = 25, and 2 + 5 = 7. (Or, if you're working with the higher numbers for the minor arcana you can use the number 59 for the Nine of Cups, then add this to 16 to obtain 75, the number of the Horseman of Swords).

Rule 4: To interpret the sum of the cards, use the major arcanum that corresponds to the number of the sum. For instance, in order to interpret the sum demonstrated in the example explained in rule 3, you can refer to the major arcana summary list in chapter 7. The sum of 7, in other words, can be interpreted as Arcanum VII (The Victory, or in other decks, The Chariot). In this case, the meaning of Arcanum VII will describe the process inherent in this sum.

Rule 5: Since the major arcana provides meanings for all numbers from 1 through 22, there is no need to reduce any number as long as it's below 23.

Rule 6: Very often the numerological synthesis of the cards will serve to confirm a logical train of thought that has already intuitively come to you while you discussed the cards individually. When this happens, you can consider this a verification of your intuition.

Rule 7: You don't have to use all four steps of synthesis for every three-card reading. The synthesis process can be specially crafted to the flow of the whole thing, and therefore can be left up to your own spontaneous sensing of where the whole thing's going.

✦ Synthesis of a Three-Card Reading Using Numerology

The following example is taken from my tarot journal. This question pertained to a series of tarot laboratories conducted for the graduate students of our tarot classes. Several laboratory sessions had taken place prior to the this question being posed, and in an attempt to keep the labs free-flowing and viable, the tarot was consulted often for assistance.

Here's the question:

In reference to these tarot laboratories, how can we make them more effective for the students?

The three cards we turned over were 1) Arcanum XXI (The Lord of the Dance, in the past); 2) Arcanum XVIII (The Night, in the present); 3) and Arcanum VIII (The Balance, in the future).

Card 1: Arcanum XXI, The Lord of the Dance. The root of the matter shows the need to establish a definite purpose for conducting these laboratories. The number 21 always signifies prioritizing. Of course, we already know that the purpose of the laboratories is to help students understand and use the tarot, but

Arcanum XXI implies that whenever anything comes up in these laboratories that seems of lesser significance or maybe off-subject or a side issue, some matter of lesser interest, it's best to always turn the direction of the class back to the most *central* or *key* concepts we want to get across to the students, for Arcanum XXI is ruled by the Sun and signifies focusing on core meanings and the central or controlling factors of any situation.

Card 2: Arcanum XVIII, The Night. This card indicates that the laboratories need to be conceived of as a vehicle for the nourishment and sustenance of both the students and the teachers. The laboratories can provide a "home" for graduate students in which they can expand their inner knowledge of the tarot and become more secure and grounded (Arcanum XVIII) in using it. Once again we are cautioned that the purpose must lead toward inner development (Arcanum XVIII, growth) or the grounding and stabilizing of the self, which is exactly what fosters growth and provides a basis for learning the ways and language of the tarot. As Arcanum XVIII is ruled by the sign of Cancer and signifies nurturing, we need to help students feel secure reading the cards and be sensitive to where their insecurities lie so that we're better able to remedy them.

Step 1: 21 + 18 = 39, and 3 + 9 = 12. The number 12 corresponds to Arcanum XII, The Devotee. The growth from the past to the present indicated by the number 12 shows a need for commitment and dedication. In other words, the pattern of growth from assuming a firm purpose (card 1 = Arcanum XXI) to the selection and implementation of the vehicle and groundwork (card 2 = Arcanum XVIII) that will manifest that purpose reveals a need for dedication as well as intuitively flowing with energies as they unfold (card 3 = Arcanum XII).

Card 3: Arcanum VIII, The Balance. The success of these labs seems to depend on our ability to make them practical (Arcanum VIII) for students, which I infer must come from our being sensitive to the students' needs and any problems or challenges they have in doing tarot readings. As Arcanum VIII rules karma, we need to make sure there is a clear flow of giving and receiving, and a grounding of all we're doing in practical reality, for Capricorn always is on a quest for finding what works. And, of course, karma is a feedback loop, so giving and taking energy among the students needs to be the goal we work toward.

Step 2: 18 + 8 = 26, and 2 + 6 = 8. The number 8 goes with Arcanum VIII, the Balance. The number 8 here as the sum is indicative of a pattern of evolution based on utter practicality. The numerological sum in this case is identical to the last card of this reading, demonstrating that not only the future potential for the laboratories depends on practicality and generating positive energy in the forms of action and the resulting reactions (karma), but this is likewise the pattern of growth that is at work between the present and the future.

Step 3: 21 + 8 = 29, and 2 + 9 = 11. The number 11 goes with Arcanum XI, The Maiden. The dynamic balance between the root of the matter and the future outcome of the situation (as demonstrated by the sum of 11) describes the need to use subtle powers and one's intuition—to feel our way through the situation psychically. This balance can be achieved through the refinement of the labs, which may indicate a need to constantly rework and reexamine them psychically as we go. This subtlety of power and refinement of the tools can come about by being receptive or clairvoyantly open to the flow of situations and being sensitive to the intuitive impressions of all involved.

Step 4: 21 + 18 + 8 = 47, and 4 + 7 = 11. The number 11 goes with Arcanum XI, The Maiden. The sum of the entire reading, which represents the overall meaning of the situation or that which is being gained or learned from it, suggests a refinement of power and the subtle use of personal power. This reduces to the same number as in step 3, which is the dynamic balance between the past and the future. Therefore, the point of balance is strongly emphasized as the lesson to be learned. Refinement of potential (the sum of past and future cards = 11) balances, or is pivotal in this case, to the setting of goals (Arcanum XXI = past card) and

> the implementation of them on a practical level (Arcanum VIII = future card). And by adding to that sum the need in the present for the selection of the proper vehicle (Arcanum XVIII = present card), that balancing point becomes the lesson to be learned.

For additional information on the total of all three cards, you can proceed to find and interpret *the level of the sum* (see chapter 15, "Numerology"). In this method, 21 + 18 + 8 = 47, and 4 + 7 = 11. The number 11 is the primary vibration of 47, meaning that it is what we obtain when we cast out 9s, in other words add the 4 and 7 together, to derive a number we can interpret by using the major arcana (a number that is 22 or less). To find the level of this vibration we can continue with 47 – 11 = 36, and 36 ÷ 9 = 4, and 4 + 1 = 5. We can therefore say that 47 vibrates to 11 on the level of 5. The number 5 represents expansion and growth (see Arcanum V, The Pentagram), so that 11 on this level suggests that the receptivity (11) must be expansive in nature (5), or we can say it represents a growing receptivity as well as an expansive (5) refinement (11), or a harmonious (5) use of personal power (11).

✦ Exercise

Now it's time to begin casting three-card readings for yourself using this numerological synthesis procedure.

Ask yourself out loud the following question: "What is my chief asset or talent in regard to my use of the tarot?"

Now lay out a three-card spread for this question.

We have found through experience that when you're interpreting a reading for yourself, it's always best to first write your question and then record which cards appear in the reading, as well as a brief sentence or two concerning the meaning of each one. By doing this you'll be better able to clarify any vagueness that might occur in a reading that is not communicated and verified through another person.

By writing down your question, the cards you draw, and your interpretation of those cards, you're allowing your journal to be the "other person," that is, your witness. As in the example discussed earlier in this lesson (which was taken from my tarot journal), you will also want to record the various steps of synthesis and their specific interpretations, as well as the interpretations of individual cards.

I realize that much of what I've told you regarding the application of numerology to the tarot may seem like a lesson you'd find in an accounting or insurance class—pretty dry and legalistic-sounding, and for that reason, challenging. The reason I've included what I have is because I want to show you how you can approach the tarot logically and objectively *when you need to.* Taking this logical approach can sometimes jump-start your intuition. As well, if you're feeling any lack of confidence in what your psychic self is telling you, then approaching the cards in this logical and objective way can often help to bolster and reinforce your confidence.

You may be one of those people who don't want to read the cards in the logical and rational manner that's presented in these exercises. Maybe you're more a person who naturally goes on instinct and intuition, and if that's the case, then definitely continue to flow in that mode. Ultimately, we always find that all these different methods and approaches fit together and harmonize with one another—there are many paths to the Emerald City.

CHAPTER SIXTEEN

Gematria

Gematria is the kabbalistic method of converting letters into numbers and numbers into letters so as to find the hidden meanings (or vibrations) in names, words, dates, and so forth. It's yet another way of using the tarot to reveal the secrets of the world around us.

The process is simple: You must first convert letters of the alphabet into numbers, starting with *A* = 1, *B* = 2, *C* = 11, and so forth. Then take any word or name and change its letters into their corresponding numbers. Each card of the major arcana is associated with one or more letters. For instance Arcanum XIV (The Alchemist) goes with the letter *N,* the fourteenth letter of the Hebrew and English alphabets, so whenever you find an *N* in a word it can be converted to the number 14. (You'll find the letter correspondences for each major arcana card listed at the end of this chapter.)

Gematria works because there are no mistakes in reality, even if at times reality seems chaotic and confusing. Everything's called what it's called for a reason. Nothing's arbitrary. Humans live in a sea of meaning, just as fish live in a sea of water. This is even symbolically true, since humans live in a sea of air, and the air or Coin level of the tarot represents ideas and meanings.

We can look for meaning in anything and find it. The challenge in gematria is not in finding the meaning, it's being able to interpret it—to be able to see it in a clear light and then translate it into words so that it accurately fits the situation we're working with.

My name is John Sandbach. Take pencil and paper and add up the letters in my name. Find their numerical equivalent by looking at the list at the end of this lesson. You will find that:

$J = 10, O = 16, H = 8, N = 14,$

$S = 21, A = 1, N = 14, D = 4, B = 2, A = 1, Ch = 8$

So when all the numbers of my name are added together, the sum is 99. We can then reduce the 99 by adding its digits, 9 + 9 = 18, so my name vibrates to Arcanum XVIII (The Night).

Note that when you do this process on a name, you always want to make sure that when you have a *Ch* you add these two letters together as an 8, rather than adding the *C* as 11 and the *H* as 8. This is because we treat certain letter pairings—like *Ch, Sh, Ts, Tz, Ph, and Th*—as single units since we are working within the parameters of the Hebrew alphabet as it transliterates into English, rather than working directly with the English alphabet. In terms of the letter pairings that are treated as units in this system, *Ch* corresponds to Arcanum VIII (The Balance), *Th* corresponds to Arcanum IX (The Seeker), *Ph* corresponds to Arcanum XVII (The Light), and *Sh, Ts,* and *Tz* correspond to Arcanum XVIII (The Night). Some arcana also have more than one letter associated with them, also as a result of how the Hebrew alphabet transliterates into English. Arcanum VI (The Crossroads) corresponds to *U, V,* and *W;* Arcanum VIII (The Balance) corresponds to *H* as well as *Ch;* Arcanum X (The Cycle) corresponds to *I, J,* and *Y;* Arcanum XI (The Maiden) corresponds to *C* and *K;* and Arcanum XVII (The Light) corresponds to *F* and *P* as well as *Ph.*

HOW TO USE GEMATRIA

You can use gematria for readings, such as doing a reading on a name. As well, gematria can be used for creative contemplation. In creative contemplation we can take words and find their numerical equivalent. For instance, let's take the word *tarot.* This word adds up to 81, and the number 81 reduces to 9 (8 + 1 = 9). So the word *tarot* corresponds to the Arcanum IX, The Sage, which represents wisdom gained through experience.

To gain the proper wisdom from experience, we have to interpret experience properly, so Arcanum IX governs interpretation. The Sage is a person who can read signs properly, and that's where they get their wisdom. It doesn't matter to them what happens to them, they're open to everything and value all experience. The tarot is an interpretative tool, so it gains in effectiveness as it's directly experienced.

All words that reduce to the same number have similar vibrations. For example, if we have a group of words or things that all have a value of 9, then we know that they are all similar in a basic way. Of course, we may have a word that adds up to 72, and another word that adds up to 81, and another that adds up to 63. All of these reduce to nine, so they're all similar. But if we have a group of words each of which adds up to 63, then these words are even more similar to one another because their number is the same even before they're reduced.

We can also use gematria to study relationships between things. For instance, if I want to find out my relationship to the tarot, all I have to do is add together the numbers 99 (the number of my name) and 81 (the number of the word *tarot*). This yields 180, which again reduces to 9. Remember that when you reduce a number, you need not reduce it any lower than something under 22. Of course, if one number adds up to a 9, when it is added to another number, the result will often be the same as the number it was added to. This is a characteristic of the number 9. It symbolizes the idea that wisdom through experience is nothing in and of itself, but always points to the experience itself.

We can always investigate numbers further before reducing them. For instance, my name gives a 99, and 99 is 9 times 11. So, it's a mixture of 9 and 11—wisdom through experience (9) and refinement (11). One might restate this as the refining of wisdom, or experience (9) within the psychic realm (11).

The word *tarot,* which adds to 81, is actually 9 × 9, or 9 squared. A square always shows how a number operates in physical reality, the realm of form. When my name is added to the word *tarot,* we get 180, which is 18 times 10. Whenever we multiply a number by 10, we are completing it—giving it a sense of individuality and imbuing it with creativity. So my relationship to the tarot is one of expansion in a creative manner.

Arcanum XVIII (The Night) has the feeling of a laboratory, an enclosed place where controlled conditions can be maintained. The reason that it also signifies deception is that all of us are working in a laboratory (a place of controlled conditions), but the unfortunate thing is that we usually don't realize this. The controlled conditions are sometimes not for our own good, and sometimes may not be to our liking, and we sometimes don't realize we're being controlled.

Marshall McLuhan says that environments are invisible. Without knowing it he was referring to Arcanum XVIII when he said this.

So we might say that the tarot is my own personal laboratory (laboratory = 18, individuality = 10). This is the highest good that can come out of my relationship to the tarot.

APPLYING GEMATRIA

In using gematria, we have to be in tune with the quality of silence. By this I mean that if we try too hard to mentally analyze a number, it's easy to get confused or end up muddying the waters by thinking too hard. If a simple answer is understood, sometimes it's better to leave it at that. Details or too many modifiers brought into an issue can confuse it and destroy the root simplicity. We could apply gematria to every term, name, and concept we encounter, but unless we can gain something from our interpretations, this can become a meaningless activity. Also, this meaninglessness can be self-perpetuating, for unless we use the information we're gaining, we can't gain more.

But now that I've said that I'll contradict myself, because I have my Moon in Libra, and Moon in Libra people are always seesawing back and forth. So it can be good to run around adding up the numbers in every word you find, because doing so gets you more and more familiar with the meanings of the numbers.

Gematria provides a vehicle for the study of oneself in order to learn from oneself. We live in an age when people think that all knowledge comes from the internet or from books, and that if you can just find the right sources—the right book or website—learning would then be made simple. This is far from the truth. Inner learning and inner knowledge are always superior to outer knowledge and facts, and the only inner internet is the angelic one. Learn to dial that up and you've got it made. It's certainly possible, and there's no monthly fee.

Occultism has been tinged with the stuffiness and constriction of tradition for quite a long time, and luckily the internet is exploding all that into clouds of colored confetti. The fact is that occultism is for everyone, because it's within everyone's inner experience. Gematria can provide a key to that inner experience. Like most keys, it's very simple, yet its form is precise enough to open the door to the Higher Self.

It's marvelously revealing to use gematria on dates. For instance, if you were born on December 7, 1928, you can add the numbers 12 (for December), 7, and 1928. Do not add up the digits in 1928 first—add the number as a whole. The result is 1947, which then reduces to 21 (1 + 9 +4 + 7 = 21). This shows the vibrations on that particular day—in this case, the vibration concerns will, centering, consciousness, and purpose—Arcanum XXI (The Lord of the Dance). If December 7, 1928 was your birthday, then your soul was attracted to this vibration for a reason, and therefore it will show your purpose in life—why you came here.

If you add your name and birthdate together, you're adding your purpose in life (the date) and that which you have to work with (your name), and the two together will show your potential of accomplishment—how to best accomplish your goal.

You can also "progress" your birthdate by adding its original number to the number of the current year. For instance, in the example given above, the birthdate added up to 1947, and if we wanted to find out what this person's purpose was in 1976, then we would add 1947 to 1976. We must remember that the original purpose of the person was shown by the number 1947. This number stands for the general purpose of the life, whereas, when we add 1947 and 1976 we obtain 3923, which reduces to 17 (3 + 9 + 2 + 3). This shows the particular purpose of the person for the year 1976, which would be to focus on communicating and thinking, since Arcanum XVII (The Light) is ruled by Gemini (associated with cleverness, mental acuity, and using information), and on getting more in touch with their interior light, as signified by the star above the head of the woman on the Arcanum XVII card, as well as on using their imagination in a positive and creative manner—also ideas corresponding to this arcanum.

Obviously we can work to any level of detail that we want, but we must be careful only to work to the degree that we need to work. Thirsting too strongly for knowledge is just as bad as overeating and overdrinking. The occult explorer may at first think they now have a tool to explain everything, but this can be potentially negative in that it can result in a substitution of idle thinking for genuine accomplishment.

We cannot stress enough the idea that there are no bad or good cards. Every card has a positive and a negative meaning. Each card is an element from which we can make a vitamin or a fertilizer, a poison or a noxious gas.

If you add up the letters in your name and don't like the result, it's good to stop and roll this around in your mind awhile. Why don't you like it? And if on the other hand you find that you really do like the result, try to figure out what the negative side of the number might be. Whatever the number is, its negative aspect represents the things you might find challenging in this lifetime. For instance, if the number for your name reduces to a 7, you might read this as philosophy and see yourself as being very philosophical. What are the negative qualities of philosophy? Well, there've been many philosophers who have been very impractical people, dreamers who were so intent on theories and intellectual concepts that they were oblivious to the practical aspects of life. This is what a person whose name reduces to a 7 would need to avoid.

I have heard many people say that they like certain numbers and do not care for others. Are there any numbers that you feel this way about? If there are, write them down and check their meanings. A person is always attracted to something they need, something that will help reinforce certain qualities in them. These numbers that you feel especially attracted to can show what these qualities are.

Often people go through periods where they tend to see certain numbers over and over again, seemingly by chance. In a case like this you're being told something, and it may help to contemplate the number and ask what it means and why it keeps coming to you. You can add that number to your name number to see how the number in question is influencing you.

You can also use numbers in this manner: Say you want to structure your obligations more because you have a lot of obligations that are difficult for you to fulfill because they are not structured. Maybe you have trouble apportioning your time properly. Take the number that governs structure, 15, and the number that governs obligation, 11, and multiply them together to get 165. When we multiply, we are blending completely. The number 165 reduces to 12 (1 + 6 + 5 = 12), which means that to structure (15) obligations (11), we need to have dedication (12). Contemplate the number 165—see it in your mind, feel it imbuing your being, and ask it to guide you.

Because numbers are living beings, we can speak to them, and they will hear us and respond. Numbers can answer all the metaphysical questions of the universe. Maybe you're enthusiastic to make a change in your life. Enthusiasm is 5, and change (of a cyclic nature) is 13. If you want to blend your enthusiasm with the spirit of change, multiply 5 times 13, and you get 65, which reduces to 11 (6 + 5 = 11). This shows that enthusiastic change requires that you be idealistic (11), receptive (11), and have a sense of obligation (11) to working with and learning from the new things coming to you.

You can also change your name as a tool to help you change yourself, but you must remember that an act like this is but a symbolic reinforcement and won't work as a substitute for inner change.

Another way to read a name is to look at letters that repeat. For instance, if a woman's name is Linda Ball, we immediately notice the three *l*s, which emphasize a strong Arcanum XII (The Devotee) in her aura. We can also look at the last name alone and add up the numbers corresponding to its letters as a means of analyzing the character of her family in general.

A SAMPLE READING OF A NAME: EDGAR ALLAN POE

The letters of this name add up to 111 (how beautiful all those 1s!), which reduces to 3 (1 + 1 + 1 = 3). This sets a general tone of activity and productivity for his personality. The number 111 is divisible by 3 and yields 37 (37 × 3 = 111). This means that 111 has a 37 overtone, and 37 reduces to 10 on the level of 4 (3 + 7 = 10, 37 – 10 = 27, 27 ÷ 9 = 3, 3 + 1 = 4).

If you continue to do this form of numerology it will seem easy after a while, but assuming you haven't yet memorized the process for determining the level of a number outlined in chapter 15, "Numerology," I'll take you through it again.

Let's do the process for 111, which is the number that Poe's name adds up to. First, we add together the digits (1 + 1 + 1), which gives us the number 3. Then we subtract 3 from 111, which gives us 108—the number representing the sum of all the whole cycles of 9 in the number. Then we divide 108 by 9 to show us how many whole cycles there are in this number (111), which yields us the number 12. We then add 1 to 12, since the level of 111 will be *one more* than the total number of whole cycles there are in the number, and the result is 13—so 111 is also 3 on the level of 13.

So, Mr. Poe is at core a producer (Arcanum III, The Queen Mother), and also highly unique and individualistic (referring to the 37 overtone adding up to 10, corresponding to Arcanum X, The Cycle), a producer on the level of newness and exploration (Arcanum XIII, The Rainbow). His name has thirteen letters, so all this reveals a headstrong (13), aspiring (13) nature that is forward-looking (13) and crisis-oriented (13). Mr. Poe was born January 19, 1809, which adds up to 1,829 (1 +19 + 1809 = 1829), which reduces to 20 (1 + 8 +2 + 9 = 20). So his purpose in life is centered around working and dealing with feelings (20), moods (20), and emotions (20).

We can also analyze Poe's name by adding together the first letter of his first, middle, and last name, and then the second letter in each name, then the third, and so on. These additions will show how his energy vibrates with Arcanum I (The Messenger), then Arcanum II (The Guardian of the Gate), and then Arcanum III (The Queen Mother) and so on.

To do this exercise, create separate columns for each letter in the order in which it occurs, as shown in the diagram on the next page. So for example, column one contains the first letter in each of Poe's three names; column two the second letter, and so forth.

Adding up the first three letters we get 23 (*E* = 5, + *A* = 1, + *P* = 17 = 23). This shows how Mr. Poe thinks—his mind, since we are adding in the

E D G A R A L L A N P O E
5 + 4 + 3 + 1 + 20 + 1 + 12 + 12 + 1 + 14 + 17 + 16 + 5 = 111 (1+1+1) = 3

1	2	3	4	5	6	7	8
E	D	G	A	R	Column 5 + Column 1 (34 + 23)	Column 5 + Column 2 (34 + 32)	Column 5 + Column 3 (34 + 20)
A	L	L	A	N			
P	O	E					
23 → 5	32 → 5	20	2	34 → 7	57 → 12	66 → 12	54 → 9

9	10	11	12	13
Column 5 + Column 4 (34 + 2)	Column 5 x 2	Column 5 x 2 + Column 1 (68 + 23)	Column 5 x 2 + Column 2 (68 + 32)	Column 5 x 2 + Column 3 (68 + 20)
36 → 9	68 → 14	91 → 10	100 → 1	88 → 16

14	15	16	17	18
Column 5 x 2 + Column 4 (68 + 2)	Column 5 x 3	Column 5 x 3 + Column 1 (102 + 23)	Column 5 x 3 + Column 2 (102 + 32)	Column 5 x 3 + Column 3 (102 + 20)
70 → 7	102 → 3	125 → 8	134 → 8	122 → 5

19	20	21	22
Column 5 x 3 + Column 4 (102 + 2)	Column 5 x 4	Column 5 x 4 + Column 1 (136 + 23)	Column 5 x 4 + Column 2 (136 + 32)
104 → 5	136 → 10	159 → 15	168 → 15

first column the first letter of each of his names, and the number 1 (corresponding to Arcanum I) has to do with the mind. The number 23 reduces to 5, so the mind is expansive, enthusiastic, and is potentially excessive. Indeed, Poe was interested in many things—mesmerism, writing, cryptography, interior decorating, and other far-flung subjects.

The second letter of each of his names adds up to 32, which again reduces to a 5. The second column in this procedure will always show what the person has to perfect in himself—what he or she has to work on. It can also show *how* they work. Here we see that Poe needed to perfect his sense of enthusiasm and harmony with the world. This may explain why he was sometimes quite morose and at other times quite enthusiastic. The number 5 can signify extremes, and in the second column might signify dualistic extremes. Since the number 2 has to do with technical ability, we see here an enthusiasm (Arcanum V, The Pentagram) for things of a technical nature. (Remember his short story "The Gold-Bug," which is about the decoding of a secret message through cryptography.)

The third letters in all three of his names add up to 20, showing that activity and productivity (the number 3) could be potentially very liberating for him (20 = liberation), but that activity and productivity (20) would be very much conditioned by feelings and emotions (both ruled by the Moon, which corresponds to Arcanum XX (The Awakening).

In adding together the fourth letter in each of his names, we're looking at his creativity, since 4 rules creativity. In doing this we skip the last name, Poe, because it has no fourth letter. We have two *As* in his name, which add up to 2. This might show a very perfectionistic nature where creativity is concerned.

In column five, the letters *R* and *N* yield the number 34 (20 + 14). This reduces to seven (3 + 4), possibly meaning that his sense of enthusiasm (5) centers on things of a philosophical nature (7).

If we want to form a sixth column for the name of Poe, we can go back and add the sums of columns one and five; then for a seventh column, we can add the sums of columns two and five; and so on up to column ten, which would be formed by adding the sums of columns five and five, that is, doubling the sum of the fifth column. Then for an eleventh column, we can add the sum of column five twice to the sum of column one. We can continue in this manner until we have twenty-two columns that correspond with the twenty-two major arcana. The amount you do depends on the amount you wish to know. The difficulty though, with using a great deal of information is that the more we have, the harder time we might have integrating it.

The above method for a fuller analysis of a name is arbitrary, meaning that it is made up. We can just make up other systems, and all of them will work. The point is that we must always be consistent in what we're doing. It's best to always use the same system, because the mind works best when it's dealing with a system that's familiar.

Another problem commonly encountered in using gematria is which name to use. This is a question frequently asked by women, because many women customarily change their surname when they get married. It's best to always use the current name of the person. Sometimes people aren't sure whether or not to use their middle name. It all depends on whether or not the querent relates to their middle name. The easiest way to find out is to simply ask, "What's your name?" If the person asks, "Do you mean my full name?" then just tell them it's whatever name they prefer. If you want to, you can later analyze the full original name they had at birth. This will show what they were born with in terms of personality, as opposed to how it is now.

And always remember what I said before about using those higher numbers discussed in chapter 13: when you use higher numbers, it gives you a subtler, more complex picture of what's going on, and of course using a person's middle name is going to give you a bigger number to work with.

LIST OF NUMERICAL EQUIVALENTS OF LETTERS

Note that the following list includes certain letter groupings (like *U, V, W,* and *Ch*) and appears in the order it does because the numbers are assigned according to the way the Hebrew alphabet transliterates into English.

A = 1
B = 2
G = 3
D = 4
E = 5
U, *V*, *W* = 6
Z = 7
H, *Ch* = 8
Th = 9
I, *J*, *Y* = 10
C, *K* = 11
L = 12
M = 13
N = 14
X = 15
O = 16
F, *P*, *Ph* = 17
Sh, *Ts*, *Tz* = 18
Q = 19
R = 20
S = 21
T = 22

CHAPTER SEVENTEEN

A Seven-Card Layout for Problem-Solving and Personality Analysis

On the next page is a picture of the seven-card layout I often use in my readings.

The following planets rule the positions of each of the cards in a seven-card layout:

Card 1: Moon
Card 2: Mercury
Card 3: Venus
Card 4: Sun
Card 5: Mars
Card 6: Jupiter
Card 7: Saturn

To do this reading, first formulate your question, then shuffle the deck and lay out seven cards in a row, from left to right. Read the cards by blending the meaning of the card that comes up with the meaning of the planet ruling the position in which it falls.

Here is a list of the meanings of each of the seven positions of the cards in the reading:

1	2	3	4	5	6	7
PAST			PRESENT		FUTURE	
Moon	Mercury	Venus	Sun	Mars	Jupiter	Saturn
Impetus	Momentum	Conflict	Consciousness	Release	Harmony	Meaning
Emotional make-up	Mental make-up	Values or love nature	Will or purpose	Initiative or action	Area of growth	Limitations

1. **Moon:** Emotional makeup of the person when you're doing a personality reading; habit patterns; the workings of the subconscious; the past of the situation; the most unstable, changeable, or moving part of the situation; what's going on in the home and with the family
2. **Mercury:** The person's mental makeup; the area of experience where the person needs to be flexible; one's point of view; means of communication; thoughts and communications surrounding the situation; any cleverness involved in the situation, or cleverness that needs to be employed in the situation.
3. **Venus:** Values; aesthetic sense; area of experience that the person appreciates and receives something of worth for; love of nature; anywhere in the situation where the person can achieve satisfaction, benefit, or gain anything, including money
4. **Sun:** Will, the state of the person's ego and self-confidence, consciousness or what the person is conscious of, sense of purpose, area of experience where the person needs to be centered, the point of balance or core or key to the situation, what's most important in the situation
5. **Mars:** where the person needs to take initiative, aggressions and how to handle them, conflicts going on in the situation and how they might best be dealt with
6. **Jupiter:** where the person's enthusiasm and potential success lie, the expansive part of their nature, the area of this experience that's most likely to lead to growth for the person, where and how the person might overdo things or be excessive
7. **Saturn:** the person's sensitivity; area of experience where one needs to define oneself as apart from others; where one needs to limit oneself; point of self-questioning or fears, or areas of inadequacy that need to be dealt with

When you lay out one of these seven-card spreads, you can then add any two of the cards together to get all sorts of further information. And, of course, you can add all seven of the cards together to get a feel for the summary meaning of the whole layout.

There are many other layouts you can do if you'd like, and you can find these online by searching "tarot layouts." The only other layout I use is where you lay out twelve cards in a circle, and then read each one as pertaining to one of the astrological houses. When you do this spread you can put a thirteenth card in the center to signify the central meaning of the reading.

Very often, though, I just draw one card to answer the person's question, and then after I've gained meaning from that one card, usually other questions surrounding it will come to me, and for each one I'll draw another card. To me this is a comfortable and fluid way of reading the cards.

The one thing you definitely don't want to do is turn over a card and think, *No, I don't like that one,* and then turn over another, and keep on going in this vein until you get one you're happy with. If you do this, you can indeed get the tarot to tell you whatever you want to hear, but ultimately it won't help you.

This reminds me of an episode of the old TV series *Mary Hartman, Mary Hartman.* On this show, one of the characters—a country singer named Loretta—is talking to God, saying what she thinks about everything going on in her life and what she thinks she and a bunch of other people should all do. At the end of her monologue she says, "And God, if I'm wrong about any of this, strike me dead right now with lightning!" After gazing at the sky and waiting a few moments, she smiles and says, "Thanks God, I knew you'd agree!"

The cards are a powerful tool, and there's a reason the ancients used an ear to symbolize the fifth element of akasha. It's because the way to clean up your akashic record is to *listen.* The tarot loves you, and that's what it wants you to do—to listen to it as it echoes your inner voice.

SAMPLE SEVEN-CARD READING

I asked the querent, whom I shall refer to as Eli, to put his question in writing. This is what he wrote to me:

> In 1992, when I was two years old, I had my strongest and perhaps earliest memory: an out-of-body experience (OBE). I felt myself floating upward, and then I went out through the window. I sensed five entities looking at me from down below. I can't clearly remember

> their faces. I then floated into a gray spacecraft, which later that night I described to my mom as a helicopter. As I approached the craft, I believe a small hatch or door opened in four sections, reminding me of a black cross as the dark interior was revealed.
>
> I had another experience a few weeks later—what I consider to be my second-earliest lucid memory, in which a pale man with large, unblinking eyes and wearing what I recall as a bowler hat stared at me from the closet. I don't recall any physical contact. He was staring into my soul, and it felt as though he sensed my fear. Attempting to calm me, he projected into my mind a video of himself performing like a Vaudeville dancer. Unfortunately, he forgot to implant a change of facial expression, so the experience became even creepier rather than feeling friendly.
>
> I'm not sure if these two scenarios are related. However, my question is this, especially in regard to the first experience, where I had a sense of losing part of myself (as in lobotomy) or even being exchanged (entangled memories or experiences): what is the spiritual energy surrounding the situation, and what does that suggest about the purpose of the interaction?

The seven cards I drew in order were: Arcanum XII (The Devotee, in the Moon position); Arcanum XX (The Awakening, in the Mercury position); the Seven of Cups (in the Venus position); the Three of Swords (in the Sun position); the Six of Wands (in the Mars position); the Three of Wands (in the Jupiter position); and the Princess of Coins (in the Saturn position).

Card 1: Arcanum XII implies a giving up, giving in, or letting go, which ideally puts a person in a state of maximum receptivity. That this card is in the Moon position seems to say this is what Eli needs on an emotional level, which is to be open to these situations and not resist or try to control them, for resistance and control completely go against the openness and receptivity of Arcanum XII. This card can also signify vague or undefined worries, so in the Moon position it could mean emotional cloudiness and apprehension, which Eli says he has had about this memory.

Card 2: In the Mercury position we see Arcanum XX, meaning that what is being communicated by these experiences is certainly subjective, as Arcanum XX is ruled by the Moon. The Moon always implies vulnerability, and Eli confirmed that what happened in these two experiences made him feel vulnerable. It can also mean that it would be difficult to clearly define what was communicated, and that to really get into the nature of the communication, Eli must go with his feelings about it, his gut instincts.

Card 3: The Venus position in any seven-card reading shows what is beneficial, valuable, and therefore satisfying in the matter. If you go back to chapter 11 you will see that one of the meanings given for the Seven of Cups suggests the state of being emotionally riled-up. Remember, though, that since this is in the Venus position it implies that if these contacts with beings from beyond our level of reality had an emotionally upsetting effect, if they caused him to become emotionally riled-up, this could actually be beneficial or valuable for him. Such experiences might show him the value of actively setting out to fulfill himself. It is also implied that there is value in stirring up his subconscious and benefit to be derived from doing so.

Card 4: The Three of Swords in the Sun position shows that the essential meaning and purpose (Sun) of these encounters is to substantiate (Swords) Eli's psychic abilities. The Three of Swords can also imply a blockage (Swords) of one's intuition, and the Sun's position of meaning and purpose seems to say that these encounters can help him become more aware of that blockage and the need to unblock it, though whenever Swords are present it can mean that the situation is only going to work out slowly and gradually.

Card 5: The Six of Wands in the Mars position means that whatever these experiences compel him to do (Mars), they are going to cause him to make his actions more purposeful (6 represents purpose) on a creative (Wands) level.

Card 6: The Jupiter position always shows how a person will learn and grow from the question or situation at hand. Here we find the Three of Wands, meaning a stimulation (Wands) of idealism and of psychic energy (3).

Card 7: The last of the seven cards, the Page of Coins, is in the Saturn position, which always shows the deeper meaning or most enduring benefit to be found in the situation. The Page of Coins is ruled by Gemini, so Eli is being challenged to find new ways to communicate and connect, for this is what Gemini does. Eli certainly wants to connect with these experiences more deeply so he can understand them, but as Saturn is the planet most like the element earth, its energy tends to unfold gradually. There is a communication block going on in this situation, and as Eli grows to see himself more and more as a person who can communicate, he has the potential of eventually getting beyond those blockages that are preventing him from fully and clearly seeing what these situations are about. As I know Eli personally, I know he already does see himself as one who is adept at communicating—and he is. But still, there are limits to these skills, and I believe these encounters with nonphysical beings are serving to move him beyond those limits. There is a communications block going on in this situation, and as Eli sees himself more and more as a person who can trust what he communicates, he will eventually get beyond those blockages.

When we use the higher numbers for the cards of the minor arcana (see chapter 13) and add up the values of all the cards, we get the following: 12 (Arcanum XII), 20 (Arcanum XX), 57 (Seven of Cups), 67 (Three of Swords), 28 (Six of Wands), 25 (Three of Wands), and 50 (Page of Cups). These add up to 259. When we do an online search for the factors for 259 we get 7 × 37 (Arcanum VII [7] × the Ace of Coins [37]). I see this as bringing in a new cycle of communication (Ace of Coins) that is of a cosmic or transcendent nature (Arcanum VII). Making these kinds of powerful (ace) connections (Coins) can give him a broad overview (Arcanum VII) of the nature of reality. Sagittarius, astrological ruler of Arcanum VII, can also imply foreigners, and here the "foreigners," that is, the nonphysical beings, have powerful (ace) ideas (Coins), or transformative (ace) information they wish to communicate (Coins).

FURTHER RUMINATIONS . . .

I feel two ways about writing up sample readings like this one. On the one hand they can be an effective tool for learning if the student reads them carefully and takes the time to study them and take them in. I've thought about doing a whole book of them, or maybe several books of this nature. On the other hand, reading such analyses can be tedious and boring due to everything being so carefully and objectively spelled out.

When doing such analyses, when I show how the cards logically relate to the reading, I feel that I have to take a rational approach to them, but in an actual reading I'm far more prone to getting into the feel of the cards and letting the ideas about them flow through me. I always keep the objective meanings in mind, but if I feel compelled to tell the querent things I can't logically explain via the meanings of the cards, I go ahead and do so, for the intuitive mind can think far faster than the rational mind. The thing you really don't want to have happen is to allow your set, conscious ideas about the meaning of the cards to suppress what your intuition is telling you.

So to sum up this reading in a subjective manner, I will say that Eli has a need to tap directly into these experiences, and rather than trying to objectively explain and understand them, it's better for him to let them speak directly to his intuition and feelings.

The card I have the most difficulty understanding in the whole layout is the Seven of Cups in the Venus position. Eli is an artist, both in the field of writing and music, and I feel that these experiences are somehow stirring up or firing his passion about being an artist, since Venus rules the arts. Certainly the Seven of Cups is a brash and impulsive card, and so these events could be showing him the value of being more spontaneous and immediately acting out his passions.

The following is a conversation I had with Eli after he read the above analysis of the cards.

Eli: I find it very interesting that Arcanum XII is in the Moon position because I have a difficult time simply allowing experiences to be what they are without analyzing them and trying to be objective.

John: So what I hear is that you use analyzing as a way of supporting and protecting yourself.

Eli: Yes, I tend to be paranoid and mistrustful of events and even my own thoughts. Sometimes I wonder if perhaps they aren't my own thoughts at all.

John: That takes me back to the Page of Coins in the Saturn position, for Saturn is the planet that questions everything, and since the Page of Coins rules Gemini, the sign of thinking, it certainly makes sense that you would feel this way.

Eli: I feel very vulnerable about these experiences because they are so unusual and outside of my control or understanding.

John: I notice that there are two 3s in the layout, and 3s are ruled by Neptune, which has a formless quality. Neptune certainly goes beyond the rational. I think these experiences are challenging you to think in a new way.

Eli: I wonder how different I would have been had I not had these early experiences. I feel like my personality was changed by them.

John: In what way?

Eli: I feel that if I hadn't had them I would have been even more analytical and logical.

John: Would you have preferred that?

Eli: I have an inventive streak and I love creating new things, but part of me admires the cold engineer type of person.

John: Is that in contradistinction to giving in [Pisces] to your emotions [first position of seven-card reading]?

Eli: I admire the purely rational and skeptical because it seems so grounded in objective reality.

John: That helps me understand why Arcanum XX is in the Mercury position, which is really the opposite of rationality and skepticism. Actually, I think subjectivity and an instinctual approach are more of what you need, even though it might feel difficult or uncomfortable to you.

Eli: But what was the practical purpose and benefit of the changes made to me by those beings for those beings? What did *they* gain? What did *they* get out of it?

John: [I drew another card to answer this and got the Queen of Wands.] They were expressing themselves and helping you to express yourself. They are not into hiding things as we humans are. [The Queen of Wands is ruled by Leo, probably the most overt sign of the zodiac. Leo is the actor on stage under bright lights. It wants to express itself and shine its light on everything.]

Eli told me after the reading that it had helped him gain deeper insight into these happenings and had given him much to digest.

The key to working with the tarot therapeutically is to send the intent to further the evolution of the person for whom you are reading. Doing this, and then following your intuition about the cards as they come up, are the two main things that can make a reading a healing experience. As Dr. Randolph Stone (1890–1981), osteopath and chiropractor and the founder of polarity therapy, says, "Energy follows intention and attention." Being attentive to the reactions you have to the cards as you see them is the ultimate way to read their meaning.

CHAPTER EIGHTEEN

The Language of Space (aUI)

In the beginning was the Word,
and the Word was with God.

John 1:1

Dr. John Weilgart's symbol for the Language of Space (aUI). The circle in the symbol stands for a meaning "space," the triangle stands for U signifying "mind," and the curved line that looks like an s lying down signifies I which in aUI means "sound."

This chapter will serve to enrich your knowledge of the tarot by seeing its relationship to aUI, the Language of Space.

What I have told you about all of the tarot cards in this book is only a summary. As the tarot reflects the whole universe, it can be delved into endlessly to discover more and more facets of truth, and to find ways that the vibrations of the cards manifest in physical reality. aUI expresses core understanding in a simple, clear way. Looking into aUI can enrich and expand your knowledge of the arcana and open up new ways of experiencing them. You need not learn aUI as a language to benefit from it—just knowing what the different aUI letters mean and which arcana they relate to can light up your perceptions of the cards.

THE LANGUAGE OF SPACE AND MEETING DR. WEILGART

Dr. John Weilgart, a philologist and psychoanalyst and the official chief psychologist for the United Nations, developed the language known as aUI (pronounced ah-OO-ee), or the Language of Space,* in order to establish a way to communicate that is intuitive, honest, and universal.

In a period starting in the 1950s and for a number of years he developed this language, which he claimed was given to him by an extraterrestrial source. Each sound in aUI has a specific meaning, and words are created by putting these various meanings together. There is no other language that does this.

Some time before his death in 1981 we invited Dr. Weilgart to Kansas City—he was a professor at Iowa University in Decorah, Iowa, at the time—to teach a workshop at our school there. It was wonderful to meet him and be in his mystical aura.

I think many people thought of his having received aUI from extraterrestrials as a fairy tale, a pretty story he'd made up. But as we spoke with him of these things it was clear that he most certainly believed that denizens from beyond Earth had come to him and given him this language, which, they said, had been spoken by Adam and Eve in the Garden of Eden.

Dr. Weilgart himself was most definitely a being of the fairy realms. His psyche was chameleonlike, and his speech was saturated with poetry.

---

*To learn all about the Language of Space and how to use it, and more about Dr. Weilgart, see the website www.auilanguage.org. Two books by Dr. Weilgart that I recommend for further study are *aUI, the Language of Space* and *Cosmic Elements of Meaning.*

At the time he presented his workshop he brought along with him a young man, his helper, and the two of them only spoke to each other in aUI when together. As we didn't have enough room to board both of them, the young guy stayed nearby at the home of one of our students. Early every morning the young man came by to help Dr. Weilgart with anything he needed, such as taking care of practical arrangements concerning classes or driving him wherever he wanted to go.

One day Dr. Weilgart asked me, after washing his clothes, if he could spread them out on the bushes around our apartment complex to dry. I told him I thought that if he did so I'd get in trouble with the management.

A linguist, Dr. Weilgart spoke many languages. One day our Japanese neighbors arrived home and Dr. Weilgart happened to see them in the hall. He struck up a conversation with them in fluent Japanese and then proceeded to disappear into their apartment for a couple of hours. At night, when he went into his bedroom and shut the door, we always heard him carrying on conversations with someone, though he didn't own a phone.

To this day I have a deep passion for aUI and would love to spread the knowledge of it to the world. It has a clearing and calming effect on the mind, and it is a fabulous language for writing poetry, since you can make up your own words that can be readily understood by any reader who knows the meanings of the different aUI letters. Of course the world is now coming more and more into using English as the world language, but aUI, by comparison, is extremely simple and easy to learn, as compared to cumbersome English with its unpredictable spellings and gigantic vocabulary. Dr. Weilgart used to go with missionaries to Africa and could teach aUI in just one day to both the missionaries and Africans, and they would be able to then communicate with each other in a rudimentary way within just twenty-four hours, so the language is quite practical. As for this language being given to Dr. Weilgart by space aliens, to me the primary significance of this is that it means that aUI is freed from human historical and cultural connotations—it comes from far outside our realm and connects us to our universe in a profoundly wholistic way. I feel certain that at some point in the future many more people will come to know of this language and its beauties and will use it in many creative ways.

APPLYING AUI TO THE TAROT

The following lists show the twenty-two cards of the major arcana together with an explanation of their aUI sounds, the symbols for which can be seen in the lower right-hand corner of each of the major arcana cards used to illustrate this book. The symbols shown are the letters in aUI. (For example, the symbol of a triangle stands for the aUI letter *U.*) They are depictions of the energy of the letter they correspond to. Note that in aUI the first letter of a sentence is not capitalized unless maybe it's a vowel, since uppercase and lowercase vowels mean different things. Uppercase and lowercase vowels in aUI are actually different letters and signify completely different concepts, such as *u* meaning "human" and *U* meaning "mind," or *i* meaning "light" and *I* meaning "sound." Uppercase consonants are not used in aUI.

Note that all but one of the vowels in the aUI system correspond to arcana that are astrologically ruled by planets rather than signs. Vowels are activators of words, just as planets are the activators of the astrological signs as the planets move through the zodiac. The only vowel sound in aUI that corresponds to an astrological sign rather than a planet is *q,* which is not a vowel sound in most languages, but it is in aUI, and sounds like the "or" in "word," or like the double dot over the *o* (called an *umlaut*) in German.

Some more things to note before proceeding: The Language of Space spirit names given in the following section are the names of spirit beings connected to each one of the major arcana cards. They were channeled by me, and they are represented below using English letters (with their pronunciations given in parenthesis). Saying, thinking, or even just looking at these names can help to tune you into the wavelength of the associated card.

Also, the accent of each aUI word is on the next to the last syllable unless there is a capital vowel in the word. If there is a capital vowel in the word, that syllable becomes the accented syllable. All the letters of the accented syllables of the aUI spirit names in parentheses are capitalized for the purpose of showing you where the accent in the word is. In addition, if there is no pronunciation given for an individual aUI letter below, it is because the pronunciation is the same as in English, as in the letter *b.*

ARCANUM I: THE MESSENGER (THE MAGUS)

A ⬭ a O

Letters: *A, a*
Meanings of letters: time (*A*), space (*a*)
Pronunciation of letters: *A* = "aaah" (a long sound), *a* = "ah" (a short sound)
Language of Space (aUI) spirit name: vavUkU (pronounced "vav-OO-koo," accent on the second syllable)

In aUI, capital *A* means "time," and lowercase *a* means "space." Space is a more primary concept than time. You'll find in aUI that the vowels written with small letters represent more rudimentary concepts than the ones written with capital letters. The capital vowels are pronounced long and the small vowels are pronounced short.

Time is always defined through space. For instance, a day is the length of time it takes for Earth to revolve once on its own axis, and a year is the time it takes for Earth to revolve once around the Sun. *A* is the widest-open of the vowel sounds and hence is the best representation of the idea of space, for it makes the most amount of space in the mouth. Both space and time move in circles—nebula, galaxies, solar systems, atoms, and the temporal cycles of death, birth, creation, destruction, involution, and evolution. This is why *A* and *a* in aUI are represented with round symbols—an oval and a circle.

A long intoning of the *a* vowel, pronounced "aah," attunes you to the whole tarot, as it's the seed of all the cards.

ARCANUM II: THE GUARDIAN OF THE GATE (VEILED ISIS)

Letter: *b*

Meaning of letter: together

Language of Space (aUI) spirit name: ykwUkU (pronounced "yik-WOO-koo," accent on the second syllable)

In aUI, *b* means "together," because when we pronounce this letter, we press our two lips together.The letter *b* in aUI is represented by two dots joined together by an arc. The closed lips of *b* are like the veil of Isis, which conceals that which is behind it. Note the two columns on the card and the veiled woman who is the hidden link between the two.

ARCANUM III: THE QUEEN MOTHER (ISIS UNVEILED)

g ⊙

Letter: *g*

Meaning of letter: inside

Language of Space (aUI) spirit name: ytlUkU (pronounced "yit-LOO-koo," accent on the second syllable)

The *g* sound is the deepest one the voice can make. It's way down inside the throat and so is an apt sound for the concept *inside.* All activity comes from inside. The symbol shows that meaningful movement is centered, as the dot is centered in the circle in the aUI symbol for *g*.

ARCANUM IV: THE COMMANDER (THE SOVEREIGN)

d ⱡ

Letter: *d*
Meaning of letter: through
Language of Space (aUI) spirit name: kwUvU (pronounced "KWOO-voo," accent on the first syllable)

In aUI, *d* means "through," but also "by means of," "instrumentality," "tool," and "medium." This signifies that the four lower elements (the number 4 corresponds to Arcanum IV) are the tools of Creative Intelligence, a medium for the expression of consciousness. Humans evolve by means of awareness. (Note: the Hebrew letter for *D* is *Dalet,* which means "door." Again we find here the idea of "through.") The aUI symbol for *d* is a foreward slash crossed by a vertical line, the two lines moving "through" each other.

ARCANUM V: THE PENTAGRAM (THE HIEROPHANT)

E □ e ©

Letters: *E, e*
Meanings of letters: matter (*E*), movement (*e*)
Pronunciation of letters: *E* = "ay" (like the *a* in *lane*), *e* = "eh" (like the *e* in jet)
Language of Space (aUI) spirit name: kvetgUvU (pronounced "kvet-GOO-voo," accent on the second syllable)

E in aUI means "matter," implying "material," "substance," "essence," "stuff"; and *e* means "movement" and "motion." To the occultist, movement and matter are basically the same thing, since matter always emanates a vibration. The four lower elements are always pushing and pulling against one another in a state of dynamic tension, hence Arcanum IV is depicted as a warrior. Arcanum V, though, as the quintessence or akasha, the fifth element, has the power to bring harmony to this conflict without diminishing its positive aspects. The difference between living tissue and dead tissue is that living tissue sustains itself, whereas dead tissue decomposes. What is it that keeps living tissue living, that is, vitally moving? It is the life force, the quintessence, prana. The aUI symbol for *E* is an empty square or box, which shows that all matter is formed from the four elements, plus a hidden, nonvisible fifth element—the quintessence. This fifth element is represented by the space, seemingly empty, inside the box. The symbol for *e* is a spiral, which shows that all movement is spiral in nature.

ARCANUM VI:
THE CROSSROADS (THE TWO PATHS)

U △ u ∧ v ϟ w ⌁

Letters: *U, u, v, w*

Meanings of Letters: mind (*U*), human (*u*); action, do, make (*v*); power (*w*)

Pronunciation of letters: *U* = "oooh" (like the *oo* in *moon*), *u* = "uh" (like the *oo* in *hood*), *v* and *w* are pronounced the same way as they are in English

Language of Space (aUI) spirit name: kedaykeda (pronounced "keh-da-yik-EH-da," accent on the fourth syllable)

Here we have four concepts: *U* means "mind"; *u* means "human"; *v* means "active," "to do," "to make," "to create," "to procreate," and "the male sex organ"; and *w* means "power," "force," "strength," "ability," potency," and "possibility."

Arcanum VI represents the macrocosm, which may seem strange in that *u* signifies "human." And yet almost all reports of alien sightings have said that extraterrestrials have two arms, two legs, and a head. Could it be that the form of the human is as universal as the stars and the galaxies?

The *u* symbol in aUI looks like two legs. Note how the symbol echoes the idea of two paths in the manner in which the lines converge. Human beings' ability to make conscious choices separates them from other animals. The capital *U* is written like the dualistic symbol for "human," except now the circuit is closed, representing "mind." The symbol for *v* is like a vertical thunderbolt. The symbol for *w* is a horizontal thunderbolt. The horizontal thunderbolt shows potential or stored energy and ability, whereas the vertical thunderbolt shows something happening, an action.

ARCANUM VII: THE VICTORY (THE CONQUEROR)

z ◖

Letter: *z*
Meaning of letter: part
Language of Space (aUI) spirit name: kUtvUkU (pronounced "koot-VOO-koo," accent on the second syllable)

In aUI, *z* means "piece" or "part of something" and signifies a cutting apart. The sound is like a buzzsaw. *z* means transcendence—cutting oneself away from fear, materialism, ignorance, and any and all curtains of darkness. The aUI symbol for *z* is a half circle. (Note that the person on this card, Arcanum VII, always carries a sword, an instrument for cutting.)

ARCANUM VIII: THE BALANCE (JUSTICE)

h ch ʔ

Letters: *h, ch*

Meaning of letters: question (*h, ch*)

Language of Space (aUI) spirit name: jyktEvs (pronounced "jyikt-EVS," accent on the second syllable)

Only the *h* is used in aUI—there is no equivalent for *ch* in the Language of Space. I still include *ch* here because you might find it in a name, for example, and when you do you can think of it as having the vibration of 8, just as *h* does alone. *h* in aUI means "question." The spirit of Justice answers questions concerning what to do and how to proceed. To answer a question effectively we need discrimination—the ability to judge. The aUI symbol for this letter is a question mark without the dot at the bottom.

ARCANUM IX: THE SEEKER (THE SAGE)

th (no equivalent)

Letters: *th*

Meaning of letters: *t* (Arcanum XXII) + *h* (Arcanum VIII)—here the meanings of these arcana are combined to describe the meaning of the letter of this card (Arcanum IX), since there is no separate letter for the sound "th" in aUI

Language of Space (aUI) spirit name: hUtevu (pronounced HOO-teh-voo, accent on the first syllable)

The *th* combination as a separate sound is not found in aUI. The "th" sound is not found in many languages and is therefore one of the reasons why many non-English-speaking peoples have trouble with the English pronunciation. If we wish, though, to analyze the *th* combination, we can say that the *t* corresponds to Arcanum XXII (The Traveler, more on this below), and the *h* corresponds to Arcanum VIII (The Balance, see above). Arcanum XXII signifies intensification, and Arcanum VIII means karma, so *th* (Arcanum IX) means "an intensification (Arcanum XXII) of karma (Arcanum VIII)." And, of course, when karma is intensified, it is paid off, dispersed, neutralized. Arcanum IX (The Seeker) means wisdom through experience, and it is through this that we learn right action and hence intensify (Arcanum XXII) our ability to discriminate (Arcanum VIII). (In Hebrew, the *Th* is called *Teth,* and means "serpent," as in "serpent of wisdom.") Since *th* is not a separate letter in aUI, it has no aUI symbol.

ARCANUM X: THE CYCLE (THE WHEEL)

I ~ i ꝋ j ⊃ y —

Letters: *I, i, j, y*

Meanings of letters: sound (*I*), light (*i*), equality (*j*), negative (*y*)

Pronunciation of letters: *I* = "eee" (like the *ee* in *speed*), *i* = "ih" (like the *i* in *hit*), *j* and *y* are pronounced the same way as they are in English

Language of Space (aUI) spirit name: kUled (pronounced KOO-led, accent on the first syllable)

Arcanum X (The Cycle) and Arcanum VI (The Crossroads) are the only arcana that have four aUI letters associated with them. In aUI, *I* means "sound"; *i* means "light"; *j* means "equal," "equivalent," or "same"; and *y* means "negation" or "opposite of." It is very significant that this arcanum is associated with light and sound, because in many occult teachings the concept of God is expressed as divine light.

Sometimes all the masters of the various occult schools have been referred to as the "White Brotherhood," the term (specifically the word *white*) referring to light and not to race or gender, since there are many female masters and masters of different races. As for the idea of sound, John 1:1 tells us, "In the beginning was the Word." Manifestations of God have always been associated with names, and in Eastern cultures the discipline of spoken or silent mantras or sounds has been used as a means of attaining higher levels of consciousness. This equates with inspiration, a key concept of Arcanum X.

The other two concepts, represented by *j* and *y,* are opposed to each other. *j* means "equal," and *y* means "opposite." The Wheel is an equalized symbol, meaning all points of its rim are equidistant from its center, and yet on it we find opposite figures, one moving up and one moving down. The idea concealed here is that any pair of opposites are, at root, equal.

The aUI symbol for *I,* meaning "sound," is a sound wave that is identical to the grapheme known as a *tilde* often found in Spanish words. The symbol for *i,* meaning "light," is a bent line whose two upper points cross themselves, signifying a contained space which is the source of light, with rays spreading out from it. The symbol for *j,* meaning "equal" or "equality," is an equal sign from math with the two lines jointed at their right ends. The symbol for *y,* meaning "negation," is a minus sign.

ARCANUM XI:
THE MAIDEN (THE ENCHANTRESS)

k c (hard)

Letters: *k, c* (as in a hard *c* sound, which sounds like a *k,* as in the word *candy*; the soft *c* sound, which sounds like an *s,* as in the name *Cynthia,* should be counted as an *s* in this system, corresponding to Arcanum XXI)

Meaning of letters: above (*k, c*)

Language of Space (aUI) spirit name: jEkYvU (pronounced "JAKE-yiv-voo," accent on the first syllable) *k* is found in aUI, but *c* is not. This is because the English *c* either sounds like an *s* or a *k*. However, I include *c* (as in the hard *c* sound) here, with *k,* because it also corresponds to Arcanum XI; when hard *c* is found in a word, such as in a name, it will have the numerological equivalent of 11, which is the number of this card (Arcanum XI). *k* in aUI means "above." The concept is not just above in the spatial sense; it also implies anything of the highest or most superlative nature. Ideals, a concept associated with Arcanum XI, raise humans to higher and higher levels. As a person is raised to higher and higher levels, their being becomes more and more refined. The word *above* signifies liberation from earth-boundedness, freedom from the pull of gravity. The aUI symbol for *k* and hard *c* is a vertical line with a dot connected to the upper right side at the top, to signify something that is above.

ARCANUM XII: THE DEVOTEE (THE MARTYR)

Letter: *l*
Meaning of letter: round
Language of Space (aUI) spirit name: brOtwUsevU (pronounced "bro-TWOO-seh-voo," accent on the second syllable)

l in aUI means "round." The number 12 is associated with the zodiac, which is a great circle. The word *zodiac* comes from the Latin and means "belt." Roundness implies wholeness and completion, which is what humans feel when they are truly dedicated. Rings, too, are associated with protection, and it is this mystical sense of protection, the idea of being surrounded by a ring of power that gave the early Christian martyrs (the alternate name for this card is The Martyr) courage to brave their tortures.

Of course, roundness also carries the negative connotation of neurosis, since neurosis is thinking that occurs in round terms, circular thoughts that don't lead anywhere and that become a hang-up (that is, upside-down). Note how the word *hang-up* so aptly describes the picture on this card. Many times people say that others who have great religious fervor or who are obsessed with an ideal are "hung up" on something. It isn't bad to be hung up, only bad to be so without wanting to be so. In that case we have the idea of addiction, which is also circular in nature and a common trait of Pisces, the astrological ruler of this arcanum. The aUI symbol for *l* is a complete space contained within universal space.

ARCANUM XIII: THE RAINBOW (THE REAPER)

m ◡

Letter: *m*
Meaning of letter: quality
Language of Space (aUI) spirit name: minkatlak (pronounced "min-KAHT-lahk," accent on the second syllable)

m in aUI means "quality." Any time anyone is impressed with the quality of something, they'll say, "mmm." This is a common expression when we eat good food or see something that pleases us. The idea of quality relates to Arcanum XIII in that at the beginning of every new cycle of anything there is a better quality. This is why everything tends to repeat itself, for the more something is done, the better it gets—and if it's something negative, then through repetition it wears itself out, which is also good—"mmm."

From every cycle we learn something, and we carry this learning over into the new cycle. This makes the new cycle, in some way, no matter how small, better than the previous one. So death (which is always birth) is an uplifting experience because it promises better quality, just as the rainbow is an optimistic symbol, God's promise to humans. Evolution strives for higher and higher quality, and as we evolve, we are reborn.

The aUI symbol for *m* is like a shallow bowl, or a smile. It is rounded, which is feminine, the feminine being concerned with quality more than quantity, whereas quantity relates more to the masculine approach to reality.

ARCANUM XIV: THE ALCHEMIST (TEMPERANCE)

n ⎵

Letter: *n*
Meaning of Letter: quantity
Language of Space (aUI) spirit name: krErOwUvu (pronounced "kray-row-OO-vu," accent on the third syllable)

n in aUI means "quantity." The sound of the letter *n* is the most nasal of all the consonants. The lower animals, when they can count, always tend to count with their nose, hence the reason for the most nasal sound ruling counting, which is the determining of quantity. The word *number* in English begins with the *n* sound, and numbers are the most tangible way we have to measure quantity. The symbol for *n* in aUI is a horizontal measuring box, used to measure lots of different things.

Arcanum XIV concerns the proper combining of things, so it is quite apt that the sound should be *n,* since proper combinations are based on how much of each thing is used. *n* also means "many" or "much" in aUI, and of course Taurus, the astrological ruler of Arcanum XIV, is or can be quite possessive and gains-oriented in a material sense.

ARCANUM XV: THE MUSICIAN (THE BLACK MAGICIAN)

Letter: *x*
Meaning of Letter: relation
Pronunciation of letter: guttural *h* (as in the Scottish word *loch,* or like the pronunciation of *x* in the Spanish word *México*)
Language of Space (aUI) spirit name: krIOvu (pronounced "kree-OH-voo," accent on the second syllable)

x in aUI means "relation." Arcanum XV rules structure, and structure is a means of relating parts together. Limitations are always brought about through things relating to one another. If a thing has no relationship to anything else, then it is unlimited. The symbol for *x* in aUI is a simplified double arrow that points both ways—from me to you.

Arcanum XV depicts the nature god Pan, and all of nature is based on relationship. We call this relationship "ecology," or "balance of nature." If the birds, fish, mammals, water, soil, and air all relate to one another in the right way, then we have natural harmony, and Pan plays the most exquisite music on his pipes. If balance is destroyed and the relationships between beings are strident, that is, not supportive of life, then we have natural catastrophes.

ARCANUM XVI: THE PYRAMID (THE POWER)

Letter: *O, o*
Meanings of Letters: feeling (*O*), life (*o*)

Pronunciation of letters: *O* = "oh" (like the *o* in *omen*), *o* = "ooh" (like the first *o* in *zoology;* these two letters sound very similar—the difference is that lowercase *o* should take a shorter time to say)

Language of Space (aUI) spirit name: kuga (pronounced "KUH-ga," accent on the first syllable)

o means "life" in aUI, while *O* means "feeling." All life feels, and so it's easy to see why these two things are related to each other. The aUI symbol for *o* (life) is like a small leaf, and the symbol for *O* (feeling) is like a heart. All feelings come from either growth or destruction. Birth is accompanied by an intense feeling, and pain is the sensation of some stress either working itself out or causing us some destruction. We say that something is alive when it has a sense of feeling. Note that the English letter *O* looks like the rim of a cup, the cup being a symbol of feeling.

Arcanum XVI depicts lightning, and some biologists believe that life first came into being on planet earth as a result of lightning repeatedly striking the ocean.

ARCANUM XVII: THE LIGHT (THE STAR)

f ph p

Letters: *f, p, ph*

Meanings of Letters: this (*f, ph*), before (*p*)

Language of Space (aUI) spirit name: Uki (pronounced "OO-kee," accent on the first syllable)

f in aUI means "this," *p* means "before" and "in front of," and *ph* is merely another way of vocalizing *f*. Dr. Weilgart says that the *f* hisses outside toward its object, calling it "this." The aUI symbol for *f* seems to point to something. This pointing of the way goes with Arcanum XVII, since this arcanum is a guiding light. *p,* meaning "previous" or "past," signifies, in light of this arcanum, returning to an original state of purity, a clearing or cleansing.

The *f* symbol in aUI is a downward pointing arrow, pointing to "this," and the *p* symbol is a dot connected to the right side of a vertical line, showing something standing *before* the line.

ARCANUM XVIII: THE NIGHT (THE MOON)

sh ts tz |

Letters: *sh, ts, tz*

Pronunciation of letters: *sh* is pronounced the same way as it is in English, *ts* and *tz* are pronounced like those same letter combinations in the Russian pronunciation of the words *tsar* or *tzar*

Meaning of Letters: exist, be (the same meaning applies to all three letter groups)

Language of Space (aUI) spirit name: yiA (pronounced "yee-AH," accent on the second syllable)

sh in aUI means "to exist" or "to be." The other two letter combinations for this arcanum are compounds. *ts* means an intensification (*t*) of purpose (*s*), or a new influx (*t*) of consciousness (*s*). *tz* means a cutting apart (*z*) from something in a very intense manner (*t*). All of these ideas go with the astrological sign Cancer, which this arcanum rules.

The primary meaning of existence or being (*sh*) alludes to the idea that nothing can be without a shell, a home, a location for its operations, an environment, or a matrix. Existence always implies the possibility of nonexistence, and it is a shell that separates the two, keeping one out and the other in. The crab, of course, which is associated with Cancer, is a creature with a shell. The aUI symbol for *sh, ts,* and *tz* is a vertical line that stands upright, affirming a state of being.

ARCANUM XIX: THE DANCE (THE SUN)

q

Letter: *q*
Meaning of Letter: condition
Pronunciation of letter: like the *or* in *worm* or *word,* functions as a vowel
Language of Space (aUI) spirit name: riOe (pronounced "rih-OH-eh," accent on the second syllable)

q in aUI means "condition," and, unlike in most languages, in aUI it is a vowel. Since Arcanum XIX governs role-playing, this letter alludes to the idea that all roles are always born out of the conditions surrounding them. To play the role of a teacher, one needs students and some sort of school, whether obvious or hidden. In this way we can define roles by describing their conditions. Also, the roles that we play create conditions, so roles and conditions have an intimate and symbiotic relationship. To change the conditions of one's life we have to change the role, or roles, that we play. The two interlocked parentheses of the aUI symbol for *q* signify the limitations that conditions impose. The two parentheses touching each other at their centers make an enclosure, alluding to any *conditions* offset from the rest of a sentence.

ARCANUM XX: THE AWAKENING (THE SARCOPHAGUS)

Letter: *r*
Meaning of Letter: positive, good
Language of Space (aUI) spirit name: vAmevs (pronounced "VAH-mehvs," accent on the first syllable)

r in aUI means "good" or "positive." It's the sound of affirmation. Arcanum XX symbolizes the subconscious, which is "good," as it contains a treasure trove of riches that humans can creatively draw on. The subconscious is only "bad" when the gifts are allowed to go to waste, unused.

This card signifies liberation, which is best (the superlative of *good*) of all. It also signifies feeling, and of course we all want to feel good, but human beings often go about trying to feel good in the wrong way, and then find out later that what they thought was good isn't.

The aUI sumbol for *r* is a plus sign, alluding to the idea that all that is good adds to our lives. The cross which is the aUI symbol for this letter can be thought of in terms of the Crucifixion, which liberated Jesus from the world of matter to become the Christ, an act that has helped humankind do the same.

ARCANUM XXI: THE LORD OF THE DANCE (THE ADEPT)

S ●

Letter: *s* (as noted above, the soft *c* sound, as in *Cynthia,* should be treated like an *s* in this system)

Meaning of Letter: thing

Language of Space (aUI) spirit name: riOevkU (pronounced "rih-OH-ev-koo," accent on the second syllable)

The symbol for *s* in aUI is a dot. It means "thing," "object," "article," "item," "it." Arcanum XXI signifies consciousness, and when consciousness is perfected, we become a "thing" unto ourself. The aUI symbol for *s* is a point of light, a star, and of course this arcanum is ruled by our Sun, which is a star. The Adept is one who has become one-pointed.

ARCANUM XXII: THE TRAVELER (THE FOOL)

t ➝

Letter: *t*
Meaning of Letter: toward
Language of Space (aUI) spirit name: kUmdavU (pronounced "KOOM-dah-voo," accent on the first syllable)

t in aUI means "toward." What is The Fool moving toward? The same thing we are all moving toward, the thing that Buddhists tell us all sentient beings are moving toward: enlightenment. In some tarot decks The Fool seems to be walking off a cliff. Because Arcanum XXII is the intensifier, it pushes us toward realization. This can come in the form of destruction. At any rate, the intensity compels us to move toward enlightenment, which is the realization of our true nature. The aUI symbol for *t* is an arrow pointing to the right, or it might be a hook pulling us in that direction.

Since Pluto, the astrological ruler of this card, is the planet farthest from the Sun, it points toward another, larger center: the Galactic Center, which is the center of our Milky Way galaxy. Scientists have found very strong radio waves emanating from this point in space, which is a black hole.

USING AUI

The letters of aUI and their sounds can be used for contemplation and to make up your own magical words. Words and sounds have healing power and can be used to focus and reinforce particular vibrations that a person needs. If you desire to tune in to a particular card, turn your attention to its sound. Say the sound and listen to it. You can also add the sounds together to form personalized words of pure meaning.

The most fascinating aspect of the relationship between the

language of aUI and the tarot is that since the aUI meanings are so simple, they help us see the cards at a very rudimentary and basic level, thus we have a veritable alphabet of building blocks that repeat and recombine into all the various forms, thoughts, and forces of the universe.

CHAPTER NINETEEN

Kabbalistic and Therapeutic Levels of the Tarot

The book that drew me into studying the tarot is C. C. Zain's *The Sacred Tarot,* which I discovered in the early 1970s. It explains the relationship between numerology and astrology, and by associating the letters of the alphabet with numbers it is possible to recognize the numerical vibrations of words and names. For me, Zain's tarot book represented a grand synthesis of so many of the ideas I'd been working with as a practicing astrologer. It deepened my metaphysical awareness of the signs and planets and gave me an excellent tool for divination. Zain's book is filled with many gems of wisdom.

Later I met Ronn Ballard, a fellow metaphysician, and we moved in together and started a school of metaphysics. We put out a newsletter every month and taught classes in astrology, numerology, color therapy, and, of course, tarot. These were times of constant discovery for us as we creatively explored the systems we were working with, so we decided to write a book on the tarot and do it as a correspondence course. We started selling the course before we had even completed writing the lessons, advertising them in the *National Enquirer.* We had a good number of people who took this course, and eventually we finished writing the twenty-six lessons in the book, coming up with many ideas for it along the way, which we put into our lessons.

Our classes had a social and communal feel to them that for me was deeply satisfying. Our students were extremely varied—young people, older people, and people from different backgrounds. I think they enjoyed meeting and relating to one another just as much as they enjoyed our teachings. On many evenings after class we'd all go out to a restaurant to eat, drink, and share our thoughts.

One of our students was Wilma Albert, a highly eccentric and singular woman. I would say she was the queen of metaphysics in Kansas City at that time, hosting all sorts of lectures and gatherings of cutting-edge New Age people. Over the years she did many kind and generous things to support me in my work, such as directing astrology clients my way and helping to get me to astrology conventions. One of the greatest gifts she gave me, though, was to introduce me to Dr. John Weilgart, who then held the honorary title of Chief Psychologist for the United Nations. At the time we were teaching our tarot classes neither Ronn nor I had delved much into the deeper meanings of the Hebrew letters, but we felt strongly that Dr. Weilgart's work would reawaken and extend the linguistic aspects of the tarot, as we were to discover in the years that followed.

Ronn and I self-published our tarot book once we finished writing the twenty-six lessons. The first edition was photocopied on 8 1/2 × 11" sheets of paper with a plastic spiral binding. Later it was picked up by Aries Press, a publishing house in Chicago, which is now defunct and had issued it in a limited edition.

Another one of our students was a woman named Teresa Anderson. She loved delving into the tarot and soaked up all we had to teach her. One evening after class she said to us, "Gee, I wish I could just move in with you guys so I could be learning from you all the time." After she left, Ronn and I talked it over, and the next day I called her and asked her if she wanted to move in with us. It was a two-bedroom apartment. Ronn and I used one of the bedrooms and the other one was set up as an office. We gave her the office for her bedroom and she moved in. I loved having her there.

I don't remember how or why she moved out (I think she found a boyfriend), and I don't even remember how long she lived with us. But I do remember that the three of us had a lot of fun sharing ideas and sparking each others' creativity.

After she moved out, Teresa began studying tarot with a man who was a witch. He explained to her that the system of numerology and astrological rulership that Ronn and I were using for the major arcana was different from the one he used. He told her that most people used his system. She carefully explained to him all the rationales for our system, for we had taught her countless reasons why the system was set up the way it was, and the reasons for the patterns it made were highly compelling. He countered by saying that if she were to persist in using our system she would have difficulty communicating with most people who used the tarot, as our system was used by so few.

Teresa stuck with our system, but the conflict got me to thinking, and as I looked into it over the years I realized that the other teacher's system was derived from a famous and very old book of mysticism called the *Sepher Yetzirah,* the "Book of Formation" or "Book of Creation," the earliest known work on Jewish esotericism and the Kabbalah. According to the tenth-century rabbi Saadia ben Yosef Gaon (the name Gaon means "philosopher"), this book explains the entire creation and how the Sefirah of the Tree of Life function to bring consciousness to the world of form. I intuitively felt that the ancient and time-honored ascriptions found in this book could not possibly be wrong, but I also felt that the sources that Ronn and I were using, which had come from C. C. Zain, could not be wrong either.

And then I read an essay on Kabbalah that informed me that in essence, Kabbalah is not a single system, but rather aims at being the grand compendium of all systems. The issue, according to kabbalistic thinking, is not whether a certain system is right or wrong, but rather what that particular system means, that is, *why it is the way it is and what knowledge does it convey.*

And then it came to me: the system that Ronn and I had been using, the one from C. C. Zain, is a therapeutic or healing system, whereas the one found in the *Sepher Yetzirah* is the root, or actual system.

Let me give you an example of how this works: Arcanum XVIII (The Night) is ruled, according to the *Sepher Yetzirah,* by the sign Aquarius, whereas in the C. C. Zain system it is ruled by Cancer. This means that the energy of the sign Cancer is the one that has the greatest healing effect on the sign Aquarius. And so my insight provided me with a clear and simple picture of how these two systems relate to each other. This revelation opened up a whole new world of knowledge for me.

The following list of the twenty-two major arcana shows the two rulerships for each card: the root ruler found in the *Sepher Yetzira,* and the astrological sign or planet that heals it—its therapeutic agent, which is found in the book *The Sacred Tarot* by C. C. Zain. The root ruler is given first and its therapeutic agent second, plus a brief description of how and why the therapeutic agent heals the root.

ARCANUM I: THE MESSENGER (THE MAGUS)

Root ruler: Air
Therapeutic agent: Mercury

Air signifies the mind. What heals the mind is Mercury, which is the ability to communicate and to be flexible to allow a free flow of information and ideas. It may be that all pathologies of the mind come from mental rigidity—a lack of Mercury's flexibility. Also, when ideas cannot find the needed cohesion that is provided by Mercury if they are to be communicated, then the mind becomes isolated, unable to connect.

ARCANUM II: THE GUARDIAN OF THE GATE (VEILED ISIS)

Root ruler: Saturn
Therapeutic agent: Virgo

Saturn rules our restrictions, fears, and limitations. When these are worked on, purified, perfected, refined, clarified, and analyzed until they are understood deeply—as brought about by the energy of Virgo—we grow spiritually, which is the goal of Saturn. It might well be that in a natal chart any problems connected to Saturn could potentially be resolved by working with whatever planets are in Virgo in that chart, or by focusing on the house on whose cusp Virgo is found.

ARCANUM III: THE QUEEN MOTHER (ISIS UNVEILED)

Root ruler: Jupiter
Therapeutic agent: Libra

The energy of growth, which is Jupiter, is brought under control and into harmony by connecting it meaningfully with all that surrounds it. Jupiter, negatively speaking, is the planet of excess, and excess is healed by the balancing and linking energy of Libra. If we find out how excess throws us out of balance, we then can have a better idea about how to restore balance.

ARCANUM IV: THE COMMANDER (THE SOVEREIGN)

Root ruler: Mars
Therapeutic agent: Scorpio

Mars is assertion, construction, and destruction. Scorpio is creativity. When our assertive urges are given creative direction, it heals them. We can also say that anger is healed by the transformation (Scorpio) of its energy into a more positive, creative, and constructive form.

ARCANUM V: THE PENTAGRAM (THE HIEROPHANT)

Root ruler: Aries
Therapeutic agent: Jupiter

Aries is the power to begin again, to start over—the new moment forever dawning. These new beginnings might be mere running in circles, however, unless there is learning and growth from experiencing them. Jupiter is this learning and growth.

ARCANUM VI: THE CROSSROADS (THE TWO PATHS)

Root ruler: Taurus
Therapeutic agent: Venus

No other sign is more desirous of comfort than Taurus, and because of this it can resist evolution. But when it experiences true and pure love (Venus), it then wants to progress and let go of those aspects of its stubbornness that do not serve it. Whether we choose evolution or our own stabilized comfort at the level we're currently at depends on magnetism—what pulls at us the most. And Venus is magnetism, with the pull of evolution always winning out in the end, as it is the strongest force in the universe.

ARCANUM VII: THE VICTORY (THE CONQUEROR)

Root ruler: Gemini
Therapeutic agent: Sagittarius

Gemini can flit from thing to thing, and in doing so can be at worst a purveyor of chaos. But when directed by a higher perspective and a sense of wholeness (Sagittarius), then its communications can take on clarity and meaning that can serve the forces of harmony and progress in the universe.

ARCANUM VIII: THE BALANCE (JUSTICE)

Root ruler: Cancer
Therapeutic agent: Capricorn

Cancer can become too steeped in its own subjectivity and too immersed in its fears and insecurities. But when given the objectivity and discernment of Capricorn, its negative emotional complexes are encouraged to clear. The Cancerian tendency to be defensive is healed when Cancer perceives what is ultimately practical (Capricorn) in spiritual terms.

ARCANUM IX: THE SEEKER (THE SAGE)

Root ruler: Leo
Therapeutic agent: Aquarius

Leo, as an actor, needs an audience, which is Aquarius. At best the audience brings out the actor's finest creativity. The self-expression of Leo is healed by being used to support others; Aquarius signifies this support, and gives Leo a positive direction toward an uplifting future.

ARCANUM X: THE CYCLE (THE WHEEL)

Root ruler: Virgo
Therapeutic agent: Uranus

At worst, Virgo engages in mere toil and busywork, but when Uranus brings inspiration to it, then Virgo's work becomes creative, unique, and original, no matter how outwardly mundane it might seem to be. Virgo's work is progressively lifted up spiritually and refined the more it gets in contact with its own individual and special abilities, which is what Uranus is all about.

ARCANUM XI: THE MAIDEN (THE ENCHANTRESS)

Root ruler: Sun
Therapeutic agent: Neptune

The Sun manifests egotism more than any other celestial body, but Neptune can inspire it to be self-sacrificing, to truly care for others, and to serve the good of all. The Sun rules purpose, and when purpose becomes high-minded (Neptune), it is healed. Also, the energy of the Sun can be harsh—it creates deserts, for instance; it can overwhelm with its brightness. Neptune can teach it to be more gentle and refined, more subtle.

ARCANUM XII: THE DEVOTEE (THE MARTYR)

Root ruler: Libra
Therapeutic agent: Pisces

The way Libra relates to others and to situations might often be only superficial, but when imbued with the cosmic depth and intuitiveness of Pisces, its energy can grow deeper and more oceanic. Also, what heals the process of relating to others is sympathy and empathy (Pisces), which opens a channel for true spiritual exchange flowing directly from the soul.

ARCANUM XIII: THE RAINBOW (THE REAPER)

Root ruler: Water
Therapeutic agent: Aries

Water can sit around and grow stagnant. Water is the emotions, which can be dammed up, repressed, and blocked, which causes them to fester. But when the new beginnings of Aries ignite sparks to break up these obstructions, it flows in fresh cycles, which cleans and restores any stagnation. How wonderful that water is magically re-enlivened by these eternal new dawnings!

ARCANUM XIV: THE ALCHEMIST (TEMPERANCE)

Root ruler: Scorpio
Therapeutic agent: Taurus

Scorpio is creativity. What heals it is stubbornness (Taurus), for to engage in any kind of creative endeavor requires faithfully holding on to one's vision in an utterly uncompromising manner. Also, Scorpio is death, and what heals death—that is, what makes it meaningful—is recognizing the true value and worth (Taurus) of all that was learned in one's lifetime.

ARCANUM XV: THE MUSICIAN (THE BLACK MAGICIAN)

Root ruler: Sagittarius
Therapeutic agent: Saturn

Sagittarius craves to live in the realm of the cosmic, which can potentially create great frustration or impracticality, or cause Sagittarius to deny reality and avoid anything limiting. But when Sagittarius comes to terms with limitations (Saturn), then its cosmic perspective becomes truly spiritual.

ARCANUM XVI: THE PYRAMID (THE POWER)

Root ruler: Capricorn
Therapeutic agent: Mars

Capricorn rules authority. It's either an authority figure or one who knows about and understands authority and how laws work. In any case it must act, it must assert itself (Mars), either to positively wield its authority, to support (Mars) true authorities, or to tear down and destroy (Mars) false ones. It is action that brings meaning and purpose to its strong opinions and therefore heals them.

ARCANUM XVII: THE LIGHT (THE STAR)

Root ruler: Venus
Therapeutic agent: Gemini

Love (Venus) finds its highest expression and is healed when it is communicated (Gemini). Venus also signifies art, and art is healed—that is, fulfilled—by achieving the total aliveness of Gemini.

ARCANUM XVIII: THE NIGHT (THE MOON)

Root ruler: Aquarius
Therapeutic agent: Cancer

For groups and friendships (Aquarius) to achieve their highest potential, there must be mutual nurturing (Cancer) among their members. We fulfill the greatest possibilities of our future by taking care of and helping one another.

ARCANUM XIX: THE DANCE (THE SUN)

Root ruler: Pisces
Therapeutic agent: Leo

Pisces embraces all, but in so doing can sometimes become lost in the infinitude of time and space. But Leo gives it direction and the assurance needed to express itself. Leo is joy, which can disperse the often dark moods of Pisces.

ARCANUM XX: THE AWAKENING (THE SARCOPHAGUS)

Root ruler: Mercury
Therapeutic agent: Moon

Thinking (Mercury) always tends to be based on and colored by feelings (the Moon), so as the subconscious is cleared of its dark, dysfunctional places, then thinking too has the possibility of growing clear.

ARCANUM XXI: THE LORD OF THE DANCE (THE ADEPT)

Root ruler: Fire
Therapeutic agent: Sun

Fire can be wild, crazy, and destructive, but when it becomes centralized with purpose and direction and true self-confidence (the Sun), then it can metamorphose into a viable powerhouse.

ARCANUM XXII: THE TRAVELER (THE FOOL)

Root ruler: Moon
Therapeutic agent: Pluto

Feelings (the Moon) are healed by intensification that leads to transformation (Pluto). One of the survival techniques we often learn as children involves repressing our emotions—turning down their volume—which dulls us. We are taught that intense feelings can be dangerous, that they're not socially acceptable. As their volume is turned up, though, we can discover many things about our inner life and can then purge ourself of the emotions that obstruct our spiritual growth. Of course, as Arcanum XXII is also numbered 0; this arcanum is both the beginning and end of the cycle of the major arcana—the zero, or egg from which all else is born.

I would someday like to write a book to further explain how each planet and sign is healed by another, as shown in this list, and possibly I will do so. In the meantime I hope this abbreviated explanation inspires you to look more deeply into these connections, which I feel are profoundly meaningful.

CHAPTER TWENTY

Tarot Contemplations

By now you have learned much about the tarot. Where do you go from here? The amount of information contained in the cards is limitless. You may read other books and study what other authors have said, but ultimately there are ways to investigate the tarot that are beyond the limits of the conscious mind. We can gain a wealth of ideas by simply going to our inner source. Human beings did not make up the tarot archetypes, they merely noted them. The thoughtforms and forces of the tarot are quite real and can be found in all of us.

The following instructions are intended to deepen your understanding of the tarot through a contemplative session with your tarot "companions."

First, you'll need quiet and congenial surroundings. In the method of contemplation presented here it's best to work with at least one other person. One person will be doing the contemplation, while the other person (or persons) will assist. The person who is going to do the contemplation, the contemplator, should lie down, close their eyes, and peacefully listen with their assistant to some music. The selection of music is quite important—it's best to choose music that is restful and relaxing, something you like, something that sets the mood. It's generally better to have instrumental music rather than vocal music so as to eliminate any mental constructs that could arise from the experience of listening to vocal music. There are certain exceptions, however—notably, Gregorian chant. So unless you know Latin you most likely won't be distracted by this type of meditative music.

The following composers were also mystics and wrote music that was cosmically tuned to a high vibration:

Frederick Chopin: Most of his nocturnes for piano are suitable.
Claude Debussy: His Three Nocturnes are especially good (except for the middle one, "Festivals," which I think it's a little too energetic and stimulating).
Maurice Ravel: "Une barque sur l'océan."
Alexander Scriabin: *Poème-Nocturne,* op. 61.
Phillip Glass: Most of his works.
Giovanni Pierluigi de Palestrina: Just about everything he wrote.
Kaikhosru Sorabji: Most of his works are appropriate, though since so many of them are quite long you may have to fade the music out at some point. Some are also thunderous, so you might screen them first.
Tom Kenyon: *Soma.* It has three different parts, all of them suitable. He's written many other pieces that are also great.
Michael Stearns: Most of his work is great for tarot contemplations.

Of course, there are many other pieces of music you can use according to your preferences. You don't want a piece of music to be so long as to become tedious, so if you have to, fade it out. While listening to the music, follow each note and ride with the flow of the rhythm. If you find that thoughts are coming into your mind, let them be until you realize that your attention is not on the music. As soon as you realize this, return your attention to the music.

Make sure the room you'll be using for this contemplation session is clean; light candles and burn some incense. This will help create a conducive atmosphere. Make sure that the surface you or the person who is the contemplator is lying on is comfortable.

Before you start the music, have your companion pick a card from the major arcana. They can, if you both agree, tell you what the card is before the music starts. Also, as you become familiar with the music you're using you'll probably want to coordinate the feeling of the music with the feeling of the particular card chosen. Follow your intuition. There are no rules for this. The key is to be sensitive to your own feelings. While the music is playing, all the companions, as well as the person doing the contemplation, should listen to the music with eyes closed.

After the music stops, have your companion describe to you the particular card chosen. But rather than describing the card as a flat picture, describe it as a living "scene." Make this description as detailed as possible. If there's a figure on the card, describe the figure's eye and hair color and what they're wearing. Describe the figure's surroundings, and as many other details as possible. Each time you do this you'll tend to come up with a different description, depending on the time and place.

Once the scene has been described, ask the contemplator to describe what he's seeing or how the picture is changing. He might begin to mention other details that the companion left out. If there is a figure depicted on the card, you might ask the contemplator if this figure sees him. If the answer is no, then ask the contemplator if he would approach the figure on the card or in some way get the attention of that figure.

Once contact has been made with the figure shown on the card, ask the contemplator to ask this tarot personage if he or she has anything they would like to show the contemplator. From here on you can let the contemplation flow naturally.

If the contemplator is having trouble seeing the scene or if nothing seems to be happening, ask him to silently ask for guidance. If the scene he's watching seems to be vague, ask for more details. Basically, there are three levels on which questions can be asked—the physical, the emotional, and the mental. For instance, it's best to always ask first, "What are you seeing?" This is the physical level. After an answer is given, then ask, "How do you feel about this?" or "How does this make you feel?" This is the emotional level. Then you can ask, "What do you think about this?" This is the mental level. There is a fourth level, the spiritual level, and the question for this level might be, "What did this contemplation mean to you personally?" or "What part do you feel the information given plays in your personal evolution?" This question should probably be left for a discussion after the contemplation.

At first it's best to make these contemplations last no longer than twenty minutes, but later, after you've become comfortable with the technique, you can go on for as long as you like.

You'll find that as you do these contemplations they will become increasingly vivid and clear. Some people might call them fantasies, but we believe that what is actually happening is that we're contacting the elementals or other sentient energy forms or tarot archetypes. There is a whole unseen world that exists everywhere, all around us. This world is peopled by entities as varied as the human and animal entities we do see around us. Some of these invisible entities or energy forms are powerful, some are weak, some are very kindhearted, and others are mean and vicious. You needn't be afraid, though, because as long as you enter into this contemplation experience for the purpose of learning and other positive reasons you will be naturally protected from contact with negative entities.

Also, when we describe what happens during contemplations of this sort, questions invariably arise: Are our experiences happening within us or outside of us? Are these energy forms and elementals part of our being, our inner world, or do they exist apart from and outside of us? The answer is yes to all these possibilities. The Hermetic philosophy teaches that the inner world and the outer world reflect each other. Everything without can be found within.

When we do these contemplations in a group, we usually record them. Also, if you would like, you can give everyone in the room a pencil and some paper so they can write down the details or incidents that are most striking to them.

The more you know about the tarot, the better these contemplations will be. Westerners are inclined to separate the mental from the emotional, but the fact of the matter is that these two realms support each other. The images that feelings generate can be analyzed by the mind, and in this way we can make sense out of our intuitions.

If someone is contemplating a particular card—for instance, Arcanum VI (The Crossroads)—and they see a *V* formation, and if one of the companions in the contemplation session knows that Arcanum VI is ruled by the letter *V,* she can ask questions about the *V* so as to gain more information about it. In other words, intellectual knowledge of the cards serves as a kind of roadmap so that we can know more clearly where we're going or where we're being led.

In the discussion following the contemplation we use a method of questioning called *art form methodology.* This methodology aids in the interpretation of visual experience. All questions posed in art form methodology are put to the group as a whole, and each person gives their own answer.

The first two questions aim at the objective or rational level. They are:

1. What pictures, symbols, colors, shapes, people, or entities stand out in your mind from the described experience of the subject?
2. What words or phrases spoken by the contemplator during the session do you most vividly recall?

The next level of questions aims at a more reflective, emotional level. They are:

1. If you could name a specific feeling that the experience evoked in you, what would you call it?
2. Were there any specific parts of the experience that you wished at the time you could share?
3. Were there any parts of the experience you found difficult to relate to?
4. Were there any parts of the experience that you felt applied to you personally?

The final level of questions aims at an interpretative level. They are:

1. Going back to the objective or rational list, did you find any of the symbols gleaned from the experience confusing? What do you feel they could mean? Does anyone feel that an alternate meaning might be implied?
2. What do you feel was the specific value of this experience to the contemplator?

3. What do you feel the meaning of the experience was for you as an observer?
4. If you were to assign a title to this experience, what might it be?

Just as in dreams, there are certain symbols that tend to crop up again and again in these experiences. One is the image of a city. Cities always symbolize a focus of a particular type of energy, a center of activity. If the contemplator sees a city, one of the companions can ask if he would like to go to that city. The contemplator might also be asked the general color of the city, the style and type of the buildings, and so forth. If an entity is leading her to the city, once the she has arrived, it might be good for her to ask the guide if there is a specific building to which the guide would like to take her.

Another recurring symbol is cliffs or seeing something from a great height. If we can persuade the contemplator to descend the cliff, she will tend to go into a deeper experience, since the cliff can symbolize going deeper into the subconscious. Also, a cliff symbolizes an overview, so it's good to ask the contemplator what she sees from that vantage.

Some other recurring symbols are hallways and tunnels. These often symbolize transitions—going from one phase to another within the experience.

If we see personages who are funny or amusing, or if our guides seem like common people or people from history, it's not necessarily the case that we're going back into history or that we're having a superficial experience.

Elementals always tend to appear to a person in a form that the person can relate to. For instance, there might be a woman in your group who has all French Provincial furniture, and who has been to France and loves French culture. An elemental of Arcanum VI (The Crossroads) might appear to her as a grand dame from the court of Louis XVI. When a companion asks the elemental to reveal its name, the elemental might say, "Marie Antoinette." This doesn't mean that the elemental is really the soul of Marie Antoinette. It may just be that since the woman doing the contemplation knows something about Marie Antoinette, the elemental has dipped into her memory bank and pulled out this costume image or role to illustrate a point.

Elementals of the higher realms are almost always friendly to human beings, ready and willing to help in whatever way they can. So if you get an elemental who seems to be loath to do anything, you can ask for its help or ask it why it's doing whatever it's doing and any other questions. If the elemental doesn't respond to your requests or seems uncompromising, tell it that you would like to talk to someone else who might be able to help you.

It seems best to always have an elemental guide in these sessions, and sensitivity on the part of everyone in this contemplative exercise will tell you whether or not the particular elemental is the right one for the session. Most usually are, as long as the atmosphere is warm, friendly, and calm. Elementals like nothing better than to commune with us humans. The reason they don't do it more often is because they're afraid of the destructiveness of humans and tend to shun anything disordered, nervous, or chaotic.

These kinds of experiences in working with the tarot can be very healing, and we've immensely enjoyed doing them. We've journeyed to many places and seen many things, all in the privacy of our own homes. Also, these experiences can deeply influence your knowledge of the cards and imbue your work with the tarot with greater richness and meaning.

It's best that the contemplator keep talking throughout the session. You might think that incessant talking would prevent her from going more deeply into the experience, but we've found that this is not the case. The purpose for continuously speaking is to make the experience a group experience and to maintain a thread of communication with the conscious waking world while journeying. This is a safeguard that allows your companions to enter into the experience too.

At times when we've done these contemplations, the contemplator has described what has happened to her so vividly that all of the companions felt like they were right there with her. If there seems to be a pause in the contemplator's talking, it's good to ask questions. This keeps the experience moving along. If the contemplator's answers seem to be slow, wait patiently, because she's probably too busy experiencing something to say anything about it right at that moment. You will have some sessions where few questions are asked, and the contemplator does almost all the talking. Other times the contemplator will need to be led and prompted more. Sometimes it's good to let the contemplator pick the card that she wants to journey into. At other times you might try picking the card that corresponds to the sign the Moon is in at that time. This tends to aid the intensity of the experience. You can also pick cards according to the contemplator's Sun sign.

Another method you can apply to this kind of session is to start with Arcanum I and go through the whole major arcana in a cycle over a period of several days. You'll tend to get as much out of these experiences as you put into them. As you do this, it might be a good idea to keep a record of the sessions so that you can follow the progress of your group. The approach to every session should be gentle and innocent. Never force anything.

It's probably best at first to keep your group small so participants can overcome any feelings of timidity or self-consciousness. Also, you should tell the contemplator to describe exactly what she sees, whether or not she understands it or sees any meaning in it, as it might have meaning for someone else. Anyone is capable of doing these contemplations, provided they take a relaxed and open attitude toward the experience.

When it feels like the experience has come to an end, it's a good idea to take a few moments to come out of it rather than ending abruptly. Also, do not end the experience if something is up in the air—a question, a thought, or a vision that wants to emerge. If something is going on, let it finish, don't interrupt. You want to aim at having the experience finish on a positive and peaceful note.

Sometimes the elemental contacted will express the thought that they are open to questions. If so, allow all the companions to voice any questions they might have. As a contemplator, you will find that an elemental will often not communicate directly to you in words but will express their thoughts to you directly through your mind. Since elementals operate at a higher wavelength, they needn't use words—they are capable of communicating faster than speech.

The techniques presented here are quite simple. It's not hard to contact these invisible realms—in fact, it's the very simplicity of doing so that prevents it from happening more often. We live in an extremely complex world (as if you haven't already noticed!), and so many of us think that to achieve anything we have to work very hard at it. This isn't true. The inner voice is always there to guide us, and it will if we simply tune out the surrounding static so that advice and help is clear.

When you meet with your friend (or friends) to do these contemplations, you might want to begin the session in complete silence. This helps everyone focus their minds. Try to avoid preliminary small talk, which can distract from your focus.

You may want to open your session with the reading of a favorite piece of poetry or a passage from a book. Remember, the quality of the group experience directly depends on the state of mind of each person in it, so try to enter into these sessions with sufficient rest and make sure you have enough time and that you're not hungry or uncomfortable in any other way.

The world has given rise to many schools of occult knowledge. The genuine ones are usually unique in terms of the techniques they employ, but all schools of the occult are alike in terms of their inner work and primary aim, which is to enhance and promote the evolution of their students. And though they may say it in different ways, they always communicate the same message: the greatest teacher is one's Higher Self. If you hold this as your focus, you will always be guided and protected.

FINAL MUSINGS

A Tarot Garden of Thoughts

1

I have been reading Aleister Crowley's *The Book of Thoth: A Short Essay on the Tarot of the Egyptians,* and I find it murky, confusing, and fragmented as a textbook on the tarot. I think a more apt name for it would be *Gothic Collage.* To me, Crowley's writing is always striving toward poetry. When I consider it solely as poetry, I find it exceptionally fine, but since we live in this Aquarian age, in which everything is held in pigeonholes, simplified to fit into neat categories, there are few poets or literati who would read Crowley as poetry, as it's already been categorized as magic and metaphysics.

2

If you draw two squares at forty-five-degree angles to and on top of each other and then inscribe a circle around them, you will have divided the circle into seventeen areas. This shows the relationship between the eight-pointed star and Arcanum XVII (The Light, or The Star) whose sky it is in. Karma, as represented by the number 8, is our guiding light, and the easiest way to clear negative karma is do the simplest sort of meditation, which is to enter into the silence of the present. Then karma falls away like old skin from a molting snake. This is the kind of meditation that Maharishi taught.

If you inscribe a five-pointed star in a circle you will have created eleven areas, showing the relationship between the kelipot and the 5, or, we might say, between intuition, 11, and expansion, 5.

3

The first prime number is 1 (not according to the mathematical definition, but in this system for interpreting the tarot), the second is 2, and the third one is 3. So up to the number 3 the ordinal placement of the primes is the same as the primes themselves. But at 5 this changes, since 5 is the fourth prime. The number 5 is the unifying and synthesizing of the energy of 4, and likewise the number of the ordinal placement of any prime shows how that prime unifies and synthesizes the ordinal number it corresponds to. So the next prime after 5 is 7, the fifth prime, meaning that Sagittarius (ruler of Arcanum VII, The Victory), which signifies transcendence, organizes and synthesizes growth, represented by the number 5.

I find it both clarifying and revealing to contemplate numbers in this manner, though I know that many people experience numbers as cold and impersonal. I had a dream one time that I was handed a magnifying glass with which to look at the robes of an angel, and as I closely peered into the glass I found it was woven of all sorts of numbers both great and small. You needn't know what a number means to receive its benefit. If you allow yourself to, you can feel into the vibrations of numbers and sense the inner beauty of each one.

4

I have been looking at Alejandro Jodorowsky's book *The Way of Tarot: The Spiritual Teacher in the Cards,* and I think it's one of the best I've ever encountered. What's amazing to me about Jodorowsky is how grandiose he can be without the slightest taint of pretentiousness. His work is imbued with a glowing sincerity I find most attractive. I will say, though, that I have no desire to study his system more closely—not because it doesn't merit it, but because I'm an artist doing my own thing, which takes up the greater portion of my attention. Hopefully, after I die, there will be a great deal more time to read and explore the ideas of other people, and certainly Jodorowsky's book is high on my list.

5

My friend Elisabeth told me recently that she tapped into this tarot book—the one you are currently holding—psychically, which at the time she told me this the manuscript was almost finished. She said she saw it was inhabited by a being. I was overjoyed at this. When kabbalists say that all matter is alive, it is also true that all ideas are alive, and more than anything else I wanted the ideas of this book to come together as one. Elisabeth's vision told me that this had happened. I will say, though, that I feel there is more than one spirit who inhabits this book, and the number of these beings changes continually, depending on who's reading it. It's much like Archangel Michael, who is one angel and yet also an army of them.

I would prefer my book to be a hotel with many rooms.

6

Maharishi said that you can't imagine a higher state of consciousness than your own, because if you could, you would already be in it. I think this has something to do with the kelipot, those shells or veils of evil that throughout the eons have separated humanity from the truth of our divine light. These shells or veils are very thin, and there are countless transparent layers of them that we remove as we evolve. We don't know what life really looks like until we remove those layers, and because of the thinness of those layers we may suffer the illusion at times that we aren't growing. But we are. Maharishi says that every day we are in a higher state of consciousness than the day before, even though the change from one day to the next might be miniscule and imperceptible.

I adore Maharishi for his optimism.

7

One of the best ways to keep the energy of the tarot flowing is to always do something that's based on the advice that the tarot has given you. In other words, make use of what it says, for if you do it will tend to pull more energy out of the cards—they perceive you're listening to them, and so they want to talk louder and clearer to you. If you just take in the information but don't do anything with it, you weaken the flow of the energy. The cards feel your intent. Take them seriously and they'll take you seriously.

8

An interesting way to read higher numbers is to think of the two outermost digits combined as a number, and whatever is between those two digits as the number that has come to live in or be inside the other two. For instance, the number 131 could be seen as the 3 coming to live in the 11, or activity (Arcanum III, The Queen Mother) inside intuition (Arcanum XI, The Maiden); or relating (Arcanum III) imbuing idealism (Arcanum XI). (Relating as imbuing idealism would be a type of idealism that always wants to connect or relate to the world around it, to link up to what is around it. The surrounding number in this case, 11, is the realm we are in, and the 3 is what is going on within this realm—the number inside idealism.)

Or for instance, let's take the number 2,783. This is the Princess of Swords (number 78) living in the Ace of Wands (number 23)—in other words, a hardworking and meticulous person (Princess of Swords) immersed in intense creativity (Ace of Wands).

My street address number is 3704, which is the number 70 inside the number 34, or the Six of Swords (number 70) immersed in the King of Wands (number 34), meaning the manifestation of purpose (Six of Swords) immersed in the exploration of new territory (King of Wands).

9

Thousands of tarot decks have been made in multitudes of patterns, meaning that there are a gigantic number of variations in the different designs of the cards. There's general agreement among many writers about the meaning of certain cards, but also a great number of writers who have all sorts of different ideas about what each card means. What pleases me most about the system described in my book is that it is integrated. Its connection to astrology gives it a balanced and complete vibration, which I feel aligns it with patterns of cosmic energy.

A student of the tarot could easily become confused by all these variations among the different decks and writers. There is, though, a certain benefit to all these mountains of thought and information. I think it ultimately throws the student back on their own intuition. You can make arguments for any symbol or system—you can find or invent a justification for anything you care to invent and incorporate into the tarot. Arguing about which system is superior does not bring one closer to the most important thing the tarot can accomplish, which is to bring forth and refine your intuition.

I have seen beautiful decks of fortune-telling cards that have no numbers on them, called oracle cards. These are sets of dreamlike images meant to stimulate the imagination of the reader. These sorts of cards are just as valid as the tarot. One can gaze into the bottom of an empty cup of tea and see patterns in the wet leaves, and these certainly can draw up insights from the psyche of the reader. In many ways the wet leaves are refreshing, as they have no centuries-old historical precedent or authorities arguing over their astrological rulerships—they're just tea leaves in a cup.

I do feel, though, that there is something permanent in the cards, something unchanging. For me it's the different numbers associated with each one of them, and the astrological signs and planets they correspond to. But the cards are kind of like houses in that even though houses are substantial and durable, they have occupants that move through them, as well as seasons. Things come and go in houses, just like all the various tarot decks all have different pictures, as well as talismans and symbols in them that the artist who drew them felt had special meaning for that card.

The year is now 2023, and it seems to me that humanity is suffering from more alienation from each other and from their spiritual source than ever before. Everything feels fragmented and obstructed. People are not coming together nearly as much as they could or as needed. I think the one thing that could most bring people together is if more and more of them got more deeply in touch with their intuition. Because when you do this, you are bound to feel your connectedness to other people and to all of life. I feel we are focused too much on our rational, logical minds, and because of this we've repressed our instincts to the extent that we are mentally compartmentalizing everything. The flow is gone, and it needs to come back, and it is tools such as the tarot that can help us all to get flowing together again. This, I feel, is why right now there's a growing interest in the tarot.

10

I would love to meaningfully correlate the tarot with the I Ching, but I've never found a way to do it, though I'm sure there is one. I think the reason this correlation doesn't easily work is because the basis of the I Ching is a square: $8 \times 8 = 64$, whereas the basis of the tarot is a triangle: the numbers from 1 to 12 all add up to 78. The tarot strongly vibrates with 3—there are twenty-one major arcana cards, and the number 21 is 3×7. Also, 21, as stated earlier, represents all the numbers from 1 to 6 added together. The number 21 is 3×7, but 22 divided by 7 (I'm now increasing the number 21 to 22 by adding The Traveler card) gives a number that is very close to pi. So the tarot vibrates with 3s and circles, while the I Ching vibrates with squares.

And, of course, astrology vibrates with both circles and squares.

11

Some fantasies: I'm imagining a website where you design your own tarot deck. The site has thousands of different objects and symbols, as well as pictures of people and various clothing and jewelry you can put on them. You can choose from any of these by dragging and dropping them onto your card. You can also ask the site to go to the net and find any other images that aren't already in its bank. Once you have finished creating all your cards, the site has the power to make a print-on-demand deck and send it to you. Many of the pictures on this site that you can choose from come with explanations of what the symbols mean and what they're traditionally related to. The site has drawn images as well as photographic ones, so that you can mix the two in the deck you create, or create a deck that's just one or the other. You can also input pictures of yourself and your friends if you want them to appear in your tarot.

I also think it would be interesting if you could buy a tarot deck in which each of the seventy-eight cards is from a different tarot deck of the past. When we become more technologically advanced it would be nice to have these cards change spontaneously and randomly, so that when you do a reading you might turn over cards you've never seen before.

Of course, cards with moving pictures would also be intriguing—just to have the scene change a little bit, maybe have clouds moving overhead in the sky, or the Magician yawning and turning his head to look at you.

There might also be advanced software that you could put on like earphones, and when you turn cards in a reading, if nothing comes to you right away about what the card means your own voice comes over the earphones and it forms into words the impressions going on in your intuition. After using these earphones for a while I imagine that many people would be able to eventually hear their intuition without them—kind of like training wheels on a bike.

In the future I see special decks that are used therapeutically. These could be bought as complete decks of seventy-eight cards, or they could be purchased one by one, so that maybe if you need a lot of the energy of Arcanum XIV, The Alchemist, for instance, you could go into a store or online and buy a dozen or so of these, or however many you need. Then you could place them in strategic places in your house and workplace, or wherever you think you might need them—say, stuck with tape under the counter of your favorite bar where you most like to sit and have a drink after work. There would be people who are experts at energetically charging such cards, and if after a time you feel that the charge in one or more of your cards has weakened, you could take it back in for a tune-up.

Also, in the future there will be people so attuned to the cards that they're like highly adept psychotherapists. You would go to them and get healing sessions, and they don't even use a deck because cards come to them in their mind and they can see and read them without having to shuffle or even having to count their deck to make sure they haven't lost a card.

Some of these people will see cards everywhere no matter what they're doing. They will sometimes walk up to a stranger and say, "Three of Swords," just because they know the person needs it. Those who are the most evolved could make cards appear in places and would often give them away or make one of them appear in a book that someone's reading, or under their bed. Eventually, we would go through periods where there is too much of this going on. The cards will have overproliferated, and so there will be cards lying around everywhere, and no one will throw them away because everyone will think that someone might need them.

But then a fad would come along and people would start taking classes on how to make things disappear, which would eventually clean up all the piles of cards lying around. Disposal of the tarot cards could even become an environmental problem, but if it does, we will solve it!

There might also be a time when tarot decks become more minimalistic, the pictures simpler and simpler, until there were decks of seventy-eight cards with nothing on them. When you do readings with these cards eventually you'd start feeling what the card is, for each one of them would have been charged by experts with invisible pictures that you will either see or feel in your mind if you keep using them.

This would be close to the time when researchers find nanoparticles in the bloodstream that, when seen under an electron microscope, turn out to be tarot cards! Then people would realize that no one invented the tarot—it has always been here, like the stars.

Acknowledgments

Many thanks to Ronn Ballard who helped developed this first incarnation of this book. He also was instrumental in putting together the correspondence course we developed to teach the material in it. Ronn and I taught tarot classes together for a number of years, as well as classes pertaining to knowledge connected to the tarot, such as color therapy, numerology, and applied metaphysics. His knowledge and support have been invaluable to me in manifesting this current book.

Thanks also to Adam Rush who was encouraging to me at every turn as the present incarnation of this book emerged. He helped with such things as layout, design, and structuring of the book, as well as by stimulating me always to think of metaphysical ideas in new and different ways. He has given me support always in just the places I needed it.

Thanks also to Sandra Sandy who has been a constant source of insight and encouragement, also to Elizabeth Perry for the fine work she has done editing and restructuring this book, and to Paul Swann and Margaret Jones for their meticulous editing and refining of the text.

Thanks as well to all the students along the way who have offered their insights and encouragement, and who have brought a richness of meaning and purpose to my life. May the spirit of the tarot bless you all and continue to provide you with sustenance from its endless fountain of knowledge.

Index

About the Author

John Sandbach was born in 1948 in San Francisco, California, and moved to Kansas City at age three. He has been living there ever since. At eighteen, he began his career as a professional astrologer, and since then has written a number of books on that subject. Several of these works broke ground, in that they explore completely new approaches to astrology, while others offer new insights into traditional methods. He is the person who channeled the Chandra Symbols of the 360 degrees of the zodiac system, which are continuing to come into more and more widespread use by astrologers worldwide. In the early 1970s he began an extensive study of the tarot and was deeply impressed by the tarot work of C. C. Zain. He is particularly fascinated with the way that author integrated the tarot with so many other metaphysical systems, including astrology.

John Sandbach has also written fiction and poetry, both of which express in imaginative form the same ideas and concepts found in his nonfiction works. These writings are similar to the mystic texts of the Medieval and Renaissance alchemists; they are meant to communicate the play of metaphysical energies that are understood more via emotions than by the conscious mind.

Most of all Sandbach is interested in therapeutics and has dedicated himself to imbuing all of his writings with healing energy. Along with this he maintains a practice as an astrologer and tarot reader, while also using Reiki and other healing modalities in one-on-one work with others, both face to face and in long-distance sessions.

Through his website, johnsandbach.net, you may ask questions of his astrological oracle, explore different types of metaphysical information, and schedule personal appointments.

OTHER BOOKS BY JOHN SANDBACH ON ASTROLOGY AND METAPHYSICS

The Dwadashamsas: Degree Analysis and Deeper Meanings
Volume I: The Dwadashamsas
Volume II: The Chandra Symbols
The Circular Temple
Volume I: Aries through Virgo
Volume II: Libra through Pisces
Planetary Containments: A Study of 990 Combinations
Manual of Astrology
How to Use Harmonics: What Astrological Harmonics Tell
Midpoints: A Kabbalistic Compendium of Meanings for Astrological Midpoints
The Mysteries of Color
Astrology, Alchemy, and the Tarot